INSIDE THIS PLACE, NOT OF IT

INSIDE THIS PLACE, NOT OF IT

NARRATIVES FROM WOMEN'S PRISONS

COMPILED AND EDITED BY
ROBIN LEVI AND AYELET WALDMAN

ASSOCIATE EDITOR
REBECCA SILBERT

FOREWORD BY
MICHELLE ALEXANDER

Research editor
ALEX CARP

Assistant research editor
JESSIE HAWK

VOICE OF WITNESS

Assistant editors
OONA APPEL, JOHANNA FOSTER, CLAIRE KIEFER,
DANIELLE LANG, JULIET LITMAN, CAITLIN MITCHELL,
SUSAN MOON, M. REBEKAH OTTO, BRIAN RUTLEDGE,
WHITNEY SMITH, MARBRE STAHLY-BUTTS, TONYA YOUNG

Transcribers/drafters
ABIGAIL EDBER, SANDI GAYTAN, VANESSA ING,
BRIDGET KINSELLA, THI NGUYEN, ELIZABETH SOUTTER

Additional interviewers
GILLIAN CANNON, ABIGAIL EDBER, VALENCIA HERRERA

Expert consultation and assistance
GAIL SMITH
CHICAGO LEGAL AID TO INCARCERATED MOTHERS

DEB LABELLE
ATTORNEY

TINA REYNOLDS
WOMEN ON THE RISE TELLING HERSTORY

SPARK REPRODUCTIVE JUSTICE

YALE LAW SCHOOL HUMAN RIGHTS CLINIC

Researchers/general assistance
ALEXANDRA BRODSKY, SANDI GAYTAN, VANESSA ING,
MICHELLE KNAPP, THI NGUYEN, GELYNA PRICE

Copyeditor
ORIANA LECKERT

Fact checker
ANGELENE SMITH

To the many people who shared their time and lives with us, including those whose stories we were not able to publish in this collection. And to all those people living inside whose voices are never heard.

VOICE OF WITNESS

MᶜSWEENEY'S BOOKS
SAN FRANCISCO

For more information about McSweeney's, see *mcsweeneys.net*
For more information about Voice of Witness, see *voiceofwitness.org*

McSweeney's and colophon are registered trademarks
of McSweeney's Publishing.

ISBN (Hardcover): 978-1-936365-49-4
ISBN (Paperback): 978-1-936365-50-0

VOICE OF WITNESS

The books in the Voice of Witness series seek to illuminate human rights crises by humanizing those most closely affected. Using oral history as a foundation, the series explores social justice issues through the stories of the men and women who experience them. These books are designed for readers of all levels—from high school and college students to policymakers—interested in a reality-based understanding of ongoing injustices in the United States and around the world. Visit voiceofwitness.org for more information.

VOICE OF WITNESS BOARD OF DIRECTORS

VOICE OF WITNESS BOARD OF ADVISORS

CONTENTS

STANDING WITHOUT SWEET COMPANY

by Michelle Alexander

The stories in this book may haunt you, follow you like a shadow. Once you read them, you may find you can never escape them. You may find yourself awakening in the middle of the night from a dream of being shackled to a hospital bed while giving birth, prison guards whisking your baby away and denying you the right to make a phone call to share the news: my child has been born. Other stories, of abuse, medical neglect, and frightening retaliation, may stay with you long after you think you've left them behind.

At first, I found myself resisting the narratives in this collection, not wanting to deal with the reality they described. Perhaps it is natural, and thoroughly human, to recoil reflexively when one encounters extreme suffering. Perhaps it reminds us of our own vulnerability, and then fear or denial kicks in, leading us to turn away. But then a voice in my head asked me: If you find these stories difficult to read, how much harder would it be to live them? And then I realized that if I slow down enough to listen, really listen, I will find there is nothing to fear here; there is only a blessing to be found. I realized that these stories are a gift.

These are personal narratives not only of suffering, but of human dignity and survival against all the odds. Hope flickers, even through recollections of painful childhoods, poverty, and domestic and institutional abuse. It is this hope that allows us to envision a way out, a path toward a more forgiving, compassionate, and caring society, one that attempts to solve social ills and improve the lives of our most vulnerable rather than sweeping them behind bars.

Our nation is awash in punitiveness, for reasons that have stunningly little to do with crime or crime rates. Most criminologists and sociologists today will acknowledge that crime rates and incarceration rates in the United States have moved independently of each other. During the past thirty years, our nation's prison population has quintupled, while crime rates have fluctuated and today are at historical lows. What explains the sudden surge of imprisonment in the United States, if not crime rates? The growth dates from the beginning of the War on Drugs in the 1980's, and the movement to increase prison sentences and reduce the possibility of parole—for example, life sentences for third strikes. These policies had their biggest impact on communities of color, as police began sweeping ghetto communities and stopping, frisking, and searching young men, especially black men, en masse. In fact, today there are more black men under correctional control—in prison or jail, on probation or parole—than were enslaved in 1850, a decade before the Civil War began.

The staggering rates of imprisonment of black and Latino men in recent years have led many, including myself, to focus their advocacy work and research on addressing the plight of men profiled and brutalized by the police, and put in prison. Women inside the criminal justice system, meanwhile, are often mentioned as an afterthought, if at all. The omission is inexcusable. Today, women are the fastest growing segment of the prison population, and the most vulnerable. The overwhelming majority—over 90 percent—of women in prison have suffered sexual and/or domestic abuse, and have lived in extreme poverty. In 2004, more than 90 percent of imprisoned women reported annual incomes of less than $10,000, and most hadn't completed high school. They find themselves behind bars primarily for minor drug offenses and for crimes of poverty and survival. Sometimes they are locked up for crimes of violence, typically when they dare to fight back against their abuser.

The result is that our women's prisons are filled with people from the poorest, most vulnerable and marginalized segments of our society, whose offenses are often a consequence of their circumstances: lack of access to employment, familial stability, drug treatment, and protection from sexual and physical abuse. And once in prison, abuse often continues for these women, who face sexual, physical, and mental abuse at the hands of prison staff.

For those who are released, they join the ranks of millions of poor people of color who have come out of prison to find themselves locked out of society, branded criminals and felons, and ushered into a permanent second-class status. Once labeled a felon or a criminal, an individual may be stripped of the basic civil and human rights fought for in the civil rights movement, including the right to vote, the right to serve on juries, and the right to be free of legal discrimination for employment, housing, access to education, and public benefits.

Collectively, our nation has turned away with cruel indifference, leaving the millions of people behind bars both out of sight and out of mind. Some of us have imagined that someone else will fix the system or extend loving arms; someone else will do the work of caring. The women in the pages that follow—mothers, daughters, sisters, wives—will tell you stories that are nearly unbearable to read, and yet their courage, dignity, and perseverance compel us to imagine how their lives would be different—how *we* would be different—if we responded to their experience with genuine care, compassion, and concern.

The poet June Jordan once called us to stand with our sisters of every race, nationality, and creed, to lift our voices with those who have "stood without sweet company." Let the voices and stories contained in these pages inspire you to see, with clarity and compassion, how this country's system of mass imprisonment is devastating the lives of women of all races and backgrounds, and is denying them the basic dignity and humanity deserving to all people. That, in the end, is what these stories, in their breathtaking candor, will never allow you to forget.

And who will join this standing up
and the ones who stood without sweet company
who will sing and sing
back into the mountains and
if necessary
even under the sea
we are the ones we have been waiting for
　　　—June Jordan, from *Passion* (1980)

Michelle Alexander is a longtime civil rights advocate and litigator, and holds a joint appointment at the Kirwan Institute for the Study of Race and Ethnicity and the Mortiz College of Law at Ohio State University. Alexander served for several years as director of the Racial Justice Project at the ACLU of Northern California, and went on to direct the Civil Rights Clinic at Stanford Law School, where she was an associate professor. Michelle Alexander is the author of The New Jim Crow: Mass Incarceration in the Age of Colorblindness.

INTRODUCTION

A BATTALION
OF SURVIVORS

by Robin Levi & Ayelet Waldman

The long drive out from the San Francisco Bay Area to Valley State Prison for Women in Chowchilla, California, is always a stressful one. The anxiety begins early, when we get dressed, making sure to comply with the ever-shifting, always onerous dress code for visitors to the prison. There is a long list of banned colors and fabrics: no denim or chambray, no lime green or orange, no tan, no attire similar in any way to military fatigues. In regulations reminiscent of Catholic girls' schools of the 1970s, skirts must end no more than two inches above the knee, and "spaghetti" straps are forbidden. Jewelry is limited to only two rings, and one set of earrings. And then there is the most bizarre rule of all, given how closely all interactions between prisoners and visitors are monitored: female visitors are forbidden to wear underwire bras.

The closer we get to the prison, by the time we have driven through Tracy, Modesto, and finally Turlock, with its almond orchards and fields of cows, a pall usually descends. There is something about the prospect of submitting to the absolute and arbitrary authority of the prison Corrections staff that intimidates and depresses even the most seasoned prison visitor. Although we've sent in the names, social security numbers, and driver's license copies of the interviewers, although we've managed to track down a working tape recorder that complies with prison regulations—no digital recorders are permitted, only MiniDisc recorders (of a specific brand and type no longer produced)—we know, from experience, that it is still possible that we will be turned away. It's possible that the women whose visits we requested might have broken one of the myriad prison rules and ended up in segregation, and thus banned from our visit. We know that we could be turned away for this or any reason, or for no reason at all.

When we pull into the prison parking lot, we grow quiet, careful of listening ears and watchful eyes. We pass through the metal detector and stand before a twenty-foot-tall barbed fence, waiting for it to slide open. Then we cross the field to the prison building, greeted by small bunnies hopping through the short grass—an incongruity in the otherwise barren environment.

Once we've passed through the rigmarole of metal detectors, barbed wire, and pat-downs to get to the visiting room, and the women whom we are visiting make it through their own gauntlet (strip, squat, cough), our malaise always lifts. Our spirits are raised not by the topics of the interviews, which are always and inevitably painful, but by the women themselves. Despite being incarcerated under grim conditions, they demonstrate dignity, courage, and generosity as they recount their often traumatic experiences before and since their incarceration.

The narratives in this collection, as told by these individuals and others in correctional facilities across the country, highlight human rights abuses in the U.S. prison system. Narrators describe their lack of access to adequate healthcare, including mental healthcare and pregnancy care. They also recount experiences of questionable medical procedures—Olivia Hamilton was forced to have a cesarean section, while Sheri Dwight had her ovaries removed without her consent or knowledge. Our narrators describe sexual and physical abuse suffered inside the prison, and the daily indignities they face just trying to ensure they have enough toilet paper, soap, and menstrual pads. In addition, they recount the myriad abusive situations that led to their imprisonment and to recidivism.

These include the lack of adequate treatment for drug addiction, domestic and sexual violence, and discrimination based on sexual orientation and gender identity.

The women featured in this volume come from all over the United States, represent a variety of ethnicities, and their offenses range from the minor (check forgery, drug possession) to the most serious (murder). These are women who have been silent for most of their lives, whose desires and needs were ignored by often abusive families and spouses, and, later, by prison authorities. They tell us their stories here because it is, for many of them, the first chance they've had to be heard.

According to the U.S. Justice Department's Bureau of Justice Statistics, 2.3 million people are currently imprisoned in the United States—more per capita than any other country in the world. People in U.S. prisons are routinely subjected to physical, sexual, and mental abuse. While abuse in male prisons is well documented, women in prison suffer in relative anonymity. This disparity is especially troubling, since women in prison are in many cases more vulnerable to rights violations for three main reasons: women's prisons are generally more geographically isolated and thus less subject to outside oversight; women are predominantly incarcerated for nonviolent offenses; and, due to their histories of sexual and physical abuse, women are both more likely to suffer serious health consequences and less likely to complain of abuses within the prison system.

As Michelle Alexander points out in her foreword, people of color are vastly over-represented in the American criminal justice system. According to a 2009 report by the U.S. Census Bureau, one out of every nine black men between the ages of twenty and thirty-four is behind bars. This racial disparity is also reflected in the women's prisons in this country. Nearly half of those imprisoned are women of color. Thirty-four percent are black, despite the fact that black people make up only

6.7 percent of the general population.[1]

Though women make up only a small minority of the prison and jail population, slightly less than 7 percent, their numbers are increasing at rates that far surpass men. In 1977, 11,212 women were in prison. As of 2007, that number had increased to 107,000. The number of women in prison has grown dramatically since the 1980s due to several factors: mandatory minimum sentencing for drug crimes which preclude judicial discretion, the dismantling of the U.S. mental health system, and increased prosecution of "survival" crimes, which include check forgery and minor embezzlement. Over the last four decades, hundreds of thousands of women have been sentenced to jail and prison for nonviolent and first-time offenses, for offenses that arise from drug addiction or mental health problems, or as a result of minor involvement in offenses perpetrated by their husbands or boyfriends.

Because women are a minority in the prison system, they face particular challenges. A prison healthcare system designed for men that mandates, for example, shackling during transportation to and from the hospital, suddenly rises from the unpleasant to the horrific when the transported prisoner shackled at the ankles is a woman in the late stages of active labor, as experienced by Olivia Hamilton.

One of the most striking things about our experience in collecting these narratives has been the overwhelming prevalence of histories of sexual abuse. According to the U.S. Department of Justice, two-thirds of women in prison have experienced sexual and physical abuse in their lives, a statistic that was reflected in our interviews. Francesca Salavieri was sexually abused from the age of six by family members, while Teri Hancock was given as a "gift" to a step-uncle to abuse as he liked. The sexual abuse and violence that women in prison endure usually comes at the hands not of other prisoners, but of guards and staff. Not once in

---

[1] Throughout this volume, we use the inclusive term "black people" to describe all people of African descent, including those whose families have lived in the United States for generations, and those who have arrived more recently and may not identify as African American.

creating this volume did we come across a woman who described being sexually abused by another prisoner. On the contrary, when women are raped, or when sex is demanded as payment for "privileges" such as medical care or family visits, the perpetrators are guards and staff.

Because prisons are managed under a patchwork of state regulations and are increasingly privatized, there is variation across the country in prison conditions and access to remedies when abuses occur. In Michigan, for example, until the groundbreaking work of attorney Deborah LaBelle, women were subject to horrific and near-constant sexual abuse, while in other states, because of more enlightened prison practices, sexual violence is nearly nonexistent.

Despite state-to-state differences, overall commonalities across the country are striking. Healthcare is rarely adequate, and usually requires a co-pay that is difficult for women to manage on their paltry incomes, which for most women in prison is less than $1 a day. Their daily lives are often characterized by degrading treatment and routine privacy violations. Women across the country experience enormous difficulty in maintaining family relationships, or even relationships with their legal representation, because of the erection of barriers to communication with the outside world.

Eighty percent of women in prison in the United States are the primary caretakers of children, but women's facilities are few and far between, and are often located far from families and communities. This makes it difficult, if not impossible, for mothers to maintain relationships with their children. Marilyn Sanderson, for example, has not seen her children in fifteen years, and yet she thinks of them constantly. Women are isolated in these distant facilities, separated both from families and from advocates, and are forced to navigate often draconian regulations to maintain letter or phone contact. Even then, they are subject to the whims of prison officials, who sometimes refuse to deliver mail without legitimate reason, as happened to Teri Hancock. Women must jump through a myriad of bureaucratic hoops to receive visits from family and friends, if visitation is allowed at all. For six years,

Emily Madison lost all her visitation rights because she was found in possession of pills: a Motrin and an iron capsule. Most egregiously, even telephone contact is strictly limited, with collect calls priced far beyond the norm in the outside world, and access is often dependent on deposits as high as $50.

Generally, it has become ever more difficult for people in prison to assert their basic human rights to protection from violence, to decent conditions of confinement, and to minimal healthcare. In 1996, Congress passed the Prisoner Litigation Reform Act (PLRA), which erected procedural barriers to litigation that preclude civil rights lawsuits in the vast majority of instances. Women in prison are forced to rely on internal prison-grievance systems, which vary widely from state to state, and are often inadequate to remedy even the most blatant violations. For many like Maria Taylor, attempts to hold officers responsible for their abusive behavior result in frightening acts of retribution. In addition, many prisons bar the media from freely communicating with people inside prison, which keeps the public from ever knowing what goes on behind bars.

In reading this volume, it is important to realize that, while the narratives here are skewed toward people who have been sentenced to long terms for serious crimes, this does not reflect the actual population of women in prison and jail. Of the over 100,000 women who are currently under the jurisdiction of the criminal justice system, more than half are imprisoned for nonviolent or victimless crimes such as drug possession, prostitution, or check forging. However, it was impossible for us to gain access to women in the network of county and city jails, where nearly half of women serve their time. Our work was limited to various state prison systems, and within those, the women who were most likely to participate had served sufficient time to build up the reserves of strength necessary to discuss the intimate and often traumatic details described in these narratives, as well as to develop the relationships with advocates such that we knew to contact them.

Furthermore, it is these women, who are serving sentences of decades or life without parole, who have the least to lose from exposing the truth of their conditions of confinement, and the most to gain from risking the often terrible retaliation to which such honesty exposes them. If, as a result of this volume, awareness is raised and change is made, they will still be inside to benefit from it. Additionally, telling their stories has led many women to experience feelings of personal empowerment, control, and a restoration of dignity.

There were many more women who wanted to participate in this project but were unable to because the prisons in which they are incarcerated are too far away or difficult to gain access to. In response, we set up a system whereby women could send in letter narratives. Sarah Chase, a young woman serving twenty years to life, was sexually abused by a guard who was then fired. The other guards then began a campaign of harsh retaliatory abuse, which ultimately led to Sarah being moved to a prison thousands of miles from her home, allegedly for her own protection. This prison was physically inaccessible to us, but Sarah participated in the project primarily through letters, and her narrative is thus included in the volume.

Inside this Place, Not of It is the result of more than seventy interviews with over thirty individuals, conducted over the course of ten months. For this project, we assembled a team of nineteen interviewers, who fanned out across the country, visiting women inside prisons, halfway houses, and in their homes. Fact-checking was conducted to the best of our abilities, but did not come without its challenges.

We used court records, human rights reports, medical records, and multiple external sources, but it is important to bear in mind that the narratives in this volume recount instances of abuse at the hands of the very system that controls the paper trail. In cases where litigation resulted in depositions and testimony, or where medical records existed, it was relatively easy to verify a woman's story. However, in many instances, the barriers to litigation discussed earlier not only precluded any redress, but also left on the record only the prison authorities' refusal to investigate allegations of abuse.

Additionally, the women who shared their lives in this volume experienced significant levels of trauma, both before and after their imprisonment. It is well documented that post-traumatic stress disorder, especially when complicated by depression, affects memory. Our narrators have done their best to verify their own memories, but oral history is by its very nature subjective. As the great author and oral historian Studs Terkel wrote in *Hard Times: An Oral History of the Great Depression*, "This is a memory book rather than one of hard fact and precise statistics… The precise fact or the precise date is of small consequence. This is not a lawyer's brief nor an annotated sociological treatise. It is simply an attempt to get the story from an improvised battalion of survivors."

In contemporary American society, we so often think of people in prison as entirely different from ourselves. When politicians want to gain easy points with voters, they get tough on crime, or on "criminals." This is a population, after all, that is politically disenfranchised. Unlike in other Western countries, individuals convicted of crimes in the United State lose their right to vote not only while imprisoned, but in many cases for the rest of their lives. When considering these individuals' paths to imprisonment, we cannot lay fault solely at their feet. Through failure to address poverty and lack of access to education, through failure to effectively combat domestic abuse and abuse of children, our society fails these women. And then, rather than investing in communities to redress these problems, we instead invest in prisons to warehouse far too many of our people.

Editing this volume has been a great privilege, not only because we are helping to bring to light stories that otherwise might not have been told, but because we were so fortunate to have met these remarkable women. These are women who have forged bonds of community and friendship under the most trying of circumstances. That a feeling of community can develop in these circumstances may be surprising to people used to thinking of prisons as only violent and terrifying places. But the women inside do develop warm and loving relationships. They form support groups, such as the Two Spirits group, founded by Charlie Morningstar, for lesbian, bisexual, and transgender people. They help one another to survive, and even to flourish, when isolation and despair would have been far more obvious a response. We are grateful to them for their example, for their inspiration, and for the remarkable courage it took to tell their stories.

—Robin Levi and Ayelet Waldman, 2011

OLIVIA HAMILTON

25, formerly imprisoned

Olivia lives with her husband and three sons in an apartment that FEMA (Federal Emergency Management Agency) provided for her family because they evacuated New Orleans after Hurricane Katrina. We sit at a table in her breakfast nook as she shares her story: abandonment by her mother, teenage pregnancy, forced evacuation from her city, and imprisonment. Olivia gave birth to her youngest son while she was in prison serving a six-month sentence for embezzling money to pay her bills. During the birth, she was chained to an operating table and given a forced and medically unnecessary cesarean section. Olivia gave birth to another child in July 2011, but because of Olivia's c-section in prison, her local hospital was unwilling to allow her to try for a vaginal birth and she was forced to have another c-section. The son she birthed while imprisoned, now three years old, bounds around the apartment wearing only a diaper, occasionally interrupting our interview to squeeze his mother's leg. During the interview, Olivia describes her distrust of both the prison and the healthcare system, and describes her precarious journey toward reestablishing her life post-incarceration.

AND THEN THE HURRICANE HIT

My grandma tells a story about when I was a little girl, that one day I got a broom and started beating my doll with it, saying, "That's what my mom does." After that, my mom sent me to live with my grandma in Louisiana, St. Charles Parish. My relationship with my grandma was really good, but she was strict with me.

My brother and sisters stayed in Georgia with my mom. I talked with my mom some, not a lot. I had a lot of resentment, I guess, for her sending me to live with my grandma when I was so young. I think the problems began when I was around twelve. It was never my grades, it was just that I was in trouble with the juvenile detention people all the time for fighting and running away; I was trying everything to get my mom's attention. I think I realized I was doing it the day I got sent to juvenile hall. Usually I'd just go to the ADAPT Center[1] when I was in trouble, but the last time I ran away, when I was about twelve, I was sent to the St. James Parish Juvenile Detention Center in New Orleans for ten days. I was hurt and mad the day my mama came to see me in juvenile hall. But then I finally realized I shouldn't be doing all this, and when I went home to my grandmother's I just got myself back together.

I got pregnant at seventeen, and my boyfriend and I got an apartment together. I had my first son, Emmanuel, when I was a junior in high school, but I still graduated with a 3.8 GPA. I got help. For instance, there was this lady from Africa who'd opened a school for teen moms. She got government funding to open it, and she'd look after the students' babies, all the way till they were able to go to Head Start.[2] I didn't have to bring diapers, food, nothing. All I did was drop him off every day, and that was a blessing.

After I graduated high school in 2004 my then-boyfriend and I headed to Augusta, Georgia, in a raggedy car to live with my mom. But my mom let me down, and six months later I moved back to Louisiana to start all over again. I started Bryman College at the beginning of 2005 and I met my new boyfriend, who is now my husband. And then, that August, Hurricane Katrina hit. Before the storm reached us, I got in a car with my boyfriend

---

[1] A social work and child resources organization.

[2] A federal program promoting school readiness for young children (ages three to five) in low-income families by offering educational, nutritional, health, and social services.

and baby, and we started heading toward Georgia. We stayed with a friend of my brother's, which was a hectic situation every day. It was only a two-bedroom apartment, but at least it wasn't a shelter. During that time, I wrote a lot of bad checks because it was hard for me to get a job. I didn't have money for food, and you know, it was just a lot that we were dealing with. It was the only way really at the time that we could get anything.

Eventually I got a job at McDonald's. My brother was working, and my dad was coming up with some money to send us so we could maybe rent a trailer or something. But then three or four weeks after we got out here, I spoke with my mom, and eventually she let us stay with her.

I'D MADE THIS HUGE MISTAKE, AND I REGRETTED IT

By the end of 2007, I had two kids and was four months pregnant with another. I was living in Marietta, Georgia, and working two jobs, at Kmart and Pep Boys.

Well, one day I got an idea. I had a friend at Kmart who used to do fake refunds. She'd say a customer was coming in and she was refunding stuff that wasn't really being refunded. So I did it the first time and I didn't get caught, but of course I was scared. I said to my friend, "We didn't get caught. Let's not do it again." But we really needed the money. I was behind on a lot of bills, and I was trying to catch it up.

One night, my friend came through my line to check out little items like diapers and different things—some of the things I needed—and I didn't charge her for everything; diapers and stuff like that I would never ring up. We would do that a lot.

That night the Kmart loss prevention officer was outside smoking a cigarette, but I didn't see him at the time. When I got ready to close up, he called me and my friend to the back, and of course they'd caught it on tape. He asked us how long we'd been doing it, and I lied, "This is my first time." And then he basically told me, "Write what I tell you to write, and then I'll let you go home."

I think the total he had us taking was $1,200 worth of stuff, and I said, "I didn't take that much," because we'd only taken $300 worth. But he said, "But we have other stuff that's been taken," even though I told him I hadn't taken any of that.

Then he said, "Well, we're gonna press charges." I think he was trying to save his job at the time, 'cause they've got to catch people, and I don't think he'd been doing too good in that department. I got arrested and taken to jail that night, but I bonded out.

About two months later, I got a letter in the mail saying there was an arraignment. I honestly thought it was for Kmart, but when I got to court, I found out it was for Pep Boys—I'd been doing the same thing there. The judge was sending everybody to jail that day, and I was totally scared. So I got up there, and the Pep Boys loss prevention officer said he'd called his manager because he really felt bad for me. He said I was a good worker, and that he knew the situation I was in. He said, "Well, I asked my manager if there's a way that you can make payments, but he's not budging. He says it's too much." It came to something like $700. The judge put me on a bond on my own recognizance. She basically let me go home that day without my needing to post bail, and told me that I needed to turn myself in the following night. It was like her trusting me that I was going to come back. She said, "I think you made a very bad mistake. I want you to go home, pick your kids up from daycare and make sure they're stable. Tomorrow at nine o'clock, you need to turn yourself in."

In my mind, I was thinking, *Okay, well, I've never been in trouble before, so the only thing they can do is put me on probation.* And that's all I kept saying to myself. But when I finally got to court, I got a court-appointed lawyer, and he said, "Well, the judge is saying eighteen months." And I was like, "Huh? I've never been in trouble before! I can pay the money back!" At the time I had $1,500 on me, which I'd saved from my taxes. My lawyer talked to the prosecutor, who said, "No. She's got to serve time."

Then my lawyer told me, "Go home for the weekend and get yourself together with your kids." He said, "The only thing I can say is that I'll try and talk the prosecutor down. Any other judge, and I think you would've been okay. But I don't think she's gonna budge."

So I went home and finally I called my grandmother, my dad, and everybody, and let them know what was going on. Of course they were all shocked, because I had never said anything about it before. That weekend was real, real hard. I was scared, because I didn't want to leave my kids. I guess it just hurt me because I'd never been in trouble, and I was doing all I could to stay out of trouble. But I'd made this huge mistake and I regretted it. I think that was the most that I felt—regret. Leaving my kids—I didn't know how to handle that part.

And so that Monday came, February 18, 2008. I had to be in court at nine. I told my oldest son, "Mommy might have to go away for a while to help some people. But once I've helped them, I'll be home." My husband kept saying, "You're not going. You're not going." When I got to court, every part of me just knew what would happen.

So I got in front of the judge and I said to her, "I'm truly sorry. But you know, I have never been in trouble before this. I just graduated from college and I'm pregnant. This is not what I thought I would be doing right now." The judge had her head down the whole time; she looked real, real sad. And then she said, "The only thing I can say is that I have to send you to jail, because your co-defendant has already gone. But I'm sorry. I think you're on the right track. I think you just made a mistake that you've got to serve the consequences for." I was sentenced to a year, and the judge said, "Hopefully, you'll do six months on good behavior, with nine years' probation." And I thought, *Okay, so you're going to send me to jail. And then I have to pay all this money back—one hundred a month until it's paid back—and then probation for nine years. Nine years.*

THEY SHACKLED MY STOMACH AND MY FEET

When the court bailiff took me from the court to a holding cell in Georgia, a guard put the cuffs around my belly and on my wrists, like a chain. When I sat down, the cuffs were real, real tight, so I was basically standing up the whole time. For a while, I was complaining about how tight it was, and other inmates were complaining too. Finally the guard came back and loosened the chain around my belly, and then I was able to sit down. The whole process was just long, and I was hungry and tired.

I think the thing that upset me the most was that they wouldn't give me water in a cup. I was not about to drink out of this faucet where you wash your hands; it was right over the toilet bowl. So I just stayed thirsty. By the time I did finally go through the holding cell, the guards gave me a sandwich to eat. Then they took us all on upstairs to the jail, and once I got upstairs, one of the female guards told me, "I won't be able to put you in a bottom bunk until you go see the doctor and he says you're pregnant." I was six months pregnant! I said, "No, for real?! You want me to climb this bunk bed?" She said, "Well, I can't give you a bottom bunk." I just said, "Ma'am, I can't climb this." And then she just walked out. Another inmate told me, "You can have my bed." So she put her stuff on the top bunk, and I took the bottom. And finally I went to sleep.

I was there about a month before I actually saw a doctor. I didn't have vitamins there, and I had no prenatal care. I didn't really complain if I was in pain or anything, because the infirmary was real nasty. There was poo on the walls. It was just nasty. Then one day, when I was seven months pregnant, the guards called me down. They shackled my stomach and my feet and took me to see an OB-GYN. I mean, you walk like this through the front door looking as if you've murdered someone, and I just thought it was really degrading. I know I made a mistake, but I don't think I deserved to be ashamed or embarrassed in this way. And even once I'd got in the back where the actual doctors' offices were, the shackles didn't come off. They took them off my feet, but nothing else; the shackles stayed on my stomach.

The doctor complained that I wasn't getting enough water, vitamins, or fresh fruits, and that it could affect my baby's brain. The county doesn't give you fruits, and it's not like I could buy them. So I just tried to drink as much water as I possibly could.

My kids came to visit me sometimes with my boyfriend. My boys were five and three then. The first time they came was really hard. They were beating on the glass, trying to come through it. I was so mad at myself for putting them through this.

It felt like my pregnancy was the only thing that was keeping me going. I was eight months pregnant when I finally left the county jail and went to prison.

NOBODY CARES IF YOU'RE PREGNANT

When I was moved to prison in Pennsylvania, I couldn't take my books that had been sent to me in jail, or anything like that. I had one picture and I had my Bible, but all the rest I had to send home.

I was taken to prison with other inmates in a cramped, hot van. Some of them were also pregnant. When we got there and were getting off the van, the guards started yelling at us, "Nobody cares if you're pregnant! You shouldn't have got in trouble. You're a sad excuse for a mother. You don't care about your kids!" It was a mess. It was real hard. There was another girl there who was pregnant, and she'd been there before. She said to me, "Don't let them get to you, girl." But they had already gotten to me. I just felt like this wasn't the place I was supposed to be.

The guards wanted me to stand up straight, but I couldn't. I was totally drained because I hadn't slept since three that morning. I was eight months along at this point, and I was huge. Eventually, one of the male guards said, "Okay, go get her a wheelchair." The female guards were actually harder on me. So I got in a wheelchair, and they rolled me on inside. When I got inside, the guards made me strip, bend over, all that. Then they made me take a shower, and afterward they gave me a sandwich and a juice. You would think that they'd give you more food, being pregnant, but they don't. You just eat what everybody else eats.

It was a whole process. I had to learn how to talk to the guards, and that I had to address them with "Ma'am" or "Sir" and "Good morning."

Or when they walked by, I had to stop. I had to ask permission to speak. Finally they gave me all my stuff in a bag to put on the bed.

I couldn't carry the bag like they wanted me to. There's a certain way you had to hold it, a certain way to walk, and I just kept dropping it. It was about ten pounds—it's your clothes, it's everything in there—and I wasn't even supposed to be lifting that. But the guards kept yelling, "You'd better not drop it again!" And I was like, "Uh, ma'am, this is heavy. I'm trying my best."

When I got in the dorm, the inmates were pretty cool and they helped me make my bed. I think, with most of the women in there being mothers, they could imagine how it felt to go through this while pregnant. Most of them were pretty understanding, and they didn't mind helping me out as much as they could.

My family was very supportive. My grandmother made sure that I had money in my account, my dad and uncles too. My mama did most of the writing as far as letters went, and she sent a lot of pictures and just different things to help me get through. I could call my grandma any time, but it was hard for me to call my boyfriend, because you couldn't call cell phones from prison, only landlines. Also, you couldn't get a visitation until about two months of being there. It didn't make any sense for me to even start that process, because my lawyer told me that, nine chances out of ten, I would be getting out in six months. By the time I got to the prison, I'd already been in county jail for two months. I had to wait another two months before I would be allowed visitation at the prison, so it would have been four months by then. And by the time they'd gone through processing everybody, it probably would have been time for me to go home.

I SAID I DIDN'T WANT TO BE INDUCED, AND THE CAPTAIN SAID, "THESE ARE ORDERS"

My due date was May 24, 2008, just before Memorial Day weekend. A female doctor from the Atlanta Medical Center came to visit me on the 22nd. At that time, I wasn't showing any signs of labor. We did an ultrasound, and the baby hadn't moved one bit. I wasn't dilated at all, wasn't even close, and I wasn't having any pains. She said I should be fine through the weekend, and that everything was normal about my pregnancy.

Then, on the evening of the 23rd—this was a Friday evening—the guards called me, and they told me to pack my stuff. But I hadn't even had one contraction, so I asked a guard, "Where am I going?" And the guard said, "I don't know. They just called and said for you to pack your stuff." I thought, *Okay, maybe I'm going home!*

I got over to the infirmary, and the captain said, "Well, the doctor from the prison says he's going to send you in to be induced." When I asked why, she said, "Because your due date is May 24th, and this is a holiday weekend." I said, "But I'm not even in pain or anything! I don't want to be induced, I'm not even late. Nothing's wrong with me!" And she said, "Well, these are orders."

They put me in a room and shackled me. I was more upset than anything that the baby just wasn't ready, and I didn't want to be forced. They gave me Pitocin,[3] but it wasn't working. Later, in the middle of the night, the doctor came in to check on me. He came in and he started poking inside me with an instrument—I'm not sure exactly what it was, it looked like a little stick. He put it inside me and started poking the bag of water, where the amniotic fluid was, so he could bust it. It was a lot of pain, and I said, "You're hurting me." He stopped, but by then he had swollen up my insides, and the baby wouldn't move any more than six centimeters.

Then he said, "Well, if you don't move any more by tomorrow, we're going to have to do a c-section." I said, "So you come in here, and you poke me to death, and now I'm swollen! I have never had a c-section in my life. My oldest son was nine pounds—no cuts, no slits, no nothing. And you're going to make me have a c-section?"

---

[3] Pitocin is an intravenous medication commonly used to induce labor.

The next day, the doctor came back and took me in to have the c-section done. A sergeant came in and said, "She needs to be shackled. She's no different from anybody else." I was hurting, and I was tired. I said to the sergeant, "Ma'am, there is no way I need these shackles. I'm not going anywhere; I'm in pain. You've got a guard in my room. And I don't know if you have kids, but this ain't something fun to have your hands shackled for." But she made them keep the shackles on me when I went in for the c-section.

The doctor gave me an epidural. I went through with the c-section, and finally, the baby came on out. It was a boy. The guard held him up to show him to me. Even then, they never took the shackles off me.

This c-section I was forced to have—I doubt that it's legal. I don't remember signing any paperwork, but I never looked into finding a lawyer. I was hoping there was something I could do, but I was told that I had no rights. The guard said to me, "You lost your rights the day you walked in here."

I named the baby Joshua. I wonder about him; does he remember all that we went through? The guards made me put the prison address on the birth certificate. That's something you have to deal with for the rest of your life.

I was fortunate, you know. One of the guards there gave me her cell phone because she didn't agree with a lot of what was going on. She said, "Call your boyfriend. Let him know you had the baby." She let me talk to him until the phone died. It was a blessing.

IT FELT LIKE MY BABY WAS DYING

After I left the hospital, my boyfriend picked up the baby and took him home. I guess for me, walking out of that hospital, knowing I was leaving my son—it killed me inside. I felt like I was being punished for the one mistake that I'd made in my life. I just remember looking at my baby, and kissing him, and crying, and not wanting to go. The nurse who was holding him was really hurt too. She asked me, "Do you want to kiss him again?" And I kissed him one last time, and they took me out the door.[4]

It felt like my baby was dying, that I was abandoning him. I felt like I owed it to him to be there, and I wasn't. I felt like maybe he would hate me, or resent me, or when I got home, he wouldn't know who I was. It hurt. It just hurt.

I got back to the prison with staples in because of the c-section. But I couldn't go back to the dorm until the staples came out, and so, on top of me being hurt and stressed, they put me in this infirmary with nothing but four walls. I didn't have any of my personal property, and there was no TV, nothing.

I was supposed to stay there through the weekend. During that time, I had nobody to talk to, and all I could really do was cry. I didn't want to eat, I didn't want to do anything. And then one of the guards told me, "Well, if you don't eat, we're going to make you stay here longer." So I made myself eat because I didn't want to stay in there that long. All that was going to do was drive me more crazy than I already was.

By then I was mad at everything. I was mad at myself. I was mad at my mom. I was mad at everybody. I had only been back there but about five weeks from the hospital, and I got in a fight. It was with a girl who was looking for trouble, and she picked a fight with me one night. She hit me and hit me, and I fought her back. So of course, they took us to

---

[4] Most prisons separate parents and their new-born infants after 48 hours. As well as causing emotional distress, the separation of mothers and their children also threatens the health of infants by posing serious barriers to breastfeeding. The Fifth Circuit of Appeals ruled in the 1981 case *Dike v. School Board of Orange County, Florida*, that the right to nurse is protected by the Fourteenth Amendment. However, the same court determined in *Southerland v. Thigpen* that the state could overlook this guarantee in prison. Some states, like New York, have taken steps to recognize the universality of this right, guaranteeing women in prison the ability to breastfeed their children for a year after birth, though in other states the reality of prison life has rendered breastfeeding impossible.

In at least thirteen states, babies can be placed in prison nurseries, though access is often limited to women with short sentences for non-violent offenses, and some parents prefer for their children to be raised outside prison walls.

lockdown. That's the worst place to be. I mean, you can't look out the windows because they're all blacked out, and you can only bathe on certain days. I was down there for three weeks. My birthday was July 18th, and I was in lockdown for that. But my mom sent me a whole bunch of cards and pictures, and I would call my grandma, and she'd be like, "You still down there?" And I'd say, "Yes."

The day I got out of lockdown was the day I got the news that I was going home on August 14. I had two weeks left! I thought, *Thank God! Finally!* I stayed up the whole night before the 14th—I was so excited, and I just wanted to leave. I was just so ready to get out of there.

ALL STORMS END

When I got out of prison, my boyfriend came to get me. At that time, his mom had the two younger kids and my grandmother had my oldest son. It took me a while to get the kids back. I missed them terribly, but things were bad. The gas in the house had been turned off, the phone was off, the cable was off. The truck I had was gone, and my credit was totally messed up. Everything was in a total wreck. I couldn't be bringing the kids back into that type of situation. I wanted to be able to have food stamps first, and I wanted to try to get the house together. It was nasty, it was dirty. I was just in a depressed situation, and I was upset with my boyfriend, who wasn't working at that time. I was mad because I'd left him with $1,500, and he got money every month from my dad and my grandmother, so I couldn't understand the house being in a total wreck when I got out of prison. I was totally mad about my money, and why everything was gone. I also felt a lot of resentment toward society.

Eventually, I was able to get a job at the food court. I saved up, and I got a car. Once I got the car, I could get back and forth to work. And finally, when we were more financially stable, we got the kids back.

Once I got out, I got in the church. I always was in church, but I strayed for a while when I first moved out here to Georgia. But once

I got out of prison, I joined a choir and I went to Bible study and Sunday school. And, you know, I got myself back together for me and God. For me and school. For me and work.

Eventually I got laid off from the food court because they didn't have enough work for me, and it's been totally hard for me to find a job since. Whenever I'm filling out a job application, I get scared when I get to that question where I have to put down that I have this conviction. I feel like I'll never have the opportunity to explain what happened. So it's like, do you lie, or do you tell the truth? And, you know, every time I get to that question, I stumble.

I think my medical treatment in prison was cruel, degrading, and shameful. Being shackled, being forced to have that c-section—it was the worst feeling, mentally and emotionally, that I have ever been through. And I feel like it would be so unfair for me to have been through all this and not say anything about it to somebody. I always felt like everything I went through was definitely for a reason, and that it made me a stronger person. So my goal now is to help prevent somebody else from making the same mistakes, with the stealing, the whole scenario. Right now I'm working with young women through my church. I want to work with these young women because when you get to a certain age, there are things you go through, there's pressure to do things that you may not want to do. I've also been without a mom, and I know how it feels to want that. There's a gap in your heart where you need it. A grandmother's love is awesome, but a mom's love is something totally different.

Through God, all things are possible. Even though I was mad at my boyfriend and my mom, God has built those relationships again. Now my mom and I share a beautiful relationship, and my boyfriend is now my husband. This shows that all storms end and the sun will shine again.

SHERI DWIGHT

35, formerly imprisoned

Sheri was interviewed in a small, empty park in Inglewood, California. As she shared the details of her story, she frequently looked over her shoulder to scan the other benches, ever vigilant from her years in prison. Sheri was seventeen when she met her husband, and their marriage quickly deteriorated into mental and physical violence. A year into the marriage, Sheri shot and killed her husband, and was sentenced to fifteen years in a California state prison. During her time inside, she was diagnosed with ovarian cysts, and agreed to have them removed via a cystectomy. Then, for the following five years, Sheri found herself unable to menstruate, and experienced menopause-like symptoms. An investigation led by the legal nonprofit Justice Now revealed that the surgeon who had performed Sheri's cystectomy had also given her an oophorectomy without her knowledge or consent. Sheri has been home for a year, and is working to rebuild her life and help other survivors of domestic violence.

SCHOOL WAS NEVER HARD FOR ME. IT WAS AFTER SCHOOL WHERE I GOT INTO MOST OF MY TROUBLE

I grew up in Watts, South LA. My parents cared for me, but we weren't an affectionate, interactive type of family. My dad was always working, and he wasn't around the way me and my mom both needed him to be. My momma, because of the strain that was going on between her and my dad, she isolated herself. I felt very unloved, unprotected, and very lonely.

School was never hard for me; I was always in some kind of gifted program. It was after school where I got into most of my trouble. I was angry, for a lot of different reasons. My home life was very strained, very hurtful, there was a lot of pain, a lot of loneliness. At school I would always be sent to the principal's office for one thing or another, get written up or have some kind of detention, yet still I aced every test. The teachers wanted to kick me out, but my test scores and my academics were high enough that they kept me in. I was one of those kids who were really smart but tough, they've got that attitude.

Fortunately I never got into the heavy stuff, but I smoked weed. I smoked it from the time I woke up to the time I went to bed. The weed just balanced me out; it calmed the anger inside of me. I don't think my mom knew the difference.

I first became pregnant at fourteen, and by the time I was in eleventh grade I had two kids already. After eleventh grade I dropped out of school because my oldest son was constantly sick. He was born with a respiratory illness and was always running a high fever or congested, so once a month I was in the emergency room to bring his temperature down.

My mom helped me with my sons. But I felt that, because I was still a child and we were all under the same roof, they were like another two of her children. So when I said no, she said yes, and her yes went. That sparked a lot of heated arguments, which led to power struggles.

MY HUSBAND BECAME CONTROLLING
OVER ME AND MY SONS

I was living with my mom up until I was seventeen, and then I moved out on my own. I met my husband at that time. One of my friends from high school was married to his relative, and so we exchanged numbers and began communicating over the phone for several months. Eventually, we arranged a formal date, and the rest is history. We were together for two years, married for one, before I shot him. I shot him twice in the upper torso and he died. I did fourteen years for that.

My husband was abusive almost from the start. At first I took it as him being protective, loving, and caring, but he became controlling, dominant, and possessive over me and my sons. At first he was physical, but he didn't hurt me. He basically would stop me if I tried to walk in the door, he'd block it. If I tried to take off, he'd grab my arm, not too hard, just enough to stop me, and he'd say, "Come here, don't go nowhere, I'm not done talking to you." But it didn't become painful, physical, until after we got married.

It started at a family event. I didn't get up and do something he asked me to do, and so he began to talk down to me and bad-mouth me in front of his family. His family tried to interject. They were saying things like, "Hey, leave her alone, man, we're all watching the game. It's cool, get up and do it yourself." And then he immediately challenged them. He said, "Anybody has a problem, I'm gonna whoop your ass! Leave my wife alone!"

So I got embarrassed and I left. I hadn't taken more than a few steps away from the house when he charged me to the ground. We began wrestling and tugging and fighting. His family didn't stop it; a stranger off the street came and broke it up. It was the first of many, many fights that came very rapidly after that.

Thirteen months it lasted, with him abusing me. It just got worse and worse. I've been raped and sodomized by him, I've been tied up and held hostage, I've been choked to the point where I passed out numerous times. He'd strip the clothes off my back, sometimes leaving me half-naked in the street. He'd take all my clothes and destroy them or hide them, and then I would walk around for a week with just the clothes on my back. He would take all the money out of my bank account so that I couldn't move. He would take the battery and disconnect the stuff out of my car so I would be stuck.

It was a very degrading, humbling, shameful, embarrassing time in my life. I was not easy in my own home; I would wake up feeling like my breath was being cut off. It was very stressful, very painful. But nothing was as painful as looking in my sons' faces after I got beaten up. One day, in the fall of 2005, something happened that woke me up to the reality of the danger me and my children were in. I'd told my sons to go put their toys away, but they were just jumping up and down on the bed. My husband snatched them off the bed, and when he did that, panic just struck in me, like this protective nature, and I jumped all over him. I knew at that point that, by any means necessary, I was going to get myself and my children out of that situation. I saw that it would only get worse. My sons were so precious to me, and they were just so beautiful, so loving, and it wasn't fair for them to endure what was going on.

I HAD GIVEN UP ON THE LAPD TO PROTECT ME

By that point, I had given up on the LAPD to protect me. I'd already had numerous police reports from previous fights. I'd had emergency room reports, reports from my doctor about the wounds from the abuse. I had given up on God because I felt God was allowing this thing to happen to me. What had I done to deserve this when I had turned my life around and was going to church and living a spiritual life? And my mother and father, with them I always felt unprotected, unloved, so it was not my first instinct to run to them for protection. So I went to the streets.

The streets are always there waiting for you. The streets always have what you need, and I needed a gun. And just like that, I had a .38. My sons and I had started staying with parents, but I got the gun just in case my husband came and caught me off-guard. I was also going to use what little money I had to get away from him. I had some friends that had moved to Nevada, so I was thinking of going there.

At this point my husband was doing all kinds of stuff—constantly calling my mom's house, threatening me, telling me that we were going to die together. So one day—it was November 15, 1995—I went to move my stuff out of the house. My husband was there, packing all of our stuff; he had the kids' stuff all packed up in this U-Haul truck. I knew there was a reason he was packing up all that stuff, and not because we were moving. I was afraid he was taking my sons' things so he could manipulate them later, like, "Hey little man, here's your toy, come get it." I just knew him and I knew some of his tactics. I knew he was treacherous, he was very calculating.

When I looked in the house, it was all messed up. Everything I'd worked hard for, my husband had destroyed. I was trying to get our things, and he was steady threatening me under his breath. After a while, I just lost it. Everything in my identity, my integrity, everything was lying on the floor, shattered and cut up and destroyed. It triggered something inside of me and I pulled out my gun.

But then my husband, he got that smirk on his face, like he knew he was going to win. He kept looking at the gun, looking at me, and in my heart I felt that if he'd got a hold of the gun it would have been me dead. I was crying, just hysterical.

He said, "So, you gonna shoot me?"

I said, "I'm tired, I can't do this any more."

Then he said, "All right," but it wasn't like, "All right then, I'll back down," it was "All right, well, let's do this." When he charged toward me I fired. And it felt out of body, it felt unreal. But when I came to, he was lying there on the floor. Somehow I got back to my parents' house because I just felt like I was never going to see my children again. I held my children until the police came.

I had a neighbor who'd heard the hollering and the screaming between me and my husband. She'd just had that gut feeling that something was not right and she called the police. I thank God for every time she's ever called the police, whether it was for me or against me. I thank God for her, because we need people like that, because it is life and death. It was my life or his death.

When the cops picked me up at my parents' house I was numb. The detective began to try and build a case, not even understanding me or what I had come out of. Every time I would begin to tell him about what had happened or what I was thinking, he'd shut me down. He only wanted something that could give him evidence to stand upon.

THE JUDGE DIDN'T BELIEVE
I WAS A BATTERED WOMAN

After just coming out of a relationship where I'd fought for my life, I began fighting for my life again in the judicial system. I don't believe the system handled my case fairly. I had neighbors testifying for me, I had family members testifying for me, I had police reports, I had medical records, but none of that meant anything to the prosecutor. Their job was just to convict me, it was like a show. The prosecutor was trying for a sentence of thirty years to life. I had to fight to not go into a prison for life.

I believe that domestic violence representation now is a little better than fifteen years ago, but fifteen years ago, let's keep it real—they didn't give a damn. I was a young African American woman, I was from the ghetto, I didn't have money or anything else like that, so of course my chances of going to prison and nobody giving a fuck about what happened to me was high.

At the first trial I got a hung jury. Before the second trial, that's when I was given a deal—fifteen years. The judge said if I lost in trial she was going to give me the max because she didn't believe that I was a battered woman.[1] It didn't matter to her that I had iron marks on my chest, iron marks to this day on my arms, bruises and scars all up and down my body. Back then, the battered woman syndrome was just becoming a factor. There was no consideration, no compassion for the fact that people like me were fighting for their lives in their own homes. There was no consideration of the fact that I was just like a prisoner coming out of war.

---

[1] Beginning in 1987, some states began to allow evidence of battered woman syndrome—a pattern of symptoms arising from persistent abuse—as a defense in a criminal trial. For more details, see the glossary and timeline.

I was in county jail for two years while I was fighting my case. It was like living with a bunch of college girls, but bad girls. The Bad Girls Club. I got a chance to meet a lot of high-profile cases, a lot of the cases that you've seen on TV. I've actually had the privilege of meeting some of these beautiful, talented, mentally disturbed women who just snapped—they were a lot like myself. Some are women who killed their own children, women who killed their husbands, women who were greedy for money. You get to hear the stories behind what started the greed. Some of them were locked in a closet with no food for days, some had been pimped out by their mothers, and it created a sense of hard, cold callousness. You just really get to hear the brokenness behind the people you look at in the news. Something in their heart, something in their mind, something in their spirit just snapped that day. And once they heal from that day, usually they go back to being decent, beautiful, intelligent, creative beings. It was just that day they lost it all.

Even though I was in jail, I somehow felt safe because I didn't have to worry about a man hurting me any more. But prison still is a violent, hostile place.

YOU HAVE A BAND OF SISTERS

I got to Chowchilla in 1997, when I was twenty-one years old. Up in prison, I learned a lot. If you don't have any street smarts, you learn some. You learn to read body language a mile away. I can tell by the shift in the atmosphere if something ain't right. Like, sometimes we'll sit here talking and all of a sudden it gets quiet, and you'll start looking around, because you know there's a fight about to break out.

There are certain things you pick up in prison, like sometimes when the male guards were mad at certain inmates, especially the ones that are homosexuals and look like little boys, they had a tendency to be rougher with them. They'd go up under your breasts a couple more times than necessary. They'd take the back of their hand and swipe your crotch. That was very inappropriate and it was very hard, especially for women like me. At the time I didn't want to have anything to do with any men, and so for a male guard to touch me—instantly anger and fright rose up in me. And so a lot of times I got slammed up against a wall when I said to a guard, "Get up off me!"

You've also got a lot of dope fiends in prison, so when people come to you with a sad story, you have to go by your instincts. You think, is this person really in a bad situation and she needs a little help, or is this person one of those crackheads and she's running this crackhead drama drag on you, trying to get a few noodles and a couple of candy bars up out of you? You have people who are constantly scheming to try to live off of you, or get something from you, or take something from you. It is a place where only the strong survive. They will eat you alive in there.

There were four thousand women there. Eight women to a room, thirty-two rooms in each building, four buildings on each yard. I knew a lot of people there, from school and from fighting their cases with me in county. That's where the bond is built. Nowadays I watch a lot of war movies and I can see a lot of what I went through in prison; it's the same thing. You have a band of brothers, a band of sisters. It was more settled than in county jail. Jail is more like, *Please God, help me get out of this situation. I don't wanna be here.* But once you get to prison you've already gone through that process and you have a settling in. Then it's like, *Please God, give me the strength to go through this situation. I don't wanna die here.*

I had a crew that was between the ages of seventeen and nineteen, and they all came in facing thirty-five to life, fifty-five to life, life without the possibility of parole. They became my sisters. We were fighting for our lives together. Nowadays, when I see some of those girls out on the street, I get so excited. I don't even get that excited when I see family members I haven't seen in years. But when we see each other, it's like, "What do you need?" We'd do anything for each other. The shirt come off your back, the shoes come off your feet, the money comes out of the purse. You say, "Come on girl, I got $5, let's go to McDonald's! At least we can get two hamburgers, two fries, and share some cookies."

MY BODY WAS SHUTTING DOWN,
AND I COULDN'T UNDERSTAND WHY

I think it was in 1999, when I was twenty-two years old, that I started having a lot of abdominal pain and heavy menstrual cycles. I knew that something was wrong. The cramping that I was having was just, oh my god. Not only was I in a lot of pain, but I was also having periods in between periods. I went to the gynecologist to see if something was going on, and he began to run a series of tests, a lot of different pap smears. One of the pap smears came back showing that I had abnormal cells. I went through more tests to figure out what was causing the abnormal cells, then more pap smears, ultrasounds, pelvic exams. All this testing took about a year and a half. During that whole time I was having pain, abnormal menstrual cycles, and heavy bleeding.

One ultrasound came back, and it said that I had two ovarian cysts, one on each ovary. The diagnosis was that it was probably caused from endometriosis. I didn't know what that was, but the gynecologist told me it was blood that had been circulated back out from the uterus to the fallopian tubes to the outer walls, and had collected itself. He said there would just be a simple procedure, that I would simply have the cysts removed and also have a cone biopsy because of the abnormal cells. With the cone biopsy, they would see if I had cancer or not. He said that, according to the cell readings, I was basically in the very early stages of cervical cancer.

That gynecologist was the only one we had at the prison. With all four thousand women, if there was anything wrong, you'd go and see him. Usually you form some type of relationship with your doctor, but that's not how it was there. It's more like, "Number X, lay down here, put your legs up in the stirrups." There is no getting to know you or your needs and wants.

The gynecologist referred me to a surgeon at the local hospital outside the prison. I had to wait a few more months for the pre-op so we could discuss what the treatments were going to be. The surgeon explained to me that he was going to be doing a surgery to remove the cysts, and that he was going to be doing a cone biopsy on me to find out whether or not I had cervical cancer. Based on the findings, if any forms of cancer were found within my cervix or in my uterine wall, then I would be looking at a hysterectomy or a partial hysterectomy. So I was basically consenting to the fact that if they had found cancer, they had the permission to remove part or all of my uterus.

The doctors said that the cystectomy was a simple procedure. They would cut, remove, and deflate the cysts. I was pretty comfortable and confident about the ovarian part of it, but I was very concerned and a little scared concerning the uterus part of it because the cancer was my main focus.

There is a lot of debate as to what happened to me when I woke up out of surgery, but I do remember bits and pieces. I do remember asking what happened to me, and they told me I'd just had a cone biopsy and a removal of the cysts. There was another girl in the hospital room recovering with me. She'd overheard some things that were going on, and she was a little bit more alert than I was. She said, "I believe that you had the same surgery as me, a full hysterectomy." But that wasn't what the doctors told me.

After the surgery, I started having pain in my back and going through these hot flash symptoms. I would be sweating, my heart would be beating fast, I couldn't sleep. Mentally I had started tripping. Then I hit depression, and I sunk into it real quick. I didn't know these were symptoms of menopause. At the time the doctors told me it was all in my head. They said, "There is nothing wrong with you, go back to your cell." But those doctors were going by my hospital discharge papers, so it's really not their fault. They're not pushed to go a little deeper. They've got four thousand other women to see. Prison is overpopulated, overcrowded, and they don't want to pay the money for enough medical staff. So during a medical visit it's like, "Okay, well, you don't have anything, I don't see anything, I'll order a blood test and see where your hormones are at, if they're high or low. See you in two months."

I never got my period again after that surgery. For the next few years, I was still asking at the prison why I didn't have my menstrual cycle.

I was told that sometimes these things just happen, that maybe my body shut down or went through shock, or that maybe the trauma of the surgery caused surgical menopause. All the discharge papers from the hospital said was that I'd had a cystectomy, one on one ovary this size, one on the other ovary that size, and that a cone biopsy had been done. I was waiting and hoping for my cycle to start back again, waiting for my body to kickstart. But my body was really shutting down, and I couldn't understand why.

I didn't learn what happened until four or five years later, when an organization called Justice Now[2] started looking into my case. Through their investigation, I finally found out that, during the surgery, the surgeon had cut off the blood supply to my ovaries, killing them instantly. Instead of trying other techniques, or offering me alternative measures to go about this procedure, he'd just gone in and just *snap*, left me with no ovaries. Then after the cone biopsy, he'd sewed me up and never talked to me about it at all. He never sat on the side of my bed and actually took the time to tell me what procedure had been performed on me and why. Before the surgery he'd even asked me if I wanted to have more children. I'd said, "Yeah, I'm hoping to find somebody one day who loves me. I didn't get a chance to raise my other sons, so I want the chance for a family again." He didn't listen to me.

THEY TAKE FOR GRANTED OUR IGNORANCE, THAT WE DON'T HAVE A VOICE FOR OURSELVES

What rights did I have for real? I was just an inmate. No one came in, no one consulted, no one asked if my mother or father knew, no one cared about any of those things. After the surgery I was just handcuffed back on to my recovery bed, and after two days I was released back into general population. If something were to happen, if a fight were to break out

---

[2] Justice Now is an Oakland-based nonprofit, and the first teaching law clinic in the country solely focused on the needs of people in women's prisons.

and I were attacked, I would have been in no condition to defend myself. I could barely walk then.

That's CDC[3] for you. When a woman comes back from an oophorectomy in prison, she goes to the infirmary for a week. No one comes to see her, they just come to check her vitals, make sure she has her medication, check her bandages, remove her staples, then send her back into general population. Even though she has been through a life-changing experience, she goes through it alone. There is no counseling, there is no mental health, there is nothing to help her try to deal with the fact that she has lost her ability to have children.

They take for granted our ignorance, they take for granted the fact that we really don't have a voice for ourselves. We have to fight an organization that's bigger than us, stronger than us, and that's been there longer than us, and we have to push past all of that just to gain an answer to a question like, "Do I have my ovaries?"

I was so sad when I found out about my ovaries. I'd fought for my life in my marriage, I'd fought for my life in prison—and here life was taken from me. It made me feel broken, empty, used up. That surgery took the last bit of what I thought made me beautiful as a woman. I asked myself, "Why do I keep losing when it's not my fault? Why is it that I went in trusting my life in someone else's hands, and once again someone mistreated me and just took advantage?"

I remember when I used to go out to a medical appointment, having those chains and that uniform on when the guards transported me to a community facility. I remember the fact that even though I was a human being, just that uniform itself made me feel different. It made me feel less than other people who were out there in society looking at me. It just made me feel less than a human being. That right there, it really messes with your mind.

---

[3] California Department of Corrections.

A LOT HAS BEEN TAKEN FROM ME.
I REFUSE TO GIVE ANYTHING ELSE UP

My case was picked up by a law firm. So I began to 602[4] for documents, I began to 602 for answers and to speak with the Chief Medical Officer. We eventually put in for a lawsuit against the surgeon. When I got that lawsuit started, the prison threatened me that they'd stop treating my medical problems. And I was telling them, "Then so be it. You're not taking care of me anyway. That's why we're here."

My lawyers, they got it going on. They fought for me when I couldn't fight for myself, they gave me a voice when I did not have a voice for myself, and I appreciate that.

The surgeon's lawyers tried to prove that I knew what had happened to me the day after the surgery. They said that I'd asked the nurse whether I still had my ovaries, and that this meant that I'd had an inkling that my ovaries were gone.

In the end, we lost. We walked away with nothing, mostly because of the statute of limitations.[5] That was the time from when I found out what had happened to when I actually filed a lawsuit. I had a specific time limit to file the lawsuit, and they said I waited too long. It really did something to me, it sent me into a little depression. It hurt me. After the case was over I just wanted to be done with everything, let everything go. I didn't want to think about it, I didn't want to go over it and figure out what went wrong. I thought, *I fought the good fight, it happened that way, it's over and done with. I'm ready for my life to go on.*

But still I walked away from the case hoping that maybe that surgeon would think twice next time. Because he's still working in the

---

[4] 602 is the process to file grievances in the California Department of Corrections. For more details, see the glossary.

[5] The laws determining how long after a specific event occurs that legal action regarding that event can be brought to court. Variations occur, according to type of alleged crime and by jurisdiction.

same place, he's still cutting on CDC women. He never said he was sorry afterward. There was no, "I'm sorry you felt that way, that wasn't my intention." He just smirked when the verdict was read, as if to say, *That's what you get for going up against me.* Maybe he won then, but it will all come back around later.

I found out later there are different alternatives for preserving the reproductive organs during a cystectomy that were never offered to me. My right to reproduce was never an issue anyone cared about. *Cut, snip, you ain't doing nothing, you're just a prisoner anyway.* I felt mutilated. And I noticed that a lot of African American women were going into prison in their fertile child-producing years, and coming back with these partial hysterectomies, complete hysterectomies, abnormal cells. I noticed that it was a pattern.

The hot flashes, nervousness, heart palpitations, lack of a sex drive, that all lasted about five years after the surgery. It took me about that long to get used to what was going on, and then my body started leveling off. Every now and then, though, I'll be sitting in church and I'll get a hot flash, but everybody is waving their fans so I blend right on in.

A lot has been taken from me from when I was seventeen up to thirty-four—half my life, really. My husband, the court system, the correctional facility, the surgeon—they all took a lot from me, so I refuse to give anything else up. Spiritually, I do things according to what feels good to me on the inside. In prison you're stripped of everything and you have to go by your instincts, and in doing so I learned to trust myself. I didn't trust myself when I was younger, but today I trust myself and my instincts. And so now I listen to my body, and what my body tells me to do, because I couldn't trust the doctors and I couldn't trust the people who were around me.

ME AND MY SONS, WE'RE GETTING THERE

While I was incarcerated, my kids stayed with my mom and dad. They made sure that I saw my kids once a week while I was in jail, so for the next year or so I saw them. If it wasn't once a week it was at least twice a month. I kept seeing them until I got to Chowchilla. Then they were so far away, and it's a very costly and time-consuming drive. The visits went from twice a year to once a year to every three years. I already knew that I was losing them, I was losing that bond. And I tried so hard, making cards and little arts and crafts. I had made money in prison, so I would send them cash to spend for their birthdays or stuff like that, but it just wasn't enough. They needed someone there every day. I did everything to protect them, but I ended up losing them anyway. By the time my oldest son turned twelve, he was in juvenile hall placements.

When I got out of prison in 2009 I was thirty-three, my youngest son was sixteen, and my oldest was seventeen getting ready to turn eighteen. So I got a chance to pay for things, for his prom and stuff like that. Both of our relationships are very much strained. I know they had a lot of anger, a lot of resentment, but I couldn't understand why they didn't hold on to how much I loved them. It's not like I'd disappeared for fourteen years and then all of a sudden reappeared. I actually called once a week. We did have those visits. Anything they asked me for, if it was in my grasp, I would send it to them. I would sit there and talk to them, write letters, long letters.

But me and my sons, we're getting there. It's a slow process. It's slower than I would like it to be, but it's a process. I've come to some acceptance concerning our relationship. I did not realize that I'd been removed from their hearts like that, and that my mom had taken my place. When I got out, I felt that we'd all been waiting for this time, but I realized the only person that had been waiting was me, and so I had to let a lot of things go.

I've suffered enough hurt and pain and abuse. I've already felt the pain of someone who was hurting me because they was hurting inside, or they didn't get what they felt like they needed in life. That's something that I just can't go through any longer. I don't care who it is. I don't care if it's my children, my momma, my daddy—I am never going to allow anyone else to put their pain upon me any longer. It's just the way it is. I don't have time to waste. I've lost too much as it is.

Some time after I got out, I met a man who I eventually got engaged to. One day I was with my fiancé and his granddaughter, playing with her at a park. I saw him holding her, and that emptiness really hit me—the fact that I missed out on raising my children and holding them at such a young age. And the fact that now I don't have the ability to do that again. I told him, "I'll be right back, let me go get something real quick." I had to step away and go to the parking lot area, and I just cried.

I'm hoping maybe God is giving me a second chance with my fiancé having a granddaughter, who I'll be able to give love to as a mother, something I've been waiting fourteen years for.

MY OWN SPECIAL MIRACLE

There were times where I felt like my femininity had been taken from me, times where I felt very degraded. I felt like I wasn't my own person any more. The part of me being a mother had been taken from me too. So it was a lot of having to hold on to an identity that I no longer had, or trying to remember who I was while I was surviving in this condition.

God has really restored me, more so than I could ever imagine, having gone through such experiences in my life. To come out in one piece, one mind; I'm strong, healthy, able to love, able to trust. You know, it's my own special miracle. I walk around this life looking at the trees, looking at the grass, knowing that I made it out of a place that was trying to keep me from all this.

Because really, prison isn't designed for you to leave, it's designed to keep you. And I don't care what anybody says—you don't go in there to get better. Only the strong survive, and you have to fight to get better, and you have to fight and win.

I pray for the girls in Chowchilla. I pray for them and I miss them so much. I'm trying to put myself in a position where I can help them. I would love to be a social worker. Even before that, I want to get some services for domestic violence and gang interventions to get back into the prison. Within the next two years I would like to set up some programs on the inside to get people ready for reentry, for what they're going to be facing when they come out. I'm working with a couple of people on some curriculums right now. We're looking toward taking it into the prison in different areas, also to the correctional officers.

We all have our personal obstacles, our personal wars, our personal struggles that we have to go through. In prison there were times when I felt like life was just totally against me and I wanted to give up. I'm so happy that I didn't, even when there were times I felt like I could not breathe in prison. There were times where I panicked and I said to myself, *I can't do this any more.* Somehow, some way, my second wind kicked in. Oh my god, it kicked in. Because I am experienced in this fight, that's what I'm doing now, I'm helping people. I'm in their corner, in their ring, and giving them towels and squirting water in their mouth and rubbing their shoulders, saying, "You can do it! Listen, next time they hit you like this, you bob, you weave, you move, you shuffle a little bit, now stick 'em!"

Even if nobody else rewards you, if nobody else is there to pat you on your back, if nobody else is there to say, "Job well done!" it is still a personal victory, a personal accomplishment, and that's where I'm at right now. Prison did not do what it thought it was going to do to me. I won. I *won.*

But even though it's a place I would not want for my worst enemy, it was a beautiful place for me. It's where I learned how to prioritize what matters in life. I learned a lot about who I am because I was stripped of everything. That's where I found my strength, that's where I found my value. That's where I found my voice.

MARIA TAYLOR

37, formerly imprisoned

At seventeen, Maria was involved in a drug deal that turned violent. She was convicted of second-degree murder and sentenced to twenty-five to fifty years in prison. Released in 2009, Maria is now a graduate student and a program administrator for the Benevolence Education Project, a community organization for at-risk girls and women. She lives with her two small dogs in a recently developed area outside of Pittsburgh, where rows of matching mid-sized houses and driveways end abruptly in a field at the end of the block. When we meet Maria at her home, she is in the middle of working on her master's thesis; she closes her laptop and turns off her cell phone to begin telling her story. The television murmurs in the next room, but otherwise the house is silent. Maria does not make eye contact as she speaks; she holds her arms against her chest and hunches over, her long brown hair covering her face. In her narrative, she describes her experiences of childhood sexual abuse, her repeated sexual assault by a prison guard over the course of several years, and how she eventually found the strength to testify against the prison in a successful class action suit.

Names and locations have been changed or omitted in this narrative to protect the anonymity of the narrator. In some instances, dates have been slightly altered.

HIGH SCHOOL AND COLLEGE WEREN'T
PART OF OUR WORLD AT ALL

I grew up in Pittsburgh. Our neighborhood was built in the early 1900s by immigrants who came over to work in the steel factories. The houses are nice, in my opinion; beautiful brick homes that were built to last. But they weren't kept up, so now you don't see nice lawns, and you see very few parks. If you do see a park, there are prostitutes or drug dealers there. You see graffiti too, lots of liquor stores, and a lot of abandoned homes. On some blocks there's only one home on the block left, and it's barely standing up.

Most of the girls in my middle school didn't make it to high school, especially the Hispanic girls. If you were to drive down the street you would see boys—Hispanic, white, and black—dressed in clothes that represented their gangs. They all had territories in the community, and a lot of them were into drug dealing and violence. You would see groups of girls walking down the street, maybe twelve, thirteen, fourteen years old, who'd shaved their eyebrows off and painted them on with liquid eyeliner. Their hair was all curled and they wore tight tube-tops over big pregnant bellies. Us girls got pregnant young, and we lived on welfare. You didn't see anybody around there working or going to school.

I also hung out on the street with a group of girls in the neighborhood, but we didn't wear tube-tops and curled hair. We thought we were different, and we didn't wanna end up pregnant. Even so, we didn't talk about college, or even graduating from high school. Those things weren't a part of our world at all.

I lived with my mom and my little brother. I'm seven years older than my brother, so I was like a caregiver for him too. He has cerebral palsy, so that was a huge responsibility. My mom had me when she was fourteen. My father was a teenager too when I was born, and he left my mom, so she had to raise me all by herself. He was white, and she was Mexican. Sometimes she got angry and would say things like, "You're just like that stupid white boy," or "You're just like those hillbillies."

I remember hating that I was so white, and wanting to get a tan so I could be like the other girls in the community who had darker skin because they had Mexican in them.

Growing up, I always felt like I had to take care of my mom, I had to look out for her. I remember when I was a little girl, if there was a noise in the basement, I would be the one to have to go down there and turn the light on and check to see what the noise was. I never felt like a child who had parents who took care of her.

I REMEMBER GOING TO CHURCH AND ASKING GOD TO HELP ME

I don't remember being happy. Nowadays I go back to the church that I grew up in and I'll remember being a little girl going to that church and just crying and asking God to help me.

I would say I was probably around ten when our landlord started abusing me. When I went to my mom and told her what he'd done, at that point he had only put his finger in my butt while I was in bed. But pretty soon it progressed to full-on rape. There would be a whole summer and it wouldn't happen, and then it would happen, and then sometimes it would happen every day for two weeks and then it wouldn't happen for like four months.

The first time I told my mom, she was upset. But then maybe because she didn't know what else do to, she asked me, "Are you sure?" She got on the phone and she told my grandma, and she called other people and told them, and it turned into this big debate about whether I was sure that it had actually happened. The person who abused me was drunk a lot of the time, and so they said, "Are you sure he wasn't just drunk because, you know, when men are drunk they don't know what they're doing." But I was very sure what had happened. I knew that I had been sexually molested.

Afterward, it wasn't talked about any more. I didn't want to bring it up because I knew how it made me feel. And we couldn't talk about it because the guy who was abusing me owned the house that we lived in, and we would have been homeless without him. For her to defend me, it would have turned ugly. Even back then, a part of me understood that it was better to just be quiet.

I got pregnant by our landlord when I was twelve, and my mom took me to get an abortion. I think because she wanted to protect me, she told everyone that I had got pregnant by a boy named Pete that I used to hang around with.

Talking about the abuse is hard, because it means talking about my mother. Maybe, if you're not from a neighborhood like that, you'd think it was all my mother's fault or that she should have done something different. I can see now that she didn't handle it the way she should have, but she did the best she could. She had no support, no education. In her world, things like this happened. She was raised to believe that these types of things just happen to girls, that's just how life is. Sometimes we talk now and she's so sad, and so sorry. There's a part of me that doesn't like her for letting it happen to me, and for not doing anything about it. But I don't blame her for what happened. I mean, how can you blame someone who was just a child herself, and who had no idea of what else she could do? Now, as an adult in my thirties, I know that she was scared and frustrated, and I have a lot of understanding for her situation.

I LOOKED FORWARD TO BEING
A DIFFERENT PERSON

When I was fourteen I started working at a clothing store in the mall. It was a huge mall, and I had to take the bus a long way to get there. Working there, I met girls from the suburbs. Those girls were my role models! I remember the owner of the store taking me out to eat and telling me I was the best worker they had. She rewarded me with coupons for clothing because I used to spend a lot of my money on clothes. She'd given me the keys to the store and said, "We appreciate the work you're doing and we want you to have more responsibility. We want you to be the assistant to the assistant manager." This was like my dream come true. I looked forward to getting on that bus and going to another neighborhood, working at the mall, and being a different person from the poor girl from Pittsburgh no one cared about. I used my money from working at the mall to buy clothes to make myself look like the girls that I worked with. I wanted to be a manager of a clothing store, that was my goal. No one ever told me that I could go to school and actually be something really big.

Then one day, $380 came up missing from the cash register. I never, ever would have taken money from that place. They never directly accused me, but they said, "Maria, you're the assistant to the assistant manager, so regardless of whether you took the money or not, you're going to be held responsible."

I just gave up. I felt like I wasn't wanted there any more. I felt that the only reason that I was accused was because some of the people I worked with knew my neighborhood, and that my family was poor, because one of the girls had given me a ride home one day. I remember them treating me differently after that. After that, one girl brought me a bag of clothes that she didn't want. They hadn't treated me that way before. I didn't actually tell them I wanted to quit, I just didn't go back. I was really upset because I had no way to prove that I hadn't taken the money. If they had only known how important that job and that group of women were to my life. I would have worked for them for free, that's how much I loved that job.

After that I worked at a meat market, stuffing chorizo. It was really nasty work, but they actually paid a lot more money than the mall did, and I could walk there.

THE JUDGE WANTED TO MAKE SURE I WAS EIGHTEEN WHEN SHE SENTENCED ME

I was in ninth grade when I left school—I was sixteen, almost seventeen. I was very smart, I got really good grades. I could have done well. I just stopped going, and nobody cared. I wanted money to buy things like clothes, and the only way I could get those things was through working.

After I left school I started hanging around with this girl, Teresa. She was really pretty, and very popular, and I started going to parties with her. Her boyfriend was a drug dealer, and we used to go riding around in nice cars playing loud music. That was fun, and I didn't see anything wrong with it because I thought, *I'm not selling drugs—so what if I'm sitting in a car with a drug dealer?*

But in 1991, when I was seventeen years old, I became involved in a drug deal. It was a marijuana deal. I was living in a community where people were selling crack cocaine, regular cocaine, and heroin, and honestly, I didn't think marijuana was as harmful as those other drugs. Basically, I drove my cousin and some friends to the drug deal, and I was going to be paid $50 for it. I dropped them off, and I was supposed to drive around the block and come back and pick them up. Halfway around the block I heard gun-shots, so I didn't go back to pick them up. Instead, the boys ended up catching up with me on foot, and I let them back in the car.

I didn't know at that point what had happened—that the deal had turned into armed robbery, and then murder. I was arrested and later convicted of second-degree murder, assault with the intent to do great bodily harm, and armed robbery. I was still seventeen when I was convicted. The public defender representing me said that the judge had told him she wanted to make sure I was eighteen when she sentenced me, so she waited until three days after my birthday. My sentencing guideline recommendation was eight to twenty-five years, but the judge gave me the maximum, which was twenty-five years, and then she increased my top to fifty.[1]

---

[1] Felony murder is a legal concept that assigns criminal responsibility to all participants in a felony in which a death occurs, whether or not the participants knew or intended to harm or kill anyone. Levying a murder conviction against an individual who neither intended to kill nor took any action to do so has been legally controversial, and the felony murder rule has been abolished in all common law countries except the United Sates and Australia. (Guyora Binder, "The Origins of the American Felony Murder Rule." *Stanford Law Review* October, 2004)

Several weeks later, I got to prison. It seemed, in one aspect, extremely organized and routine. As soon as I walked in with the new inmates, they stripped us of everything we'd accumulated in the county jail—our clothes, our Bibles, letters and pictures—and we had to put them in a box and send it home. And then they put us in a quarantine room with a lot of other women. You stayed in that room until you were medically cleared to be put in the general population. The room used to be a library, so it was big, but there were about a hundred bunk beds in there, and if I put my arms out sitting on the bed, I could touch people on the other bunks. It was hard. There were about a hundred women in the room and there was no air circulation. You couldn't get off your bunk unless you asked for permission.

After about thirty days I was put in general population. I actually got out of quarantine sooner than the other girls; because I had twenty-five years, I was "high-security level."

HE WAS LETTING ME KNOW THAT
HE WAS WATCHING ME

In 1993, about two years after I got into prison, the inmates had to pack up and go to a different correctional facility. The first couple of days there were unbelievable—it was much more modern than the previous prison, and much cleaner, with nice landscaping on the grounds. And it was really odd because prisoners were walking all around the grounds. At the previous prison, there were areas in the yard that were designated for prisoners to walk around, but here you could walk anywhere. It was sort of out of control. People were standing around smoking cigarettes and joints and even crack in the bathrooms. Guards were smoking joints with the prisoners. I knew right away that I didn't like this place.

There was this one officer who would tell me I was pretty, or that I had nice legs. I remember feeling like I liked him telling me these things, but that I felt uncomfortable when he'd do or say dirty things, like when he would give me shakedowns, he'd cup my breasts or say things about my butt, like, "I'd like to lick that butt." But then if he told me I was pretty, of course I liked to hear that. You know, I like to hear nice things about myself.

This officer knew about my prison life. He knew how much money I had in my account, and he would say things like, "What are you going to buy at the store? You've got enough to do a full shop." He was letting me know that he was watching me. He also knew when I had a visitor, and he'd ask me, "Who is this person? What kind of friend is that person?" Or he'd say, "Your mom came to see you."

He would come in my unit, into my room, and just stand there and watch me. I wasn't doing anything in particular; I remember many times he would just stand there and watch me, and there was nothing I could do about it. Other times he would shake me down, and then he would tell me that he liked doing it. A shakedown is where officers come into your room and go through your stuff. That's normal; they're supposed to do several shakedowns a day. A pat-down is where they come and actually search your body to make sure you have no contraband. He did both of those quite often.

When he worked in the unit, he would call me to the desk in front of people. That was the most humiliating part, him making me stand at the desk and talk to him. He was old and and he had greasy hair, and he smelled like cigarettes. He had that sly look to him like he was a pimp, like he was trying to pimp me, and all the other girls in the unit could see it. It made me look bad, and it would cause problems for me with the other prisoners. The other girls would call me "bitch" and "slut," and they would say things like, "You're letting him do that, you're letting him do this." There was nothing I could say or do to defend myself. They were older than me, and I was intimidated by them.

I didn't really want him to touch me. I didn't really want to be around him. If it were my choice, if I had anything to say about it, I would not be around that man. But there was no place to go to report him, because what he was doing to me, I had seen it happen to other women, and nobody had helped them, so why would I think anyone would help me?

About six months after I got to the prison, right around my nineteenth birthday, that officer came to my unit when it was count time. When count time occurs, everyone has to go in their room. So he came to my room, and the officer who was working in the unit that day was with him. He grabbed me out of my room and took me into the bathroom right next to my room, and he started putting himself on me and pulling my jogging pants down. He had me against the sink, and he put himself in me. The other officer was standing outside of the bathroom, watching.

That was the first time he raped me. At that time, I didn't even know that what he'd done was rape, because I'd always had a thought that rape was when someone puts a gun to your head. It was just like when I was a child being abused. The difference was that when I was a child, those things were done in private, and even if people did know, it wasn't something that was talked about. But in prison, nothing is private, and so people talk about it.

When he was done, I just walked back to my room. My bunkie was there, and she didn't do or say anything at the time because she didn't want to get involved. She had her own problems. Things like that were happening to her too, by someone else. Later we talked about it, but not all the time, because it's not something you want to talk about. Everyone knew that you couldn't go to the prison officials and give a report, because the prison officials wouldn't do anything other than retaliate against you.

That officer sexually assaulted me for years. Then he got fired from the Department of Corrections. He wasn't fired for sexual harassment, even though I later learned that he'd sexually harassed and assaulted many inmates, not just me. He was fired because he had missed too many days of work. Can you believe that? I later learned that there were several reports written about him by his bosses at the Department of Corrections, and in one of the reports they said that he should not be working at a women's facility. But nobody did anything to stop him from working there. Nobody forced him to work at a men's facility. Nobody did anything.

After that, there were other officers who would do things to me. They knew about the officer who had raped me, that I had been "his girl"—that's what they said. So they felt that they could do things to me too, like open the shower curtain when I was showering, or come into my room after I got out of the shower and molest me. They did what they wanted at that time with no consequences. The other officers scared me; they touched me inappropriately and said inappropriate things to me, but there was no other officer that full-fledged raped me the way that one particular officer did. Even the one officer who put his fingers in me, I know that that's considered penetration, but no other officer made me feel the way that one did.

When you're a prisoner in that environment, you don't feel like you have the power to say no. Your life, your every move, is controlled by these people. When you eat, when you sleep, everything is known. At the beginning of my prison term, I didn't feel like I was a human being. I didn't feel like I had any rights. I didn't feel like anyone cared. I never felt like I had the power to say no, until I met my lawyer.

I STARTED TO FIGHT

It was around 2001, when I was twenty-seven, that I turned into a different person. I had heard about this one lawyer, Amanda Taylor, from other inmates. She was known as the lawyer who would protect you, and who was fighting to bring changes to the visiting room because the Department of Corrections had taken away some of our visitation rights. This lawyer was also fighting for us to get better educational programs, and to change prison rules because there was so much sexual harassment inside. I hadn't heard the words "sexual harassment" before I met Amanda

I had never realized that people would care. With Amanda's help, I started becoming really, really strong. I finally started to love myself regardless of everything, and I started to fight.

I was one of a group of women bringing a suit against the prison for all the sexual abuse we had suffered. I was willing to go to court, to do depositions. It was very hard, because when Amanda would come to visit a prisoner, everyone knew why she was there. So when you went back to the prison after she'd left, you'd be a target. I had to walk on eggshells every day. I stayed in my room a lot because I was afraid of being written up. I was really isolated.

I became really involved with the case when I spoke out in the media a few times. It had reached the point where no staff would talk to me. By then we had a whole new regime of officers, and most of them were female. Some of them were very neutral on the subject, because they weren't working in the prison when all these things had occurred. But some of them were manipulated or persuaded by some of the older staff to treat the women involved in the lawsuit in a retaliatory way. They were really slick, and they were really careful about how they did things. They could write you a ticket and get you in trouble for any little thing. They could terrorize you so much that they made you curse them, and then they could write a ticket for it. They could harass you so much that you would go crazy. I learned not to talk to anybody. I stayed in my room. I wasn't going to let them make me go crazy. If I was going to go crazy, it was going to be from my own demons, not from them harassing me.

I felt very proud to be in this group of women who had gone through similar things and were standing up against these people who had abused their power. It made me feel strong and powerful. It also helped me to deal with my demons. It helped me to not continue to blame myself. I had worked very hard to become the person that I was. So I ignored the officers when they called me a bitch or a snitch or ugly or fat or stinky, or whatever they did or said to me to try to get a reaction. I would remind myself every day that when I left that prison, I never had to see those people again in my life.

By 2003 I had thirteen years left on my sentence, but I had a pending petition in front of the governor for sentence commutation. My guidelines were eight to twenty-five years, and the judge had given me twenty-five to fifty years. So I had been sentenced to the highest range of my guidelines, and yet I had no prior criminal record. Most lawyers who reviewed my case agreed that there was no basis for the high sentence. There were a lot of theories about why. Some people told me that the judge was ready to retire and had become bitter, angry, and cold. But I don't have any factual reason for the high sentence.

For the next five years, I was waiting every day to hear an answer on my petition. It was on the governor's desk, and I knew that all I needed was one ticket in my file and my petition would be denied. So I lived in constant fear that anything could happen at any moment, and that it would ruin my chances for freedom. My freedom was all I lived for, but who could live like that, walking on eggshells every day for years? Sometimes I felt like I would have a heart attack.

MY HAPPINESS TURNED TO EXTREME FEAR

Then in 2008 there was a big raid in the unit. It was a really hot day, one of the first hot days we'd had in Pennsylvania. And in prison, the hot days are very, very hot because there's no air conditioning and no ventilation in the housing units. The squad had come in the unit, and everyone had to go inside this small little TV room while they went in the rooms tearing everything apart. I could hear them in my room. There were three officers in there, throwing all my books around, going through my letters, destroying my belongings, just because they could, because they wanted to. They had these raids to search for contraband, and I had none in my room so I didn't care. *Let them go through my room*, I thought. But I didn't want my stuff destroyed. I was sitting there in the TV room with about fifty other prisoners, and everyone was watching the guards in my room, and I was crying because they were taking my jogging pants and my sweatshirts, and they're not supposed to take things for no reason, but they did. They were throwing all my things into garbage bags. They were violating the rules, but was it worth me filing something? I thought, *They're not raping me. Rape and taking jogging suits are two different things.* Then the counselor in the unit came down to the TV room, and she said, "I need to talk to you." I looked at her, and I thought, *Oh, what's next?*

What are they going to come up with next that I did wrong? I followed her to her office and she said, "Close the door." I sat down, and it was so hot with the door closed that I could feel the sweat dripping underneath my shirt. Then she said, "The parole board wants to see you. I have to get a report ready for them."

That was one of the happiest days of my incarceration. I had been incarcerated for sixteen years, and the parole board had never wanted to see me. When she told me the news, nothing else mattered to me. Not the rapes, nothing. All that mattered was that the parole board wanted to see me. Then my happiness turned to fear, because a staff member knew that the parole board wanted to see me. Now I was even more of a target, because before that, everyone had known that I was participating in this litigation, and that I was a bitch, I was a snitch, I was this, I was that, but nobody knew I had a petition to get out of prison. Every prisoner who goes to the parole board gets picked on by guards and other prisoners.. So my happiness immediately turned to extreme fear. I didn't want to go in the shower because I was afraid someone was going to come in and try to hurt me. I didn't want to leave my room. I would pay prisoners to watch my room when I had to leave it, to make sure nothing happened.

In Pennsylvania, the normal procedure is to see one member of the parole board at your initial hearing. Then if that member votes for release, you have to go through a hearing in front of the full parole board. I finally saw the one member in May 2008. I didn't get an answer back until March 2009, and the answer was that I had to go through a full public hearing. I was very happy, but it was also extremely hard because at the same time that all this was going on, I was put in protective custody, because at that point another prisoner was threatening to kill me. I had asked staff to move me, but they wouldn't, so I had to ask for protective custody. This meant that I lost the prison cell that I'd had in general population. I was stripped of all my property and put in a room that people go to when they assault people. I had never in all the years of my incarceration been to segregation or protective custody. But I felt that I had to. Then after protective custody, they moved me to a different unit, and that was another adjustment because now I had to figure out who I should be scared of and who I should and shouldn't talk to.

After my hearing in March, I had another long period of walking on eggshells. I was anxious. I couldn't sleep. I didn't know if I was becoming paranoid or if bad things were really occurring, so I decided just to stay in the unit and not go out at all.

Then it was August 25, and the warden came into the unit at 8:15 in the morning. She took me to the counselor's office and closed the door. It was the warden and two deputy wardens, all women. The warden looked at me and said, "I'm here to tell you that the governor signed your commutation today. You're going to be released in thirty days."

I couldn't believe it! I was so happy I had finally made it, after seventeen years. I had made it through everything that had come at me. I remember calling my mom and telling her, "Mom, I'm coming home!" She started screaming and crying, and I was so happy.

A couple of days after I heard that I was being released, one of the women who was part of the sexual abuse lawsuit came up to me, and she said, "I want to talk to you." So we sat down, and she looked at me, and I could see in her eyes that she was so overwhelmed with emotion. She was almost shaking. She said, "What makes you so special that you get to go to court and tell them what happened to you and you get to go home? What happened to you happened to me, but nobody cares." When she said that to me, I felt so bad because she was right. She was absolutely right. What happened to her was just as horrific as what had happened to me. And she asked me, "Will you help me? Will you help me write a petition for sentence commutation? Will you help me write a letter to the parole board?"

And so for the final weeks until my release, I spent my days helping other women prepare petitions. None of the women I gave help to got released that I know of. There was one woman, but it wasn't because of me. She would have been released anyway because she was in her sixties, she had a bad heart problem, and probably didn't have much longer to live.

WHAT SAVED ME WAS FINDING
OUT THAT SOMEONE CARED

I'm a student now, at the University of Pittsburgh. I finished my coursework and am working on my master's thesis. I also do program administrative support for the Benevolence Education Project, which is a community organization for at-risk girls and women. I started a program at Benevolence called Open Doors for women who have been in prison or jail. The program helps them with résumé writing and interview techniques, basically how to adjust to finding a job when you have a record. I also do community outreach, so I see a lot of teenage girls. They don't always have money, and they can't always get government money if they don't have papers. I try to help them. There was one girl who we helped get a full private scholarship so she could go to Penn; I'm proud of that. There are a lot of girls struggling in the community, and when you see someone working really hard, you can't help but want to help them. I absolutely believe that what I do keeps these girls out of prison.

I struggle to reach the girls who aren't in programs, who are out on the street. We might have a night with pizza and dancing, but more than likely I'm not going to get the gangbangers. I want to figure out how to get the hard-to-reach kids. If I could just talk to one girl who was like I was, I would tell her to stay in school and listen to adults. I would tell her to read. I would tell her to love herself. I wish I'd had someone like me, now, to talk to me then.

I made it out alive and I went home. I left that place, and every day I think about some of the women I left behind. And one day I would like to go back there and see them and help them in some way. Until then, I'm just out here telling people what those women go through. I know that what saved me was finding out that someone cared, and I know that will save those women I left behind.

SARAH CHASE

21, currently imprisoned

Sarah Chase sits in a prison several states away from her family, friends, and everything she has known. She keeps busy with books, crafts, and writing, but she is lonely. She was sent here because of her relationship with a guard at her previous prison. Because of her new prison's inaccessibility and the high cost of phone calls, Sarah shared her story with us through letters and one short phone call. She described her experiences of childhood neglect and brutal rape, and how, in 2007, she was sentenced to twenty years to life for the murder of her stepmother. In one letter, Sarah included a picture of herself. It showed a petite young woman with large eyes and very long blonde hair, wearing prison sweats and smiling cautiously at the camera.

GOD SPARED MY LIFE FOR A GREATER PUNISHMENT LATER

My father was a missionary pastor in Meridian, Nevada. We were Evangelical Christians. My mother was a stay-at-home mom, taking care of six kids—four girls and two boys. We were very poor, but my mom worked miracles. She made our clothes or found bargains at the thrift stores. She always made sure that we had food to eat. I remember making "mommy mud pies" to try and cheer her up, as she was always very sad and often in tears.

Due to our religion, life was different. My brothers and sisters and I lived in fear of everyone else, as we were taught they were doing the devil's work and we had to be very careful not to displease God. When I was six, my parents divorced. My mom decided to go to college to be a nurse, as she had dreamt of doing since her own horrible childhood. During the divorce, the courts gave custody of the three oldest girls to my mother, and custody of my two brothers and me to my father. They split us fifty-fifty, like property. I first started drinking when I was nine years old. My mom says I tried to kill myself around then. I don't have many memories of that time in my life, but I do remember being very sad and feeling totally alone.

My mom was busy with college and she really couldn't supervise all the kids. We would do dumb things, and because my mom was overwhelmed, she would become abusive, mentally and sometimes physically. Also many of the men she brought home would make passes at my sisters. Because of all that, all of my teenage sisters moved to my dad's and lived with me and my brother. What teenager wouldn't want to move back with our father—after all, he was gone for weeks at a time on work trips, and our house was the party house when he was gone. When he was home, us kids would clean up and keep the friends away. But there were times when my mom came to pick us up for the weekend and our house was so trashed that there was literally a foot of filth on the floor and no food in the house. She began to take pictures every time she came over, to build a custody case against my father. A woman my dad probably met online moved into our home and she took care of us. She says that when she met us I only had one pair of panties and no clothes that fit me. I had cavities in most of my teeth and had no clue how to properly care for myself. Unfortunately she was only around for a year, because while she loved us, she maxed out all my father's credit cards buying things we needed. It forced him to file for bankruptcy and he threw her out.

Shortly after, Child Protection Services (CPS) took all of us kids away from our father and placed us with my mother. I was ten years old when I went to live with her. By then, she'd gotten her nursing degree and was living in Carson City. I turned eleven years old that summer. We lived in a trailer park in a double-wide trailer, and my mom was usually working twelve-hour shifts. My brother and sisters eventually ran away to Meridian to live with my dad, leaving me without them. I got more depressed. I attempted suicide at least twice more, once by hanging myself and once by taking a bottle of pills. Apparently God spared my life for a greater punishment later.

After my second suicide attempt, I spent several months at a psychiatric hospital called West Hills Hospital in Reno, Nevada, where the staff tried to figure out what was wrong with me. Eventually I was sent to a long-term treatment center called the Adolescent Treatment Center in Reno, where I was diagnosed with bipolar disorder. At the treatment center I felt like a guinea pig. I was placed on different prescription medications: Zoloft, Neurontin, Depakote, Seroquel, Thorazine, Vistaril, Topamax, Trazodone, Paxil[1]—and those are just the ones I remember. None of the pills seemed to be helping, and some made me feel worse.

Later, when I went to prison, I found out that I'd been misdiagnosed. The prison psychiatrist said that there was no way I could be bipolar. That doctor said the meds were actually what messed me up to begin with. I wish I had known back then that I wasn't the one who was mentally ill. My parents had the problems.

I was neglected and abused, but I wasn't crazy. I didn't want to go back to my dad's, as he'd remarried by then and my stepmother hated all of my father's kids, but especially me and my oldest brother. She called us names, she told us that she couldn't stand us, and that if my dad had to choose between us or her, he would choose her. The games she played were endless. She would freak out like a child, throwing things, slamming doors, threatening to eat lots of sweets, as she was diabetic. Everything was about control. However, when I'd tell my counselor at the treatment center what it was like at home, it was hard for him to believe me, since

---

[1] The medications in this group are often used to treat depression, anxiety, seizures, bipolar disorder, alcohol withdrawal, and symptoms of schizophrenia.

my father was a pastor and my stepmother was a preschool teacher, and they drove to Reno every week for family counseling.

My stepmom made life hell, and I turned back to drugs and alcohol. I felt hopeless and I wanted to die. My life at this time was very chaotic, and I began using meth as well. A cellmate I had at the treatment center would sneak in meth sometimes, and we'd do lines and eat it. I'm certain I was locked up for short periods of time in juvenile detention centers for running away and stuff, but that period of my life is hazy due to all the drugs I was doing then.

At that time I was thirteen and still on probation. One of my rules on probation was to take my prescription pills, but my pills made me go from wanting to hurt myself to getting really violent and angry. School was really hard for me because I had so much going on at home, but I had to bottle it up, since my stepmom was always looking for a reason to call my probation officer.

I went to live with my mom the summer before my freshman year. I loved it. But then she began to date my future stepfather. He would yell at me and say I was possessed by demons, so I ran away. I was gone with strangers for a week or two, getting high on meth the entire time, and had no intention of ever going home again. But I was reported as a runaway, and the cops started looking for me. One night, I was taken to a gas station by a woman who lived where I was hiding. She made me promise not to tell where I was or who I was with, and then she let me call my sister, Mary, to come get me. Mary took me home that night, but the next morning she let the cops get me. I was taken to West Hills Hospital again to detox. I was really messed up. After that, my mom threw my stuff out and told me I could never live with her again, so I was released to live with my father in Meridian.

I WAS NUMB TO THE WORLD

The summer I was fourteen, after a three-day binge on meth where I hadn't slept, my stepmother told me that she was taking me to get drug tested and that I was going to jail, so I ran next door to stay with my best friend's mom. My best friend wasn't there at the time—he was in California with his aunt and uncle. I would smoke weed with her, sometimes several times a day. One day, my friend's mom also allowed her forty-seven-year-old uncle to start shooting me up with meth—I had never shot up before—and then he raped me. For the next week they shot me up and raped me over and over. Then they sold me to their drug dealer to pay for drugs. He watched my friend's mom do things to me, and I had to do stuff to him and sleep with him. As brutal as the rapes were physically, psychologically I suffered the deepest wounds that would take years to heal.

Once, when I was being raped, some friends of my rapists saw what was going on and went next door to my stepmom. They told her where I was and what was happening to me, but she just told them to leave. Then she pretended not to know where I was or what was happening to me. She even called the police asking if they'd found me yet, saying that she knew something bad was happening to me and that they just had to find me. And all the while she knew I was next door, being raped.

The people who my stepmother turned away went to the police, but unfortunately one had a warrant out for her arrest, and she was put in jail. Two days later, the police came to get me. By then I'd been at that house for six days, and I believe I was totally brainwashed or something, because when the police came, I was protecting the people who had done horrible things to me. I actually had it in my head that my rapists were trying to protect me from my dad and stepmom, and that they cared about me. I was messed up. After the police got me, I was placed in a foster home for several weeks, and finally I was released to live with my sister Mary in Sparks, Nevada. I'd just turned fifteen. I was so messed up from the rapes that I had no respect for myself. I was embarrassed, ashamed, and blamed myself for it all. I was numb to the world. I dressed trashy and would sit at bus stops waiting until a stranger would come by and pick me up. I didn't care if anything happened to me. I also started having blackouts at that time.

I was spun out when I showed up for my court date about the rapes. The judge ordered me to be detained until I could get into treatment for both the drug abuse and the rapes. So I was then taken to Western Nevada Regional Youth Center, where I stayed for three months in an empty cell. I was locked down for twenty-three hours a day, awaiting an open bed at Spring Mountain Treatment Center in Las Vegas, Nevada. Then a bed opened and I was transported to Las Vegas, where I spent the next year.

During that time, the post-traumatic stress disorder (PTSD) from the rapes caused me to have night terrors, flashbacks that resembled seizures. I had conversations I have no memory of, and blackouts where I would get violent. Other girls at the treatment center would make comments and then I would freak out and beat them up. Afterward I'd have no memory of any of it.

I punched walls and doors, bloodying my hands. At night when I was asleep, I would claw at my private parts and be screaming and thrashing around, and staff would have to wake me up. The medications were not helping.

I had one good counselor, and she had me do packets from a book on PTSD, and that really helped me. The packets were designed to help me deal with guilt, denial, blame, anger, mistrust, feelings of hopelessness and self-hate. It made me draw pictures and remember details that I desperately wanted to forget, but it made me see things clearer and feel confident that I could protect myself in the end. I pretty much had no choice but to get over it. I was tired. I wanted to be happy.

I THOUGHT THIS WAS HOW
THE REST OF MY LIFE WOULD BE

I was released at sixteen years old back to my father, and I was still on probation. For the most part I tried to stay clean and sober, but I was not happy. I really didn't have friends at that point, and the trial for the rapes was starting.

We lived in a small farm town with a few horse ranches around. When I was seventeen my dad and I got into a big fight about a horse that was supposed to be mine, but that he had put in his name. I don't think I'd ever seen my dad that mad. I left the house and went to my boyfriend's, and then I got a call from my dad saying I needed to pack up all my stuff and get out of his house. He said I needed to be home in ten minutes to do that or else. I was really, really scared. I don't why, but I had a bad feeling that my dad was going to hurt me, so I asked my brother to come with me.

I made it exactly on time, but my dad told me that he'd already spoken to my probation officer because I hadn't got there within ten minutes, and that I was going to be locked up. All that was going through my mind was the last time I was locked up and how horrible it was. I don't remember anything after that. I blacked out, like I did after I was raped. The next thing I remember is being in my parents' room inside the house, holding a gun from my boyfriend's house. My ears were ringing so bad and my stepmom was on the floor. I went to the church where my grandparents used to go, and I think I blacked out again. The next thing I remember is crawling through fences from the police.

As soon as the cops came to get me, I got to see how I would be viewed and treated for the rest of my life. I was dragged through the gravel in front of the house, even though I no longer had the gun and I wasn't resisting. The cops told my dad that they would do anything and everything to make sure that I got the max.

I was seventeen years old, I was terrified, I had no clue what was going to happen to me, and I had absolutely no one fighting for me. I was taken to county jail. In county the cops were horrible to me. For the first couple of weeks I was kept in a rubber cell, with only a mattress, a blanket, and a roll of toilet paper. There wasn't even a toilet, only a hole in the ground. I slept on the mattress on the ground, and sewage would rise up on the floor. Ants would crawl all over the ground and all over me, not to mention the bugs that would crawl up from the hole in the ground. When I was let out at night to shower, the porters would clean the rubber room with ammonia and bleach together, and the cops would put me back in there. I would be coughing and choking and I'd hear them laughing.

The worst thing was that one of the men who raped me when I was fourteen was in the jail that was housed right next to me. For two weeks, the cops would let him yell at me and taunt me.

There was only one cop who treated me well. I wanted someone to be nice to me, so I didn't care why he was doing it. He would stand out of the camera's view and he'd put his hands through the bars and touch my breasts, or put his hands down my pants and finger me. Sometimes he'd take me to another room without a camera and "pat search" me, feeling all over me and inside me, but the room was right by other officers, so we didn't have sex. In December 2007 I was sentenced as an adult for first-degree murder. Everyone told me that if I didn't take a deal I would get one hundred years for shooting and killing my stepmother, so I pled guilty. The trial judge gave me twenty years to life.

The women's prison is in southern Nevada, so women in northern Nevada who are sentenced to prison are taken to the men's prison first to await transportation to the women's prison. For eight days, me and an old lady sat in a cell with nothing. We were given dirty orange jumpsuits to wear, and we never got to change them. The room was freezing, and the blankets didn't keep us warm; they were dirty and had holes. We had nothing to properly bathe ourselves, no way to comb our hair. The cell was disgusting, and we were locked in it 24/7. The officers would ignore us altogether or call us whiny, needy bitches if we asked for anything. It really scared me, because I thought this was how the rest of my life would be.

Eventually I was taken to the women's prison in Las Vegas. The woman who raped me as a child was there for another crime, so after intake I was put in protective custody. I didn't want to be in protective custody. I felt it was a punishment—I wasn't a kid any more, and I could handle myself. Then the prison decided to place me in the mental health unit because it was locked down, and therefore they could ensure I wouldn't be in contact with the person who raped me. At least that way, I wasn't in P.C. and I could still do some programs.

I MESSED UP, BUT DID I DESERVE TO LIVE IN FEAR?

There were officers who I was close to. One touched me and let me touch him down there. He led me to believe he loved me and would help get me out if we were together. I was hoping that, by doing things he asked me to, he would get me out. Another officer would hold me, feel my body, but nothing really bad. Eventually I told the prison about them. As far as I know, nothing happened to them.

Then I got close to a forty-five-year-old officer. At the time I thought he was the only person who cared about me. I did anything for him, as I didn't want to lose him. I lived in a cell alone, and whenever he came around I would take my clothes off and he'd watch me get into different positions and do things he asked. Once in a while he'd open the door and kiss me and touch my naked body. Once he even came in during count[2] and kissed me all over my body and put his mouth between my thighs and performed oral sex on me. I wanted it, though; he didn't force me. He set up a P.O. box on the outside and we wrote letters to each other using that box.

I had no one and he acted like my knight. But as the relationship continued, I began to realize that he was taking advantage of my situation. I realized that, in the real world, I probably wouldn't have looked twice at him, and if a man his age pursued me I would probably have been afraid and got help. It was true, even if I hadn't been willing to admit it. So I tried distancing myself. When that happened, he got scary. The last night I saw him, I tried breaking things off and he tripped out on me. I was outside my cell, alone with him in the dark where no one could see us. He told me that I was dumb and I didn't know what I was doing. I was crying and he grabbed my arm, but then two superior ranking officers came out and saw us. It was pure luck, because the situation was getting worse and he was scaring me. He looked crazy.

---

[2] A regular prison security procedure where inmates return to their assigned cells to be counted by prison staff.

There was an investigation into our relationship, as by that time many things had been overheard or witnessed, but I refused to cooperate. I thought that if I told the truth, nothing would happen to me, but I knew he would lose his job. So I denied everything to protect him. But somehow his wife found our letters. When she turned in my letters to him, he was fired and I was given two years in the hole[3] for not talking to begin with. Mind you, officers are walked off all the time for having sex with the girls. And no other inmate ever did hole time for having sex with a guard. I was being punished for protecting him, not for what we'd done.

Life got a lot worse after everyone found out I'd had a relationship with an officer and he'd gotten fired because of it. Everyone quit talking to me. The officers would totally ignore me if I needed something. They started tearing up my cell every time they had "random" cell searches, leaving everything trashed so bad I'd often have to spend hours trying to clean up and salvage what photos, letters, and other paperwork they hadn't destroyed.

The officers started to taunt me so bad that the other girls in the hole began to scream and yell at them, telling them to leave me alone. Their solution was to move me to the death row cells where no one could see or hear what they did to me. The morning after I was moved to death row, I woke up with hundreds of thousands of little bugs crawling all over me, the blankets, and the bed. They were coming from cracks in the walls and they were all over the floor, everything.

Needless to say, the officers refused to move me to another cell. When I'd try to ask for something I needed, they would close the door between me and them. Even when they came around to pass out food trays through slots in the door, they would often ignore me completely.

These officers are supposed to be here to protect us, not to take advantage of us. I was being punished for being a teenage girl when

---

[3] A colloquial term for administrative segregation or solitary confinement, where a person in prison is isolated from the general prison population for disciplinary or security reasons. For more details, see the glossary.

these grown men were trying to get with me. It was unfair. I messed up, but did I deserve nearly two years in the hole? Did I deserve to live in fear?

MOSTLY I SIT AND TRY AND STAY POSITIVE

In January 2010, I was taken to a men's prison in Carson City, Nevada, to await transfer to another facility out of state. I spent five months at the men's prison, waiting for them to find a state to accept me. For the first six days I got put in a cell alone, with nothing. On the sixth day, when I asked a nurse if I could get my clothes washed or some clean underwear, an officer came back screaming at me. He told me to "leave the fucking nurses alone" and that he wasn't going to put up with my "high-maintenance bullshit."

Eventually they put me in the infirmary with women who were sick and dying. The sick women were in the men's prison because the women's prison didn't have a sufficient medical unit. Often, only about ten feet or less from our window, we would watch the coroner's van load up the dead bodies of inmates. We'd listen to officers laugh and make jokes about them, like, "Well, that's one more down."

When the officers found out about my relationship with that officer in Las Vegas, they started making my life hell. They filed false reports on me, and told me that if I gave them any problems they'd put me upstairs with the inmates who'd lost their minds. I don't know what was in the reports, but a caseworker at the prison told me that she kept getting reports on me and I'd better knock it off or I'd have everything taken from me and be moved upstairs. When I asked her what she was talking about, she said, "Quit fucking playing games. You know what you were doing." That was a typical response. They said I'd be stripped down, strapped to a bed, and drugged so no one would have to deal with my shit. My time there wasn't easy.

On May 13, 2010, I arrived at this women's center where I am now. It's in the middle of nowhere, where I have no one. I've only been here for six and a half months, but I'm still not adjusted. It's a "safe" prison. It's definitely not the environment I'm used to. Only one officer has truly been inappropriate with me, and he transferred to the men's prison.

Your crime determines the color you wear at first, and the privileges you get. The fewer points you get, the more privileges you get. For example, yellow is for intake and segregated people; blue is for inmates with eighteen points or more; red is for inmates with eleven to seventeen points; and green is for inmates with zero to ten points. If you're under twenty-six years old you get two points. If your crime is violent you also get points. For me I got five extra points for first-degree murder. Prior convictions give you points, so some people come here already condemned. Then you can get points for disciplinary behavior. We're housed by color. Green inmates get all day out and can work anywhere; blue and red get four hours out of their cell, yellow get five hours out if they're intake and three if they're in segregation. I was blue when I first got here. Now I'm red.

I'm lonely here, and I don't fit in. I can't afford college[4] and I can't apply for almost any educational and job training opportunities because I have a life sentence. Mostly I sit and try to be positive. I work, stay physically fit, write, and read—I like to read political and historical books—anything that keeps me from feeling like I am rotting away. Right now I am writing proposals to get things changed for the better in here. I want to start advocating for inmates being targeted. I'm also hoping to start a newsletter for the facility.

I feel like I'm wasting away in here sometimes, so I busy myself with little projects for my family. I call my dad often, and for the first time we have a good relationship. I call one of my sisters regularly, and some holidays I get to talk to my other siblings. My dad and new stepmom visit,

---

[4] Due to cuts in federal and state grants for prison education, the Department of Corrections has been forced to cut its free course offerings. Many women are thus required to pay local community colleges for credits necessary to obtain their degrees. The community college closest to Sarah Chase charges $103 per credit hour—$1,236 for a full semester. These fees mean that a college education is unobtainable for many people making prison wages.

and all my sisters and my mom have visited. I make my entire family gifts at Christmas. I crochet a lot of things for them, like stuffed animals, blankets. I've also made jewelry and picture frames, and some drawings. I've written down my favorite recipes to make little cookbooks for them. I can't talk to them about a lot of things, but I'm glad I'm still involved in their lives somewhat. It kind of feels like we're strangers; we aren't real close, but it's okay. I love them all very much still.

I hope to get out of here one day and have a family, a home, and a business, but I'm not sure what kind yet. I've grown up a lot. But I still have to serve a long time before I can even ask for parole.

TERI HANCOCK

34, formerly imprisoned

Teri uses box fans to prop open the windows in her small duplex, her thin blonde hair sticking to her face and neck in the heat as she shoves the fans into place. She apologizes for the rough neighborhood, and reminds us to lock all doors and windows. She talks at first about the dolphin mural she put on the back window of her car, and her prized dolphin figurine. She is relaxed and smiling, sharing recollections of riding horses on her family's farm when she was little. As the conversation turns toward her childhood abuse and the sexual abuse she faced in prison, she quickly lights the first of many cigarettes. However, she perseveres with her story until she can talk through to the present, bringing the conversation back to her hopes for the future and her desire to go back to school before she turns forty.

I ALWAYS REMEMBER HORSES

I always remember horses. My mom had a thing with them; she was a fanatic. That's what we used to do all the time together, horseback riding on our farm in Michigan. We had seventeen horses on our farm, and I'd go out to the field and jump up on this old Appaloosa with a sway in his back. I'd pull myself up and put my feet up on his neck. He was old, he would just walk around and eat, and I would lay up there for hours. At that point, life was kind of good. It got worse as I got older, though.

My mom divorced my father when she was pregnant with me, and when I was a few months old she married another man. I never called him Dad, but he was like a father to me and my older brother. I'd say my childhood was good, until I was about eight or nine years old. My mom divorced her second husband then, and started dating this other man, Steve. That's when everything went bad.

Steve was a full-blooded Blackfoot Indian, born and raised on the reservation. He was also a drug dealer, and once my mom got with him, she got into drugs. Her thoughts of me and my brother changed. I think she was more interested in the fast life and the money, and drinking and doing drugs, than the two of us kids.

My mom and Steve were going on vacations all the time—Hawaii, California, Detroit—and just leaving me by myself with all the responsibilities of the farm and the house. I couldn't go to school because I had to stay home and make sure the animals were taken care of. My mom would leave us by ourselves for weeks. I was eight or nine and she'd leave me and my brother up on the farm with the seventeen horses. I had responsibilities to take care of them, and I would miss weeks of school because there was no one to drive me.

When my brother was fifteen, my mom ended up giving him away because he stole some money from her bedroom drawer. He was just a kid, you know what I'm saying? He probably just thought, *Oh wow, lots of money! Let me grab some!* My mom was so mad she gave up her rights to him. My brother moved to my grandparents' house, which was in Florida, and then my uncle Mark took him to Texas with him, and I guess that's where he lives now.

I guess I got to a point where I was comfortably numb and I didn't care what people thought, what they said to me, what they did. I closed myself off. My mom was gone so much, and I did what I wanted, so when she tried to put authority down and tell me do this, do this, do this, I would rebel and do what I wanted to do. I thought, *I'm taking care of myself anyway. You're not doing anything.* Don't get me wrong, I love my mother, but she decided to do the things that she was doing, and I did a lot of bad things myself.

I was twelve when I first drank and smoked a joint with my mother. She said she'd rather have me drink and smoke in front of her than go out in the streets doing it somewhere else. I'd been smoking cigarettes for a while. She tried to stop me—she'd rip up the cigarettes, flush them down the toilet, try and make me smoke a whole pack—until she got to the point of thinking, "She ain't going to stop. I'd rather have her smoke in front of me than burn the house down."

Things started to go really wrong for me when I was about thirteen or fourteen. One time my mom wanted to go to Hawaii, but she couldn't leave me alone because I'd gotten in trouble by not being in school. So she dropped me off at a juvenile detention facility. When I first got there, I had a quarantine period that you have to go through like you do in prison, but it's a little different. They sit you in this chair and they have these cameras that watch you, and you have to sit there for hours. You can't move. You have to sit and think about why you're there, and every time you move or get up out of that chair they add time to it. I'm a very active person, I don't like to sit still, so that was so hard for me. You couldn't even go by the window—they had these plastic bar things on the window that if you touched, an alarm would go off. It was a mess.

I FELT LIKE I WASN'T WORTH ANYTHING

When Steve drank, he'd pull me up onto his lap and make me sit there. If I got up and moved, he would beat the shit out of me. I mean, I could sit there for twelve to thirteen hours. I would end up peeing on myself because I was scared to get up and go to the bathroom. Once, I pissed all over his leg.

From the very beginning, Steve beat on me. One time he hit me in the back of the head with a cast-iron frying pan, knocked me out, and dragged me across the floor by my hair. Another time he put my head through the wall. He held the whole back of my head in the palm of his hand, and all I could see was wood going through my eyes. I tried to cover my face with my hands, but before I could get my hands up there I could feel the wood smashing. I had a big old gash in my forehead, and my mom just butterfly-stitched it up. I begged her to do something. I asked her, "Why are you allowing him to do this to me?" She never would answer me. She would just stare off into space, and that made me feel like I wasn't worth anything.

The only thing she'd do was tell me not to press charges. My god-mother, she's state police, and she used to come and get me all the time and beg me not to drop the charges. But I couldn't do that to my mom. She was happy, you know what I'm saying? Every time Steve beat me she would promise me that she wouldn't let him do that any more. Then the next time would come around and he'd do it again. It just got worse as time went by.

My mom would take me and hide me from him in hotel rooms for a day or two, or drop me off at this cabin she had up in the woods in Gladwin County, about five miles from our house. It got to the point where Steve shot the windows out in my bedroom with a 9-millimeter and made me lay in the glass. It was February, freezing cold. I had glass all over me, all in me, all over the place. While I was laying there, he threw his boots at me, he threw pots and pans. I knew better than to get up, because the consequences were going to be worse. My mom just sat there and said nothing.

EVERYBODY KNEW ABOUT IT, BUT NOBODY WOULD SAY ANYTHING

Steve would use me as a drug trafficker all over the country, even to Canada, and once to France. He taped the drugs to me because customs wouldn't check me—I'm a kid, I've got boots up to here, and I've got drugs stuffed down them. I was taught to lie. It's a secret, you smile and act like everything is peaches and cream, when it's really not. Steve also used my name to send money to friends of his in jail, other drug smugglers like him, because he didn't want there to be any affiliation with him. I didn't know any better.

When I was fourteen, my mom and Steve bought me a brand new bed set, but then afterward they gave me to Steve's brother for sex. I couldn't understand why my mom would sit there in the next room and just allow that to happen. You know what I'm saying? I'm your baby, I'm your youngest, I'm your daughter, why would you do that to me? That went on for a long time. Everybody knew about it, but nobody would say anything. I begged and pleaded with my grandparents and my mom's baby brother, and they would turn their back on me, refuse to help me. I had never had sex until then, but to them I was a slut, I was a tramp, I was a no-good bitch. I think that's what made me so bitter about things. I mean, I'm really angry with my mother still after all these years.

Finally I ran away, but the cops found me two days later. My mom and Steve had to come get me from the jail. They were all excited to see me until I got in the car. I begged the cops to drive me home, because I knew what would happen as soon as I got in the car. As soon as we got out of that parking lot, oh Jeeze oh Petes, Steve swung back with his hand and hit me in the side of the head. I thought for sure my head was going to go through the window. My mom just sat there and did nothing.

IT WAS LIKE IT DIDN'T REALLY HAPPEN

When I was fifteen, Steve kept kicking me out and then reporting me as a runaway. Finally, I got sick of it. I said, "The hell with this. You're not beating me any more, you're not shooting windows out and making me lay in the glass any more. You're not going to make me lay down and sleep with your brother any more." I'd had enough by that point. The next time he kicked, I just took off.

I ran away to Grand Rapids to stay with my boyfriend Chuck. Chuck sold drugs for Steve in Grand Rapids, and we'd been together since I was twelve. He didn't want to sell for Steve any more because he kept seeing how Steve was abusing me. He'd been there through all of it, seeing all the bruises, the cuts, the stitches, just all kinds of stuff. He wanted to get back at Steve for all the dirt that he had done to me, and you know, it sounded good to me—I wanted to get back at him, too. So we had this idea of going back to my mom and Steve's house, breaking into the storage area where he kept his stuff, and taking it.

We called Chuck's mom, who lived about two miles through the woods to my mom and Steve's, and she told us that they were gone for the weekend at a family reunion. We thought, *Great, we'll go see Chuck's mom and sister, and then break into Steve's storage shed and take his money.* We knew he had bills in a briefcase in the back of a car that he kept in storage, plus we knew he stored his marijuana there.

It was early August 1993. I went with Chuck, his brother Paul, and Chuck's friend Mike up to Steve's storage unit. It was up in Meridian County, and it was a large place, with big units for RV storage and smaller, regular units too. We cut a hole in the fence, and I went through and pointed them in the right direction. I told them where to go, I mapped it out, showed them what number it was and how to get in. Then I came back out. When they got back and didn't have the money, they wanted to go to my mom and Steve's house to get the money out of the safe. I told them how to get into the house through a broken window, and that my mom and Steve kept his safe underneath the bed. I didn't go with them to the house; I stayed with Paul in the car, about a half mile down the street.

Chuck and Mike went into the house. They had five or six different guns that they'd picked up at the storage center, including a 12-gauge shotgun and a 9-millimeter. I wasn't there, so everything I'm saying now I only know from what happened in court. While Chuck and Mike were inside, my mom and Steve came back with my aunt and uncle. They'd all come home early from the family reunion.

Chuck and Mike shot my mom. They blew her left arm off and shot her in the face and then shot her in the stomach. They took Steve's .357 Magnum, shot him in the eye, and then unloaded the rest of it into his chest. They shot my aunt and uncle once in the face with the double-barrel. Then they poured gas all over the house and threw in a half stick of dynamite and blew it up.

I didn't find out until the next day all that had taken place, because Chuck and Mike only came by to where Paul and I were waiting for them for a moment. They told us to meet them later, and so Paul and I went back to Grand Rapids. When we got there, Chuck and Mike finally called, and told us to drive to Saginaw to meet up with them. In Saginaw, at first they didn't tell me what happened—they just said they didn't get anything in the robbery. So I drove back to Grand Rapids with Paul, and Chuck stayed in Saginaw with Mike. He said he had a few things to do, that he could get a ride home. As soon as Paul and I got to Grand Rapids we got a call from Paul and Chuck's mom saying that my house had burnt down, and that they'd found four bodies in the house.

At this point, I went numb. This is kind of the way I always respond to bad things, to strong emotions. I'd much rather shut them down so I don't have to feel anything. Part of me wished I could have taken my mom's place, so she wouldn't have to die. But part of me felt relieved that I wouldn't have to worry about Steve shooting the windows out and making me lay in the glass, or trying to run me over in his car, or kicking me out, or being forced to have sex with his brother any more.

Paul and I went back up to Saginaw, and that's when Chuck and Mike finally told us what had happened in that house. Chuck said, "I didn't do nothing, it was Mike." When Chuck and Mike were explaining it, they were joking and laughing. It was like it didn't really happen. I didn't really know what to believe. They were high and drunk, and they thought it was funny. I was in shock, I was freaking out. I didn't know what the hell to do, because I was a co-conspirator now. I'd taken them there—I might as well have pulled the trigger.

I left Chuck and Mike in Saginaw and went back home. Then I went to the police and turned myself in. I also ended up turning state's evidence against Chuck and Mike.

I was charged with four counts of first-degree murder, four counts of armed robbery, and four felony counts of use of a firearm. I was also charged with arson and breaking and entering. Because I'd turned myself in and testified, they dropped the murder charges. They dropped everything but the armed robbery and one felony use of a firearm.

I was supposed to be sentenced as a juvenile because I was only sixteen when I was arrested, but 1994 was an election year, and I was sentenced as an adult. I was given a sentence of four to fifteen years, plus another two. I had to do the firearm felony first, which was two flat, and then start the four to fifteen.

In my pre-sentence report there were all the details of the four murders, so that was one of the reasons it was so hard for me to get out of jail. Every time I came up for parole, the parole board would read this old report about the murders and just keep me in jail. The sentencing judge had told me I'd only do four years, but because of this messed up pre-sentence report, I just kept getting sent back for more and more time. Eventually, the errors with the pre-sentence report ended up being the reason I was ultimately released, though it would take seven years for my appeal to make it back to the judge. When he finally got my appeal, the judge was furious about how long I'd been in, and he let me out. But it would take seven years, and a lot would happen in that time.

HE COULD SEE ALL THE PAIN THAT I CARRIED

At first when I was in juvenile detention, it wasn't too bad. There were a lot of good people working in juvie. They tried to help me. They had threats on my life from Steve's family, and the media kept finding out where I was at and trying to take pictures, so the juvie staff had to keep moving me to different rooms. I did what they told me to do. They told me to get my GED, so I did. It took me four months. I was seventeen, but I had it. I also took their Assaultive Offender Group,[1] because they

---

[1] For details about Michigan's Assaultive Offender Program, see the glossary.

said I had to have that. I know how to draw, so I took graphic arts, and also a program for illustrations and computer design. I took classes on codependency, about HIV and AIDS, domestic violence, drugs, and self-esteem. I even took an eating disorder class, because it was pounded into my head that I was fat. Steve used to tell me I was fat, even though I only weighed 112 pounds. I tried really hard to better myself.

In the first adult prison I was put in, things weren't so bad for me. There were a few good guards. They didn't treat me like a criminal. Instead they said, "She's a kid. She just lost her mother, her home, her family." One guard in particular really tried to help me realize that just because bad things in life happen, it didn't mean that I was a bad person. He said he could see all the pain that I carried, and he tried to keep me out of a lot of trouble. He was a lieutenant, and he'd basically tell my unit officer and the sergeants that run around, "If she gets in any trouble, radio me, send her to her bunk and make her sit there until I get there." He was like my father. His daughters were the same age as me, and he used to say that they could be in the same situation that I was in. He'd say, "All it takes is one wrong turn. You're driving down the street, accidentally not paying attention, and you hit somebody." He helped me realize that not everybody's bad.

I think it's partly because of his inspiration that I took vocational training and college courses. I stopped getting in trouble, I got a job working in the kitchen, I was going to college. My days were full. I was going from one place to another all day until nighttime. Then I would go into my unit, take a shower, and then fall out until four o'clock in the morning. That lieutenant really helped me change the way I viewed things. When they told me that I had to leave, I cried. I didn't know what I was going to do. I freaked out because I'd never really had anybody just care about me as a person and my well-being before. It was a really bad transition for me to move from my comfort zone.

I FIGURED IF I SAID NOTHING,
I'D STILL GET MY FREEDOM

My problems really started in 2000, when I was transferred to Western Wayne Prison. Western Wayne had transitioned from being a men's prison to a women's, but they left all the guards there that had been there with the men. Suddenly all these female prisoners came in, busloads of them. It was like a big-ass orgy going on at the prison; the guards were fucking with everybody.

I ended up in a bad situation with the assistant deputy warden, the ADW. I was his clerk, his cleaner. I cleaned the control center, the visiting room, the ADW offices, and the security offices. Because I worked in a secure area, every time I went in and out of there I had to be stripped, so I was getting stripped three, four, five times a day.

I worked the night shift in the control center, 2 a.m. to 10 a.m. Everything closes down then, even the wardens go home, but the ADW would stay. He would always call me up there to be with him. Officers started asking questions, making jokes and stuff, which wasn't funny because I wasn't doing anything; I would just go up there, do my job, and come back.

One night he called me up, so I checked in and grabbed my cleaning supplies. Now, I had bottles in this hand, bottles in that hand, I had garbage bags and stuff hanging out of both my pockets, and I was on my way to get the vacuum from the closet. Then the ADW came and pushed me into a room and closed the door. He said, "If you make any noise, you're the one who's going to be in trouble, not me. I can cause problems for you."

He bent me over and pulled my pants down. I still had all my cleaners and stuff in my hands. He tired to push himself in me, and with me being in prison for so long and being so young, it was like being a virgin all over again. He ripped me and I started bleeding all over the place. Then he sent me back to my unit to clean up and take a shower. He told the officers that I'd had a "female accident."

I couldn't tell anyone. My appeal was still in the courts, and I wanted to go home. I'd been in prison for so long, so I figured if I said nothing and just let it happen, I'd still get my freedom.

The next time I went back up to the control center, the ADW forced me to give him oral sex. The first time that happened, I puked on him, so I had to clean that up. This became an everyday thing for two years. One day, one of the girls in the control center counted that the ADW had called me out seventeen times. Seventeen times he'd assaulted me that day. I had bruises and marks, and officers were asking me how I was getting these hand prints. I was scared of the ADW, so I refused healthcare, but how was I supposed to explain that? I think that's one of the reasons why I have a hard time with men touching me now. Because he damaged me. I feel damaged.

EVERYHING HAD CRASHED DOWN ON TOP OF ME

At the time, my case was going on. My writs and stuff would come through the control center, and when they do that you have to sign to get your legal mail.[2] But I wasn't even getting mine. My attorney would call me and say, "You missed a court date today." I had no idea what was going on. It didn't dawn on me that the ADW was stealing my stuff. I was eligible for camp at that time, which meant I was eligible to go outside the gates and work in society. But my papers kept disappearing. It turned out that he'd been shredding my legal mail, and had put a red flag in my file that said I was a problematic prisoner, so they couldn't transfer me out of Western Wayne. Every time I was up for parole, it was the ADW's job to write a statement to the parole board. What was he saying? I don't know, I wasn't allowed to see it. But they never gave me parole. He was trying to hold me there until my max day—that way he could have what he wanted.

---

[2] Mail to a person in prison from an attorney or officer of the court, or legal documents related to their case, has greater privacy privileges than regular mail. For more details, see the glossary and Appendix VIII.

I had bruises all over my body, and he would tear me up. It would make me walk funny, and some of the officers would joke about it. They'd say things like, "Oh, did you run into the mop bucket again?"

Finally, in 2001, after about a year of this, the abuse got so bad that I decided to say something. I told the counselors, and they had me file a grievance against him, but the warden rejected it. They said I hadn't done it in a timely manner.

Then the other officers started really giving me a hard time. They tossed my cell, threw away my stuff. They ripped up my pictures, took my letters. In the middle of this my father passed away. They didn't tell me for six days, so I couldn't go view his body, I couldn't go see him and say goodbye. Oh my god, I was so upset. I was so mad, I flipped out. I threw a pool ball at the window. I lit a cigarette and was walking up and down the hall with it. I was screaming that I wanted to use the phone. Then they took me to the control center to see the ADW. They said I needed to go through him to see where my mind was at, to see if they needed to call someone in to talk to me. He was supposed to decide if I was okay. Of course he said I was fine.

But everything had crashed down on top of me. Now I had nothing. My dad was dead. I had this man raping me, this man who was supposed to be protecting me and watching over my well-being.

YOU WOULD NOT BELIEVE THE EXTENT OF THE RETALIATION

The assaults only ended because I wrote a letter to a friend of mind who was at camp, and I told her what was going on. The camp then sent the letter to internal affairs. The ADW had his friends threaten me before the investigation. They told me that if I kept quiet I wouldn't be retaliated against, I would be left alone. They said I'd be able to go home, but if the investigation continued, he'd lose his job, and then everybody would come down on me.

I was afraid, and I lied to the investigators, told them nothing was happening, that the ADW was just my boss, a good friend. It was hard for me to sit there and tell them that. In the end they moved me to another facility. They took me out of his hands, and he couldn't assault me any more.

The ADW was suspended with pay for a little while, and then he went to his union and had a hearing. Me and some of the other girls had to come and testify. But they didn't care about what we had to say, and he got his job back. The one thing they said was that he couldn't work in a women's facility any more, but nothing else happened to him.

When I got to the new facility, a camp, another prisoner told me that she'd been sexually assaulted, too, and that she had a lawyer who was helping her out. The investigators were still interested in my situation with the ADW. They hadn't believed me when I'd said nothing happened. Well, it was time for me to get some help with all this. The prison wasn't going to be on my side, and I needed a lawyer of my own. So I called the lawyer the next day and she came up to see me. Getting into the visiting room to see her was my worst nightmare. The female officer stripped me in the bathroom, took my chain, my glasses. She made me strip in front of everybody who was in the bathroom, even the male officers, because she'd kept the door open. The officer then went into my room and took all my legal work. She even took the notebook that I was supposed to give to my lawyer, with the list of dates of what happened to me. I had to redo everything.

My lawyer was working toward trying to stop the officers from harassing me and physically assaulting me. Our goal was just to stop them from doing things like taking me out of my room in the middle of the night and moving me to another facility, keeping my property, strip-searching me, taking my mail, stealing my photographs. You would not believe the extent of the retaliation.

One time that female officer who stripped me just went crazy on me when I was talking to my lawyer, screaming at me and at her too. But my lawyer wouldn't have it. She said, "Excuse me. I'm her lawyer. I'd appreciate it if you don't talk to her like that any more." Then she said to me, "Teri, you can go back in there and sit, I'll be right back."

My lawyer got the attorney general to tell the officers that they couldn't abuse me, they couldn't come into my room without permission, and they couldn't strip me without permission, unless I was on a visit or I was doing a random urine drop.

I'M STILL STANDING

After I got transferred to the camp, the ADW had no control over my writs or my legal mail any more. Then, seven years after I was sentenced, I finally got into the courts in front of the judge. The judge was furious about the seven years I'd been inside. He said he'd never meant it to be more than four, and he pulled my sentence back and released me directly out of the courthouse. Usually you have to go back to prison and be processed out, but he was so angry at what had gone on with me serving all that time, and experiencing all that abuse, that he just let me go. The prison didn't want to let me go, they were freaking out. The officers that escorted me to court said they wouldn't release me—they said I had to come back to the prison first. But the judge said, "No, you have no jurisdiction over her. Release her now. I'll hold you in contempt if you don't. She is free to go; she is no longer a ward of the state. She is a civilian now."

I had been in front of the parole board so many times that I just couldn't believe it was finally happening. I freaked out, I fell to my knees. The prison officers kept insisting that they could take me, and the judge kept saying no. Finally, the court officials just hustled me into another room. It took me a while to comprehend that I was really free.

After I got out, I took the ADW to court. That was hard, having to see him sitting right next to me, smiling, when I did my depositions. The state's answer was that he's working in men's facilities now, so it's okay. From their point of view, whatever he did to me was all right because I was a convict. That really upsets me. How can women bring charges when they're abused, when they know they're just going to be retaliated against? Even the officer who was assigned to help women like me with this kind of case, she was really on the side of the officers. She lost paperwork on purpose and disciplined women who filed charges. Officers stick together, right or wrong.

With the help of my lawyer and her friends, I came back up to Saginaw. I got a job, I got an apartment. I even went on *The Montel Williams Show*. But I don't sleep at night; I have really bad insomnia problems. I have nightmares, I wake up seeing him. It never goes away. I feel frustrated and closed in.

The hard part is, when I look in the mirror, I look just like my mom. That's been a real issue for me to deal with. I'm scared I'm going to be like her if I have children. That's probably the reason why I don't have any yet. I see her in me sometimes, when I get angry, and I just have to close myself off. I walk away from people and literally close myself off for days—I won't answer the phone or anything. I guess I go into a deep depression. There were a lot of things said between me and her that I can never take back. I mean, the last words you would hate to hear from your mother are, "I hate you and I wish I'd never had you." She said that to me. She said I would be the one to cause her death.

When I found and contacted my grandmother, she told me I was dead to her, right along with my mother, and I should never call again. I don't have family to turn to for advice or anything. It hurts, and I'm scared.

I was trying to get therapy, but the therapist is in Detroit, and it's a long way to drive a couple of times a week. But I want to have a normal life. I want to get the past behind me. I know it'll never go away, it'll always be part of my life. But here I am today, still standing.

EMILY MADISON

45, formerly imprisoned

Emily is a tall, African American woman with the physique of a basketball player and a strong, firm handshake. She has asked to meet in the family restaurant across the street from the prison in which she spent most of her twenties and thirties. Visible from the restaurant is a patch of green surrounded by triple barbed wire—the prison yard. Emily likes the view because it reminds her of when she was inside, and how she would fantasize about eating at that restaurant. She says it gives her strength to remember. Over the course of the meeting, Emily tells of being raised by a crack addict mother, of her younger sister's pregnancy at thirteen, and of her decision to go into sex work at sixteen in order to support her sister and baby nephew. The conversation falters only once, when she starts talking about the crime that put her in prison. Emily describes how, in November 1986, she stabbed a man to death while defending herself against sexual assault. A year later, she was convicted of first-degree murder and given a mandatory life sentence. "I can never forget what I did," she says. She also describes her experiences of being abused and retaliated against in prison, and her decade-long fight to bring to justice those who perpetuated the abuses.

I ALWAYS TRIED TO MAKE EVERYBODY HAPPY

I grew up in Detroit. I remember always being in charge of taking care of my little sister, who's twenty-two months younger than me. I remember holding her hand and walking her to school, with the house key tied around my neck on a shoestring.

My sister and I were supposed to go over to our father's house every weekend because he paid child support. I wanted to go and see my father, and my mother took that as a slight. At first she was just verbally abusive. She would say things like, "You ungrateful bitch. I take care of you every day, I feed you and you want to run over there to him." Then in 1972, when I was six, he married a woman called Danielle. I don't have any bad stepmother stories, only positive ones, because Danielle took me in when my mother threw me out, and even to this day, I go over there. She gave me a huge barbecue when I came home from prison. She hired a DJ, and she even had a porta-potty in the backyard.

My mother was definitely meaner after my father remarried. I didn't know what to do. I didn't want her to be mad at me and I didn't want her to think that I liked my stepmother more than her. I always tried to make everybody happy, and I'd try to make my mother happy, but it didn't matter. Sometimes she would tell me she hated me and that I was the reason for all of her problems. She was fourteen when she had me, and she resented having to get married so young.

My mother began using drugs when I was twelve. She was on heroin and cocaine. When I was fourteen she beat me really bad because I'd hidden her drugs. My little sister said she'd seen me with the drug kit, and then my mother got really mad. She slapped me, she punched me, and she hit me with an extension cord, a coat hanger, and a metal curtain rod. I was bruised and bloody, and I was lying in a fetal position covering up my face. And she kept saying, "Uncover your face, uncover your face."

After that happened I went to the Children's Center,[1] which is where we got counseling. My case manager's name was Miss Quinn, and I remember when I first walked into her office she gasped at the sight of me and put her hand over her mouth. She called Protective Services and they took

---

[1] A service agency in Detroit for at-risk children and youth.

me away to a school for girls in Detroit. It was nice there; they were really kind to me, and they let me go to my father on weekends. He and Danielle would pick me up and then I got to spend time with him. But I still thought it was my fault, because I was thinking that, had I never hid her drugs, she wouldn't have done it. When my mother and I went to court, she said how sorry she was and that she really didn't mean it.

My father was trying to get custody of me, but then my sister got pregnant when she was thirteen and I just flipped the script. I really felt responsible for her. I told my father, "No Daddy, I have to go home, I have to go home." He said, "Emily, that's not the place for you. Me and Danielle'll take you and we'll help you and we'll raise you and do what we can for you." But all I could see was my sister, poor thing. She's pitiful, you know; my mother spoiled her to death. I couldn't imagine her having a baby. Still today, my sister's totally irresponsible, in and out of rehab.

My mother was out on a binge when my sister went into labor, so I took my sister to the hospital to have the baby. Mind you, I was just fifteen at the time, and my sister was thirteen going on fourteen, and I was down there with her having this baby. Afterward I knew that I had to take care of this baby and I had to make sure my sister was okay. I was the only one who could do it.

I COULDN'T GET ENOUGH MONEY FOR THE HOUSE NOTE, THE ELECTRIC BILL, THE LIGHTS, THE GAS BILL, THE CAR NOTE

By the time I was sixteen, my mother had started staying away for weeks at a time. It was just me and my sister, and we didn't have any money because my mother would take all of it with her. My sister was just hanging out in the streets. I remember diluting my nephew's Similac until it looked like skimmed milk. He'd be constantly crying, and I knew he wasn't getting enough nourishment. I'd thought about getting a job at McDonald's or Burger King, but I knew that I just couldn't get enough money for the house note, the electric bill, the lights, the gas bill, the car note. And I really couldn't leave my sister in that house with that baby for eight hours to go and work a shift anywhere. Finally I went up to the grocery store on the corner and told the man who worked there that I wanted to sleep with him for some money. We went to the local hotel. After we slept together, I didn't even know how much money to ask for. He gave me $50 and we went back to his grocery store. I got milk, diapers, the cheapest pork steak, rice, beans, cornbread, and chicken. In Detroit there's a street called Woodward where all the prostitutes go, and all I could think about was the ladies that stand on the corner with the really short skirts on. But then my mind went back to, *Now I have some milk for my nephew. I bet he won't be hungry today, and I bet he won't start crying after I give him this bottle.*

I remember running into the house and taking out a can of formula and a box of cereal. I was gonna make my nephew the best bottle he'd ever had. My sister was in the back playing loud music with some of her friends, so I went and got my nephew. Then I sat on the kitchen floor with my back against the counter and I started feeding him. If you could only have seen him looking up at me!

The next day I went up to the store and asked the man if he would introduce me to his friends who owned grocery stores and gas stations, because I knew I couldn't go and stand out on Woodward. People would see me and then they would know what I was doing. So he did just that. He introduced me to the other men in the neighborhood who owned gas stations and party stores and liquor stores and grocery stores, and that's what I started doing. We would go to fancy hotels, we would sleep together, and they would give me money.

I dropped out of school in the tenth grade. I couldn't do what I was doing and go to school, babysit my nephew, make sure my sister went to school, and be there for my mother.

I remember once when I was really happy. I was probably still sixteen at the time. Our house note was $500 a month. I was struggling to pay it, and all I could think of was, *I don't want to lose our house.* I went to the mortgage company, and I asked the man if he could decrease our payments if I slept with him. He was looking at me like, *You cannot be serious*. But I was really aggressive, and I asked him if we could go out to have a drink. So we went out and had drinks and he liked me, so he arranged to federally subsidize our house through HUD.[2] That broke our payments down to $250 a month. I feel like that was one of the best things I was able to do, because the mortgage had been such a burden.

I KNEW I WAS GOING TO TAKE CARE OF THIS CHILD

One day, when I was seventeen, a guy forced me into a car at gunpoint and he and his two friends raped me. I went to Detroit Receiving Hospital and they did the rape test kit. I had vaginal bruising and bite marks on my breast and on my thighs, and they found three different types of semen in me. The police got the guys and they had the evidence. Later, I went to police headquarters with my mother, and the female officers in the sex crime unit there were really nice to me. But my mother told them, "We aren't gonna press charges. We aren't gonna testify against them, because they're thugs. They are not throwing a Molotov cocktail through my window." When the officers said, "Well, what about her? What about what she wanted to do? Do you even know what they did to her?" my mother said, "She's fucking guys anyway. We're leaving." That's exactly what she said. I remember going home and taking a shower and crawling up in bed and just crying.

At that time, I had a boyfriend who was a drug dealer. I never told him about the rape. My boyfriend helped me out a lot so I didn't have to prostitute myself any more. One day we got pulled over by the police, and my boyfriend gave me his gun. The police officers had him get out of the car and they shook him down, and then they were looking at me. They said, "Let us know, what did he give you? What did he tell you to

---

[2] The U.S. Department of Housing and Urban Development, a federal agency that oversees public housing and tenants' rights.

hold?" My boyfriend was on the other side of the car, mouthing to me, "I love you. Don't worry about anything." Then one of the police officers found the gun on me.

My boyfriend came down to the jail with his attorney and got me out. I got three years' probation for that case, even though it wasn't my gun. At the time, I did what I did because I felt that this was what a good woman did for her man.

It turned out that I may have been maybe a month pregnant when I caught that case, but I didn't know it. Almost immediately after that my boyfriend went to prison, in 1983.

When I was pregnant I read about everything and I ate the right foods. I wouldn't even eat ketchup because I didn't want the acid in the tomato to thin my breast milk. I didn't smoke, I didn't drink, and I made all of my checkups on time. I would take a towel and rub it across my breasts really hard to toughen up my nipples, because I wanted to have my breasts in good shape for breastfeeding. Then I would massage my nipples with lanolin. I'm telling you, I was crazy.

My daughter was born on March 27th, 1984 at 9:42 in the morning. She was seven pounds and eleven ounces, and twenty-one and a half inches long. I had just turned eighteen. My boyfriend died the following year; he was killed in August of 1985. I was really sad because he'd done stuff for me that nobody else had ever done. We used to have so many meaningful conversations, and I knew that I could share stuff with him that I couldn't share with others. He was the very first man who ever told me I was smart. He told me that I was going to be something, and that I needed to go to school.

My daughter is my pride and joy. My first vow to her when she was born was, "I will never ever spank you. Never." I didn't have a good upbringing, but I knew I was going to take care of this child. And to this day—she's twenty-seven now—I've never ever spanked her and I've never called her out of her name. Those are two of the things that I'm most proud of, because I felt like what my mother did to me still affects me today, and I didn't want to do that to her.

My mother came to the hospital, and I was really happy about that, because I think by then she'd had something like thirty days clean and sober. I was so proud of her, and I thought she was so pretty. She was bright and so bubbly. She had a beautiful smile. I named my daughter Andrea, after my mother.

I had completed maybe two and a half years of the probation when I had my baby, and I was going to my probation officer like I was supposed to. When my daughter was about two, I started working in a club. I had got my own apartment by then so I needed the money, and I didn't want to go back to prostituting. My sister and my mother were living together down the hall from me, and sometimes they would watch the baby for me when I worked.

When I told my probation officer where I worked, she said, "Oh, you can't work in an establishment that sells liquor." She told me I had to quit. But I was bringing money in, I was able to pay for everything I needed. I had my stuff together and I felt like she was being really unfair. I didn't quit, and so they violated my probation. The judge sentenced me for my last six months to a residential facility called Evolution House, and my dad and his wife Danielle looked after my daughter. I didn't want to leave her, but it was one of the best things that ever happened to me, because the people at Project Transition showed me how to take care of myself.

At Evolution House I took my GED and passed it the first time. Then I went to Ross Medical Education Center and studied for seven months to become a medical assistant. Danielle was a lab tech at Sinai Hospital, and she gave me a bunch of her white uniforms. Then one of my aunts got me a job as a health aide in this really nice senior complex called the Jefferson City Apartments. I would work for four days straight and then I would come home for three days. I was being paid really good money. It felt good.

THAT'S WHEN I STARTED TO FIGHT

I met Stanley, a resident at the Jefferson City Apartments. He was eighty-one years old and I was twenty. I would stop at his place sometimes and wash his dishes up for him. He used to give me money, and I was overly flirtatious with him. We didn't have sex; we just kissed and touched. He said that he was impotent, so I felt really comfortable just being over there with him. He was really nice, but my aunt told me, "You're gonna have to stop seeing Stanley, because people will think you're trying to use him." So I said okay, and I stopped going to see him.

On the night of November 5th, 1986, Stanley called me. He wanted to know why I hadn't been to visit him. I said, "My aunt told me to stop seeing you because people in the complex were talking." Then he said, "You need to come out here and talk to me."

I waited for my father to go to bed, and I took a cab out there to see Stanley anyway. When I got to his place, he was sitting there drinking wine and smoking cigarettes. I sat on the couch and he said, "Now tell me the real reason you don't want to see me." I told him, "My aunt said that people were talking, and trying to say that I was manipulating you and taking your money." Then it was like he went from zero to sixty. He said, "No, you just used me. You don't wanna see me any more. You probably have some little boyfriend. You know, all he's gonna do is get you pregnant!"

I got up and I tried to go toward the door, but he got up and grabbed me. He was eighty-one but he was in really good shape. He might've been like six-one, six-two, over 250 pounds. We were struggling and I was still trying to go toward the front door. We went into the kitchen, which is right near the front door. He said I wasn't going anywhere, and he kept trying to kiss me. I can remember his saliva being on my cheeks and across my mouth. Then he got a paring knife out of the kitchen sink and he said, "We're gonna fuck tonight." I put my hand over the blade, he pulled the knife back, and it cut my pinky finger. To this day that finger doesn't bend like the other ones do. When I looked at it, I saw all of this blood and I just started crying. That's when I started to fight. We slipped and he ended up on top of me. He was trying to pull his pants down. I felt around for the knife and I picked it up and I stabbed him.

When I went to trial, the prosecution said I'd stabbed him between thirty-two and thirty-five times, and that all of the stab wounds were located in an oval shape under his left armpit. Stanley stopped moving, and I remember pushing his body up and trying to stand up. I looked at him and I just knew he was dead. I went in the bathroom and I washed my hands and wrapped a towel around my hand. I went back and I looked at him and he was still. I'd killed him. I put the towel in the bathroom sink and I left.

The next morning, my father saw the paper and said, "Emily, look at this." I went down to my bedroom in the basement and I just started crying. I had so much rage and so much anger and so much hurt and resentment in me, and Stanley had caught it all. He didn't deserve that.

Three months later, on February 11th, the police called all the Jefferson City Apartments home health aides and the maintenance workers in for questioning. They asked for all of our fingerprints. So I gave my fingerprints, and when I went home that night I got a fifth of Tanqueray and Rose's Lime Juice. And I drank, drank, drank. My stepmother heard me crying at 5:30 in the morning, and she sent my father downstairs to my bedroom. He found me sitting in there with my hands on my face. I was crying and I had scratch marks on my face from my nails. My father said, "What's wrong? Tell me what happened." I wouldn't say anything. I just kept crying. So my stepmother said, "Wrap her up in a blanket. We're taking her to the hospital." When I got to the emergency room I just freaked out. I started screaming, and the nurses restrained me and took me to the psychiatric unit.

My father would come and see me every day, but I would never say anything. I would just sit by the window. I was thinking about Stanley. I was thinking about all of the men I'd slept with, the drugs that I'd done, my mother, the drugs she was doing, my daughter, how I was going to survive, what I would do. Sometimes I would have crying spells, and the nurses would come and give me an injection and just knock me out. They released me after thirty days of hospitalization.

After I went home, I quit my job at Jefferson City Apartments and got a job at a clothing store. I was there April and May. Then May 9th, 1987, the police came to the store. I was in the back hanging up stock when they went to the front desk. I knew they were there for me. They said to me, "We have a warrant for your arrest for robbery and murder."

I STARTED THINKING, *THIS IS WHAT I DESERVE*

I had two trials. The first trial I testified at, so I was able to tell my whole story, that his wallet with $61 and all his credit cards in it was right on the coffee table. I could testify that he was found with a gold watch on, a diamond ring, a sterling silver ring with a precious stone on it and a large gold chain. His car keys, everything was right there in his apartment. So they couldn't say it was a robbery and a murder. The jury deliberated for three days and declared a mistrial.

Then I had to have the second trial, but in the second trial my attorney didn't want me to testify. My attorney said I didn't come across well to the jury, because most people cry when they're talking about something so tragic, and I wasn't crying. I just wanted to tell my story as clearly and as quickly as possible. My attorney said that wasn't a good idea. I felt that he was wrong, and I remember at that point I started to shut down. I had been so adamant about everything, and I felt like my attorney should have supported me, but it wasn't like that. So I didn't testify at my second trial, and I was found guilty of first-degree murder. On November 9, 1987, I was sentenced to a mandatory life sentence. The judge said that I'd leave prison in a pine box.

Once I was sentenced, they took me straight to Huron Valley Women's Prison that same day. I was twenty-one years old.

In prison I guess you could say I was vulnerable and way too trusting at first. I trusted this one officer and he took advantage of me. Every day he would come in and tell me how beautiful I was or how pretty I was. I hadn't had anybody say that to me in so long, and I fell for him.

I remember the first time he tried to touch me, I said, "Ouch, don't do that." And he said, "Oh, you know you want me to do it," and he did it anyway. It could happen anytime. If I was standing in the counselor's door talking to the counselor, he would come up behind me and squeeze my butt cheek. I couldn't say anything. I just started thinking, *I killed a man who was trying to sexually assault me, and I've been gang-raped before by three men. This is what I deserve.* I started not caring.

The officer would come into my room on a midnight shift and I would be asleep and he would wake me up and say, "I want you to suck my dick." In the beginning I was like, "Ah, no." But he would grab me by the back of my hair or something and I would do what he wanted me to do. I didn't tell anyone because they had seen us talking, so I thought, *If I go and try to tell them something, they're gonna say, "Oh, you were asking for it. You wanted that to happen."*

By 1988 I was in charge of the kitchen, and one day I got into a fight in there. I never usually fought, but I think the reason I did it was so I could get away from that officer. After I had the fight in the kitchen, I went to the segregated house unit. While I was in seg[3] I heard that the officer had raped another girl, and I felt so guilty. I thought that if I'd stood up and said something, that wouldn't have happened to her.

There was a lawyer who was trying to bring college education to the prison, and I finally told her what was going on. She told me to write a grievance, and to tell the warden, the deputy warden, and the inspector. The officer was immediately taken out of the unit, and he was put on a stop order that prevented him from coming to work in the prison. It was really hard, because then I had to deal with the women who were mad at me, because everybody liked him. They said he was cool because he would let them get away with stuff they weren't supposed to be doing. And the officers, they were pissed off at me because he was one of their own.

The retaliation was horrible. The officers made me submit urine samples on a weekly basis. They would wake me up on the midnight shift and tell me to come drop urine, even though usually you do urine drops on a day shift. It was horrible. They would come and shake my room down.

---

[3] Segregation/segregated housing, which is isolated from the general prison population. For more details, see the glossary.

I can remember some of the female officers saying stuff like, "Well, that's what you get."

I was at Valley from December 1987 until May 28th of 1992. Then they closed Valley and transferred all of us to Robert Scott Correctional Facility in Michigan. I was elated, because I felt like this was going to be a whole new start. But it wasn't so.

Some of the officers that came with us, they immediately pointed me out. They said, "Oh, that's the bitch that'll get a man," or "You gotta watch out for that one. She's a set-up queen." I'd hear what they said and I'd keep it moving.

By then I decided that I was going to think about some college. When college first came to the women back in 1989, I really wasn't comfortable—I wasn't ready, and I knew it, so I didn't go. But by 1992 I was ready to go full-fledged with my education, and that's exactly what I did.

I STARTED FEELING LIKE IT WAS
NEVER GOING TO STOP

I lost my visitation rights permanently from 1996 until 2002 because of two substance abuse tickets. I was the very first woman in the state of Michigan to ever get a permanent visitors restriction for that reason. One ticket was for an 800-milligram Motrin that I didn't have a prescription for, but I was cramping and I got one from another girl. The other one was for an iron pill. I had iron pills prescribed to me because I had low iron, and I had kept them a little bit too long, so they were out of date. Those two tickets were considered substance abuse.

The visitors restriction impacted me deeply. The inspector who enforced it—Inspector Donald—was horrible, and I felt like he was trying to set me up. He was having my room torn up all the time. He said I was selling drugs even though I wasn't. At one point he sent two officers to shake my room down, and they planted marijuana in my room. The stupid part was that one of them wrote an incident report and said that I had loose marijuana in my make-up bag. And then the other officer said it was wrapped up in aluminum foil and ready for delivery. I had to go down to Wayne County for court, and the judge threw the case out. Inspector Donald was sitting behind me, and I'll never, ever forget the look on his face. He was frowning at me so much. He was just so eager to get me. The officers even noticed it, and some of them would say, "Dang, Madison, what'd you do to him, 'cause he really wanted you bad."

Another time, in '96, some friends of mine in prison drew a chalk outline of a dead body right in front of my window. They put three bullet holes in the head and then they wrote "Donald" above it. Inspector Donald saw it and sent me to seg. Anytime you get to seg, they have to serve you with papers clearly stating what you're being held for. The papers said an investigation was being conducted to see if I was going try to have Donald killed. I thought, *You cannot be serious. All because of the chalk outline that I didn't draw?*

Then the warden came back to seg to see me and she told the officer to release me. But I thought, *What if Donald does something, or has something done to me?* So I signed myself into protective custody, which meant I stayed in seg. I was there for about four months. The officers there would bring me cold food. So if I had beans for dinner, they would be so cold they would be gel. I knew it was being done purposely. I complained, and the deputy warden told the officers that if a prisoner in seg complained about their food being cold they had to use the microwave to heat it up. So then all the officers got mad at me again. They would say, "We're so sick of you, Madison." I didn't pay any attention, because the bottom line was that I knew I didn't have to eat cold food.

After I got out of seg I had a new roommate. An officer named Edwards was sexually abusing her. After a while they split us up as roommates and moved her to another unit, but they put him back in the same unit with me. So I wrote a statement on her behalf. Then Edwards came to my door and said, "I hope you aren't going to testify, because if you do, you know what's going to happen to you." I was really scared. Then, in January of 1997, that officer came to my room and sexually assaulted me. He said, "You'd better not tell anybody. I can reach you wherever you are."

That's when I started feeling like it was never going to stop. I felt like I just couldn't take any more. Between the sexual assault, the innuendos, the verbal attacks, the retaliation, Inspector Donald—I was just ready to give up. I stopped eating. After three days of not eating any food or taking any liquids, they shipped me to HVC, the psychiatric hospital. I was there for a year, from February 1997 to February 1998.

I hoped that I'd finally be someplace where I could get some help, where I could talk to somebody. But no, the officers who took me there spoke to some of the staff at HVC and they told them all sorts of things. So it was just more of the same. I felt like it would never stop. I thought, *This is what I'm going to have to do the rest of my life—listen to them badger me, belittle me, humiliate me. This is what I'm going to have to do.*

I DIDN'T BELIEVE IT UNTIL THE DAY I WALKED OUT OF THE DOOR

I tried to hang myself in the bathroom. But I stayed in there too long and the officers found me. They stripped me and they put a little pink gown on me. There were five males in there with me, and they five-point restrained me. That's one of the worst things I've ever experienced. Then they put me on one-on-one suicide watch, but the staff person assigned to me was male. In one-on-one, the staff person goes to the bathroom with you. I thought, *Why would you do this when you already know my history?* I felt like all of that was done purposefully. I was on one-on-one for twenty-nine days, and then I just got so fed up, I stopped eating again. My blood pressure dropped down to eighty over forty and they had to take me to the Duane L. Waters Hospital. After a couple of days they asked me if I was going to start eating, and I shook my head no. That's when they put the tube down my throat to force-feed me. Then after a couple of days I told them they could take it out and I would eat. I was at HVC for another couple of months, and in February they transferred me to Florence Crane Correctional Facility in Coldwater, Michigan.

The retaliation and harassment started as soon as I hit the ground, because the warden wanted me to go to a unit with an officer who was a defendant in the sexual abuse cases. They knew I was helping with those cases.

I was at Coldwater for fifteen months, from 1998 until 2000. I was there when the third sexual assault occurred. I filed a complaint, and the prison doctor did the rape test kit and said everything was negative. By then I was on a writ for my criminal appeal, which means I was transferred to a county jail so I could go back and forth to court. While I was there, I tested positive for gonorrhea. I just couldn't believe it. I had been locked up for thirteen years and I didn't know how long I'd had gonorrhea.

After the lawsuit was over, I was transferred to Western Wayne Prison in Michigan. It was like all the other places I had been to, because the officers knew who I was and were like, "Oh, lord. We don't want her here." But I could finally see some light at the end of the tunnel. I enrolled in the Residential Substance Abuse Therapy (RSAT) program. I feel like that was the best program the Michigan Department of Corrections (MDOC) ever offered to anybody. I'm telling you, that program made such a difference in me and the way I feel. It was just amazing. Another program was the Assaultive Offender Program (AOP), which just taught me so much about who I was and why I was the way I was. Before I got into the AOP, I didn't know who I was. I was full of false pride and bravado, and I hadn't gotten to know my strength. AOP taught me to think about what I do before I do it, and to rethink it. It taught me more than anything to accept full responsibility for my behavior. It was then that I stopped getting into trouble in prison. Everything had been because my mother did something, or a man did something. I stopped blaming people and I stopped being a victim. It was just amazing. I feel like everybody going into the system should do that. It meant everything to me, and it changed the way I look at life.

I was eligible for parole in 2004. Of course they didn't let me go. But after 2004 I knew it was just a matter of time. I knew I needed to keep my nose clean, do all that I needed to do, and have something else positive to take back every year I went back. In 2000, when I was at Coldwater, I'd got my bachelor's degree in liberal arts. My major was psychology and my minor was sociology. I kept doing what I had to do, and I finally made parole in August 2009. I didn't believe it until the day I walked out the door, because I knew that they could take it back for any reason.

When I left, I felt like I was starting my life all over again; I had a second chance. Now I'm forty-four and I have a ten-year-old grandson, and three granddaughters who are six years old, three years old, and eight months old. The birth of my fourth grandchild was the first time I had ever witnessed one of my grandchildren being born, and I thought that was such a beautiful experience. My daughter had the baby on a Saturday and she was back in school that Tuesday, so I was there with the kids every day, spending the night, just being there, helping my daughter with my grandchildren. It was phenomenal.

A few months after I came home, I started volunteering with a girls' group in Ann Arbor, acting as a mentor to help at-risk girls stay in school, stay off drugs, and not get pregnant. I did that for a year, and now they've hired me as a paid mentor. I love my job so much. I'm doing good work and I feel good about it. I really feel like I'm making a difference in the lives of others. I like to talk to people about their choices and the consequences, because I know about all of *my* choices and consequences. If I can help anybody avoid what I went through, that's what it's all about.

ANNA JACOBS

56, formerly imprisoned

Anna sits on the sofa in her large suburban home, surrounded by her husband's legal papers. Her husband recently retired and is in the process of emptying his office. Anna jokes about moving all his boxes into their two-car garage when he isn't looking. Two small, matching dogs curl up at Anna's feet and repeatedly attempt to jump into her lap. When she begins to speak, she does so matter-of-factly, at first only relaying biographical facts—where she was born, when she got married, where she went to college. But once her husband leaves the house, she begins to talk about the effect of her drinking on her husband and two sons, her numerous arrests for drinking and driving, and how she ended up serving almost a year in prison. She describes the lack of medical care in prison for her diabetes and cirrhosis, and how her health deteriorated to the point where her heart stopped beating.

YOU CAN MAKE AN ADDICTION OUT OF ANYTHING

I'm fifty-six, born and bred in Palestine, Texas. That's in East Texas, home of the dogwood trails. I had one divorce and then I married my current husband; we've been married for over twenty-five years. We went to school together, so we'd known each other for thirteen years when we got married.

Somewhere along the way, I guess alcohol became the major focus of my life. I guess you can make an addiction out of anything if you just totally give yourself over to that. For some people it may be a food addiction; it can be sex for others. For me, it was alcohol. I fought it. I wanted to be a good mom, but I didn't feel worthy of certain things, so it was a struggle.

I didn't drink in high school. And when I was at the University of Texas at Austin, I was too busy studying, so I didn't have time to drink. I graduated after three years with a bachelor's in journalism, with a specialization in communications and public relations, and after that I came two credits shy of getting my teaching certificate.

After college I met a boy. And aren't they the root of almost all evils? I never should have married him; he pretty much broke my heart. After three years, he left me for somebody else, and that's when I really started drinking.

After my marriage fell apart, I stayed in Houston for probably six months. I didn't do anything, and I pretty much just lay in bed. I was depressed. I drank. And then I'd get up and just putter around the house and feel sorry for myself. Finally my mother called and said, "I know you're depressed, but this isn't good, this isn't healthy. If you don't come home, your dad and I are gonna come down there and get you." So I just packed up and picked up some clothes and stuff, and went back to East Texas, where immediately I got back in bed. And that's when I think the drinking really started to take a more important turn. That's when I started to hide bottles.

For quite a while, I was able to get away with it. I'd go to the liquor store while my parents were at work, and nobody knew I was drinking. But I started to worry that I might have a drinking problem. It wasn't the first thing I did every morning, but it was certainly the last thing I did every evening. And so I went to the doctor, and told him, "I think I have an alcohol problem." He said, "Hell, I'd have an alcohol problem too if I was going through a divorce." So that didn't give me any reason to stop, and it justified everything that I needed to hear. As an alcoholic, that kind of justification is really important.

When my current husband and I got together, my drinking got worse. His father was a doctor in our town, and very well respected. But his family were drinkers. Dr. Jacobs didn't really start drinking until he got home, and then sometimes he might just have one or two drinks. But my mother-in-law started drinking at five o'clock. They had a beautiful house with a humongous open bar. There was everything you could possibly think of, and you could mix your own anything. Just after five o'clock, we would congregate in their big house. There were always people there for dinner, enjoying the bar and the company.

I started drinking more and more, even when I wasn't with my husband. I thought I was doing a good job of hiding it. I didn't drink when I was pregnant, so therefore in my mind I wasn't really an alcoholic.

After our first child, Jacob, was born, we moved to Irving. I was totally overwhelmed. I was in a place where I didn't have any friends, I didn't know anybody. I drank, but I'd manage to keep things together pretty well until my husband came home in the evenings. Then I would go lie down in the bedroom, and he would take care of the baby. Finally I realized it just wasn't working. One day, I said, "I need to get a job." We didn't really need the money, but it was more that I just needed to get out of the house.

I found a really good school for Jacob, and I went to work at the Las Colinas Country Club. I functioned well; I didn't drink when I was at work. It just never occurred to me to drink because I was doing something that I really enjoyed doing, putting together wedding receptions and parties. But every day, I would leave work and stop at the liquor store. I would buy vodka, and I'd drink on the way home. I'd leave the bottle in my car and then when my husband went to take a shower, I'd take my bottle out and hide it somewhere in the house.

I did that for about a year and a half. But after a while, my husband began to notice that something wasn't right. I finally went to rehab in the late 1980s. That seemed to work for a while, but I guess I was in denial, so it didn't work for that long a time. We moved again, and things just escalated. I began to drink and drive, and I got arrested for it several times. I'd get arrested and sent to jail, and my husband would come and bail me out. I always got arrested in Dallas County, just on the other side of the line, so nobody at my husband's work had to know what he was living through.

I WANTED IT TO COME TO AN END

I kept thinking that another baby would save my life. So I had Henry. Once again, I didn't drink the whole time I was pregnant, and I was thoroughly happy. I did fine; I didn't go through any kind of post-partum depression. But then, just all of a sudden, I'd be someplace and alcohol would present itself again to me, and I would drink. I think there's a song that says "one's too many and a hundred ain't enough," you know? That's what it was like for me.

Every six months to a year, I'd go to rehab. I'd spend twenty-eight, thirty days there, come out, be fine for a while maybe. I was what is called a functioning alcoholic, so I don't think anybody knew, except for just my husband and two kids. I could stand and shake hands and do whatever it was that was required of me, but emotionally, I just wasn't there. I went to my own mother's funeral drunk, because I couldn't bear the pain of losing her.

All this has put a humongous strain on our family. You can't imagine what I did to my two sons. I never laid a hand on them, but I hurt them. I hurt their hearts. If there was anything I could do, I'd take all of this back in a heartbeat.

The second or third time I got a DUI, they gave me six months at Cornell Corrections of Texas, a correctional and drug treatment program. It was a goofy program, I'll be honest. And you would've thought that after going someplace, and being away from your family on your son's sixteenth birthday, after not even being able to see the car we bought him for his birthday, that I would have changed. Once Jacob got his car they would drive down to see me on Saturday mornings, but finally they decided that they just didn't like coming, and I said, "That's okay."

When I got out I was on five years' probation. I completed five years without drinking, but as soon as the five years were over, I couldn't wait to have a drink. I started drinking again. I thought I could drink responsibly, but it just doesn't work that way. Like I said, one's too many and a hundred's not enough. It really escalated. I thought I was unhappy with my marriage, I thought I was unhappy with the kids. But it really wasn't any of that, I was just unhappy with me. And I kept saying to my husband, "I think I need some help." My husband was willing to give me any kind of help I wanted, but he said, "You're going to have to do what they say."

In March 2009, he took me to a doctor, who prescribed two medications to help me go through withdrawal and, I guess, make me not crave alcohol. My husband went to pick up this prescription for me, but I was determined that I was gonna drink one more time before I started taking this medication. I'd already been drinking that day anyway, but I had run out of wine and beer. So I drove to Tom Thumb, a grocery store down the street.

Before I left, my younger son Henry said, "Mom, you don't need to be going anywhere." Then he said, "Mom, I'm gonna call the police." And I said, "Yeah right, just go ahead, you call the police." I don't even really know what I said, but it probably wasn't very nice.

I got in the car and I drove down to Tom Thumb. When I got there, as I started getting out of the car, I could see these two police officers sitting in their car across from me. Now at that point, anybody in their right mind would say, "I'm not going in there, and I'm not gonna drive myself back to the house. It's not that far, I can actually walk." But alcohol just screws up your brain. It just overtakes you. And so I went into the grocery store, and I bought two bottles of wine and some beer. I had a moment when I thought to call my husband and tell him to come get me, to just say, "Look, I'm sorry, I screwed up." But I didn't have a cell phone with me, and I didn't see a pay phone. So I just thought, *What the heck, you got yourself down here, you can certainly drive yourself back home.*

Immediately I knew the police officers were going to come and arrest me again for a DUI, and part of me wanted them to. I wanted it to come to an end. I guess if I thought anything, I knew I'd be put in jail, but I don't think I really thought it through. Sure enough, the officers followed me, all the way down the street, all the way down to my house.

They pulled me over up next to the median, and my husband drove by then with my son in the car. They had never seen me be arrested. They just stopped and stared at me.

Because the police officers knew me, they decided not to impound the car. One of them drove my car home and the other one handcuffed me and put me in the backseat, took me to jail, and booked me in. They gave me my phone call, and the phone just rang. I mean, the answering machine didn't even come on. I can understand. Not only was my husband angry, he was hurt, and so was my son. My husband was trying to protect our kids.

I was feeling really bad. It took several days, and finally one of the officers said, "You know what's wrong with you—you're going through withdrawal." I said, "I know. I have some medication at home that could ease this and help my bad stomach."

He said, "You can use my phone to call someone to bring it to you." It didn't come up on the caller ID as the jail phone, so my husband answered. When he realized it was me, he said, "Anna, I've had enough. I'm not coming to get you out or anything." He did agree to bring the medicine, but he didn't bail me out, and honestly I don't know if I wanted him to. I did want to come home, because I thought I could fix everything if I apologized. But I knew what kind of a mess I'd gotten myself into.

SO LONG AS I WAS JUST LAYING ON THE FLOOR, I COULD BREATHE

First I went to a tiny little jail, and the lights were on all the time. They gave me a mattress, and I slept on the floor. I couldn't drink, and it was extremely difficult; I was just so frightened by everything. Have you ever gone to a party and drank too much and gotten dry heaves? That's what it was like. There was no bathroom I could go to, no bucket or anything. I did everything I could not to throw up on the floor—I just hung on.

Once this officer came in, and I said to him, "I think I need to go to the hospital," but he told me, "You're just going through withdrawal. You're going to stay right here." I was there for about a week, long enough that they let me get a shower. And you know what? I think I slept for the whole week. When I left there I felt flattened, scared. But I wasn't gagging any more.

When they got me to Dallas County Jail, they checked me in and didn't give me anything for the withdrawal. It would've probably helped, but I guess I got through it okay. I was in Dallas County Jail from March 13th, 2009—it was Friday the 13th, I'll never forget that—to June 4th. My attorney visited me. My husband visited me. He also had me served with divorce papers while I was in jail. I said, "You know, I really don't think I can handle this right now. Before we do anything drastic, can we try to just manage to exist? Just give me some time to see where they're gonna put me, what's gonna happen to me."

He said, "You're the mother of my two kids. I've loved you ever since we were in ninth grade. You'll have money in your commissary account, you'll have all the medical attention you need." But he did want to get divorced. He just couldn't do it any more.

My attorney told me that I was probably looking at eleven months, but I didn't tell my husband that. I thought that, as long as he just thinks I'm here for six to nine months, maybe we can handle that and then we can work on the marriage. And I was still trying to figure things out in my own head.

Wednesdays are big nights in the Dallas County Jail, because that's when you find out what prison you're being moved to. On June 4th, the guards gave us dinner at four or five in the afternoon, and then we didn't eat again. They moved me to a cell with thirty, thirty-five other women, with only two toilets and no toilet paper. It was impossible to sleep in the cell with so many other women. I did a lot of just sitting and watching. There were black women singing hymns. There were other people just saying off-the-wall stuff. I was scared to death. I'm a talker, so I could have talked to anybody, but nobody really wanted to, so I just sat there.

We were stuck in there until they decided that they were ready to go to Plane State Jail in Dayton, Texas. When it got time, they handcuffed me to a girl named Bobby. Then they loaded us on the bus. We traveled overnight. I don't know why. I guess they think that somebody's going to, I don't know, overturn the bus or something like in that movie *The Fugitive*. The whole time I was thinking, *This is so bizarre. This is too dramatic for me.*

It took about four hours to get from Dallas to Plane State. When we got off the bus I was exhausted because I hadn't slept, so I just kind of followed Bobby. She seemed to know where she was going and what she was doing. I was feeling really weird, exhausted and not right. The worst part was the heat. The bus had air conditioning, but when we got off, the temperature outside was probably a hundred and three. As my father would say, it was hotter than blue blazes.

Plane State Jail is where they do what they call diagnostics; that's where they go through your family and health history. The big tin building where they put us for diagnostics had no air conditioning. There weren't even any fans in there. The building was divided into cages, and the guards put us into these, and then they'd bring us out one cage at a time to get our clothes. It was just so hot. I kept thinking, *Well, surely it's gonna get better.*

I didn't know at that point where we were going next, so you've got all the fear going, and it was just so hot you can't even describe it. Finally they started taking us to our dorms. Before they moved us, they gave us a little sack with a little tiny toothbrush, a little bit of toothpaste, and a bar of lye soap. They didn't give you shampoo; you had to use the lye soap on your hair. We also had a roll-on deodorant, a little bitty thing about travel-size. I went to what they call F Dorm, which was an overflow dorm. There were fifty-six to fifty-eight women in the dorm, in bunk beds. By the grace of God, I got a low bunk. I was fifty-four years old at this point, and extremely overweight; I weighed probably 300 pounds. I don't know what I would have done if I'd gotten a high bunk.

F dorm was a Quonset hut.[1] The prison was meant for 500 to 700 women, and there were at least 2,000 there at the time, so they had to use these Quonset huts. It only had industrial-size floor fans, and maybe a couple of ceiling fans. That first day they gave us a little paper-cone cup for water. I didn't know to save my cup, and I threw it away after I drank the first time. It was only later when I was thirsty again that I found out that you only get the one cup. When I asked what I was supposed to drink out of, the other girls told me that I had to look in the trash for a Coke can or something.

We had showers in our little dorm area, and people started lining up just to get under the water. I was in there with a couple of heavily pregnant women, who were just miserable, because of the heat and because of their size. It was so hot we'd sprinkle water on the concrete floor and just lay down in it. So long as I was just laying on the floor, I could breathe. It was tolerable.

We'd arrived that day too late for the sack lunch, so I didn't eat all that day. The next morning, breakfast was two to three pancakes, tons of syrup, tons of butter, some pork product. You could also get biscuits or toast. It was the same every morning. Great days were when you could have prunes.

After about three weeks, they said I could go to the commissary. I was so hungry at that point, I bought anything that was a carbohydrate. All kinds of chips. I spent some seventy odd dollars, almost all the money I was allowed to spend.

While I was there I felt really bad, but I wasn't sure what was going on. I thought it might just be depression. Usually I'm a real Texas-type girl, you can't beat me down. But I knew something was wrong, it just wasn't anything I could put my finger on. Then, after three or four weeks, my

---

[1] A Quonset hut is a prefabricated building with a long, rounded roof made of corrugated steel.

feet started swelling. They were huge, especially around my ankles. They were as big as a salad plate. All the girls kept telling me that something was really wrong. I put in a medical request and saw a physician's assistant (PA). She just said, "Get over it. Get real." I was in there with a girl who was humongously pregnant, and she got no prenatal care at all. She just kept gaining weight, which couldn't be good for her or the baby.

I DON'T KNOW IF ANYONE IN THERE EVER USED THE WORD "DIABETES"

I put in medical requests every two or three days. Once, the physician's assistant (PA) did a Pap smear on me. When the results came back, she said, "You have abnormal cells." I was freaking out, and I said, "Now what do I do?" She said, "I don't know. Come back in about six months." I guess she figured I probably would be moved by then, and she wouldn't have to deal with it. By then I was terrified. I felt so bad, I just knew something was really wrong with me, and I was afraid I'd die in prison.

After a while it was so bad I couldn't put on shoes. I've had two babies, and yet my feet have never swollen like that before. The swelling was even going up my leg, and the other girls kept saying, "Anna, you've got a problem." I got a letter to my husband, who called them and got all my medical records. I finally saw a different PA, and she actually tried to help me. I went to her and said, "I'm sick and tired of being sick and tired. Somebody needs to give me some help." She looked at me and said, "Honey, let me try to get you some help." She was really nice. By then they were fixing to put the girls in boots, but I couldn't wear a boot because my feet were so swollen. So the PA gave me a pass for plain old tennis shoes; that had to come from her, otherwise the guards would make me wear the boots. After I gave her my medical records, she gave me a diuretic and my feet went back to normal. She also told me to come and get my blood sugar tested twice a day. I would stand in line with a bunch of girls; the ones on insulin got in first. The nurses would call "Insulin finger prick," and I'd go in, even though I wasn't on insulin.

Then a nurse would prick my finger and my blood sugar level would come up on a computer. The number usually ran from 245 to 500. They'd show me the number and that was it. Now I know I'm supposed to be around 100 or 120. But in there, no matter what the number was, they didn't do anything. They just pricked my finger and that was it. I don't even know if anyone in there ever used the word "diabetes."

Once I was sent to see a doctor. He was Asian, and his accent was really thick. I was embarrassed to admit I didn't understand him, so I just said, "Yes, no." That was the only doctor I ever saw at Plane State.

I'm on insulin now, but I never got any while I was in there, and no one ever told me what I should or shouldn't eat. Now I know I'm supposed to have very limited carbohydrates, but back then I knew nothing. The thing about it is, you didn't have a choice anyway. The PA put me on a "diabetic tray," but no one would honor it, and I had to put in another request to go see her before I was given the special diet menu. On that menu, they would let me have some fruit and sometimes a piece of Spam or some kind of petrified pork. The only thing different at breakfast was that they'd give you pancakes with sugar-free syrup. That was about it. I'd try to do it on my own, but it was so hard. Sometimes I could've just killed myself because they'd have chocolate cake. When you're stuck in a prison, just a piece of chocolate cake would feel like a pat on the back. But I'd tell myself, *No, don't eat the cake. Your body is worth more, you're worth more than this. You'll survive.*

The thing is, in the women's prison, they just don't have any special food for diabetic people. Maybe they do for the men, because I spent one night in a men's prison. I looked on their board when we went for breakfast, and they had something like three different menus to pick from for breakfast, lunch, and dinner. Women don't have that. Now, I'm not exactly a women's libber, but if they've got that for men, why don't they have it for women? And if they're going to call it a diet menu, or a diabetic menu, why isn't it closely monitored? Because the food where I was nearly killed me.

I'd started a job folding uniforms in the laundry. By then I was feeling just terrible, I felt so sick, but I kept going to work. Maybe it's my age, you know, or maybe it's the way I was raised, but if you've got a job, you go to it, you do it. Boy, there'd be days I didn't feel good, but I loved going to work because it gave me someplace to be. You were out, you could talk while you folded clothes. We didn't have a whole lot to talk about, but, you know, everybody talked about their families and what they were going to do when they got out and everything. I enjoyed that. It sounds funny, but I felt like it saved me, to have that job.

But I kept on not feeling great. When we walked to and from work we were supposed to stay between these two yellow lines. Well, sometimes my foot would just slip out and I knew I wasn't doing too great. I was weaving when I walked, and my thought patterns got confused. My bunkmate and I would be in a conversation and all of a sudden I'd just stop. I couldn't think, I couldn't remember where I was, I couldn't remember what we were talking about. Once when I was trying to write my husband, all of a sudden, my writing just went off the wall. I was so confused. And my skin was turning yellow.

The PA said they were going to have me see a liver specialist in Galveston. She said, "Honey, we don't wanna lose you." That scared me. I thought they were going to send me to the doctor, but one day they just put me in a room with a computer screen and a doctor talked to me on some kind of video thing for a few minutes. He said, "We'll try to get you down here in the next few days, but we're going to prescribe some medication now." I said okay. I didn't know what was wrong, but I knew I was sick.

Two weeks went by and I didn't hear from anyone. I asked, but no one said anything. By then it was August and I'd been in prison for two months. I'd go in the pill line and ask, and they'd have no information. It got to where I couldn't speak or think correctly. But I was still working in the laundry and doing everything that they asked. I was in prison under my own doing, and as long as I could keep it up, I'd keep working. But I was just getting sicker.

I DIDN'T KNOW THAT MY LIFE WAS IN DANGER

One day I went to the pill line and they said they had lactulose for me. No one talked to me about it, and I just took it. Well, that medicine kept me running to the bathroom—I'll be honest, it was awful. And the guards would holler at me because you're not supposed to move around that much. At the time I didn't know what lactulose was for, but now I know that it's a laxative that's used to treat hepatic encephalopathy, which is toxins in your bloodstream. When you have cirrhosis, your liver doesn't process toxins; they build up in your body and go to your brain. That's what caused the weaving. That's what caused the lack of thinking ability. But no one told me that then, and I didn't even know I had cirrhosis. I didn't know that my life was in danger.

In prison they only give you two rolls of toilet tissue every week, which is not enough. And after I took lactulose the first time and I went to the bathroom, I thought, *This isn't going to work. I'm using up all my toilet tissue.* Once the prison ran out of toilet tissue, can you believe that? How was I supposed to take the medicine then? Another time I had an accident and stained my britches, and this other inmate yelled at me to get clean. She said I smelled bad and didn't want to be near me. After that I got kind of fearful of taking lactulose because of the stigma. Also, how do you go to work every day when you keep having to run to the bathroom? I wanted to keep working. But in the laundry there was only one toilet, and you never knew if there'd be toilet tissue. I'd try to take tissue with me when I went to work but the guards would strip-search me and find it. So I cut my dosage back. I guess I had a little bit of pride.

One day I passed out, I guess from too many toxins in my body, and once I passed out I lost all control of my bowels, and my bodily fluids went out with me. I was taken by ambulance to Cleveland Regional Medical Center. My clothes were all soiled, and they had to be cut off when I got there. A nurse tried to take my blood. I have really tiny little veins, they're real hard to find, and after three pricks, I said, "I've had enough." And I'd started feeling better, so the guards just put me back in the ambulance and took me back to Plane State without seeing a doctor.

When it was time to go back, I asked for clothes. They said, "You don't have them any more," and I had to go back to prison wearing two hospital nightgowns, one in the front and one in the back. I guess I still smelled bad because I hadn't been able to clean myself. At first a female guard said, "We're not riding back with you until you're clean." But I couldn't wash myself anywhere. Finally they drove me back to the prison that night. Then I had to go sit in what they called the government office until medical opened at maybe eight or nine in the morning. It was air conditioned, and I basically sat there for four or five hours, near naked and freezing. The female guard wouldn't get near me. She told me, "You stink." I said, "I'm sorry. There isn't anything I can do about this. Let me get back to my dorm so I can wash." But they wouldn't let me.

They finally walked me over to medical. One of the nurses there said, "You can't just be walking around here naked." But what could I do? The nurse took my blood pressure and said I was okay, then sent me back to my dorm.

For a few days I didn't take anything because I didn't know what had caused any of this. No one told me anything. Finally I went back to medical and figured out from the PA that I needed to be on lactulose because of the toxins. I said, "How do I work? How do I do anything?" She didn't have any answers. She was just medical. So I started taking it again, but then I guess I wasn't taking as much. I thought I could cut back, because I just wanted to work.

But something mentally happened to me, which I guess was the toxins building up in my brain. I was in an upper bunk by then, and you can't just be climbing up and down every fifteen minutes to use the bathroom after you take it. I thought I was in control by taking less. That was me being stupid. I thought I was in control of my body, but I wasn't.

I don't know if it was a week, maybe two weeks later, but from there things didn't get any better. I kept asking for medical help, but the guards wouldn't let me see a doctor. This one night, it was so hot, and I said to my bunkmate, "I don't feel good. I've just got to lay down." And I took my top sheet off my bunk and laid it on the concrete floor, and I just laid down. And then the guards came around to do a check and one of them said to me, "You have to get up on that bed." I said, "I can't, I can't get up." He said, "You're either going to get up on that bed or I'm going to write you up." I said, "I don't really care what you do."

That's when I really cratered. I don't remember much after that. I guess I remember going to work and coming back over the next couple of days, but one of my bunkmates said I wasn't making any sense at all, at talking or anything. I guess I decided to take a shower, but I have no recollection of any of this. My bunkmates followed me and sat outside the shower, but I never turned the water on. They opened the curtain and found me lying there. The girls dressed me and got the guards, and then I got airlifted out.

YOU CAN EAT OR NOT EAT, WE DON'T REALLY CARE

I woke up in Galveston at the University of Texas Medical Branch (UTMB). Part of that's a prison, and part of it's a teaching hospital. In my records it says that I coded on the flight to the hospital. Basically, my heart stopped beating. Those helicopter paramedics saved my life. They said I'd coded because of all the toxins in my body. They said I was lucky I didn't die.

After four or five days I was moved to Carole S. Young Medical Facility at Dickinson. This was the beginning of September. It was a medical unit, but they put me in a single cell, and I kept banging on the door saying, "I'm supposed to see medical!" But no one paid any attention to me. I never saw a doctor there either.

At that point I had begun to take insulin. I was supposed to be on a special diet, but they didn't have one at Galveston. At breakfast one morning I asked for the special diet, and this guard looked at me and said, "You can eat or not eat, we don't really care." I tried to pick out what I could eat, but I mean, if you're stuck in a situation, you can only do so much.

I had this little yellow band around my left wrist that said "fall risk" because I teetered and tottered when I walked. This one guard tried to make me work. She took me to the warden and said, "She's worked in the laundry at Plane State, you know, she could work in the laundry here." The warden looked at me and said, "Ma'am, I don't want to hurt your feelings, but you look like a yellow Post-it note. I don't want you working anywhere. Ma'am, you need to go lie down."

I got two injections daily for my diabetes. But the day that I was due to go to Huntsville to be released, they didn't know if they were going to be able to send me home because my blood sugar was at 600. And do you know what they had given me to eat that day? We were on lockdown, and when they do lockdown you get nothing but sandwiches. I had one ham sandwich and two peanut butter and jellies. The nurse was afraid to let me travel, but finally we got my blood sugar down a little, and she let me get on the bus for Huntsville.

I was released early for medical reasons, because of the diabetes, and because I was in the last stages of cirrhosis when I was at Plane State. In three months I had gone from 300 pounds to 185. That's a loss of over 100 pounds in three months. It wasn't right.

I don't think anybody knows how demoralizing and how humiliating it can be to be in prison. The men get better treatment in Texas than the women do, and I don't understand why. I understand that what I did before was wrong, but I damn nearly died in prison, and truly I don't think anybody deserves that.

FRANCESCA SALAVIERI

48, formerly imprisoned

On a sunny fall afternoon in northern New Jersey, Francesca and her husband Michael meet us at the Unitarian Universalist church in town. The couple has driven over an hour for the interview, and both are friendly, although shy at first. Michael has agreed to walk around the town for a few hours so Francesca can tell her story. Francesca grew up as the youngest of six in a working-class Italian-German family, and is now the mother of two adult children who refuse to see her. A survivor of chronic childhood sexual abuse, domestic violence, and drug addiction, Francesca has battled mental illness since she was a young girl. She has been home from prison for not quite a year, having served six years for armed robbery. For the entire first year of her sentence, Francesca was housed in solitary confinement.

I JUST KNEW I WANTED TO BE NUMB

I was born in a little town in the Northeast. When I was growing up there was nothing but farmland there, but now there are million-dollar homes, with the rich and the lovely and all that stuff.

I'm the youngest girl in the family. Back then, as long as you were old enough to make a bottle for your younger brother or sisters, you were old enough to take care of the family, so we never had babysitters. There were six of us all together, and my brother and sisters basically raised me. We were all eighteen months apart, and very tight—actually too tight. We didn't know how to separate from each other, and there was a lot of violence between us. Both my father and my mother got violent too.

During my childhood, starting when I was six years old, I was sexually abused by siblings and cousins. I had a pattern of just following anybody who would give me a little bit of attention. I just had this innocence then. I just wanted to believe that everybody was good, and if you were nice to me, I would just go with you. I couldn't take tension and anxiety well, so I just wanted to make everyone happy. I wanted to make everything calm.

I started cutting when I was ten. I began cutting because I didn't know how to deal with painful and terrifying emotions. In my home, it wasn't permissible to show emotions, so the only time emotions existed was when they exploded into violence. Cutting allowed the evil feelings, the guilt, the remorse, and the anger to flow out of my body. The feeling of release from torture and satisfaction always followed the cutting episode. It got really bad when I was twelve, and that was when I started going in and out of psychiatric wards. At first, my family would put a bandage on the cuts and figure it was just what I did, and would tell me to cut it out. But eventually, I got in trouble for the medical bills. I was diagnosed with borderline personality disorder and dissociative symptoms, and I was on a lot of psych meds for most of my life.

When I was twelve, I met James. He was nineteen and had already dated two of my sisters. There were four of us sisters, and we were all allowed to have male or female visitors in our bedrooms at night. We were also allowed to drink and use drugs in the privacy of our rooms. My mother felt it was safer for us to do bad at home than to get hurt out in the real world.

James started coming into my bedroom at night when I was twelve, and then we eventually started dating. Even though he was of age, he was still immature, and he was an alcoholic and a drug user who hadn't finished high school. After a while I became a user too. I did a lot of pills, and when I turned sixteen, I sought out heroin because I just knew I wanted to be numb.

I ended up marrying James when I was nineteen, and a year later I gave birth to my daughter. James never lifted a finger. He never changed a diaper, never took a dish out of the sink, never did anything. He wasn't really physically abusive at first, but he used to throw things, and he was a screamer—very intimidating, just like my father. It was really very scary. I was always cringing, it was like my insides were shaking.

It took me fifteen years to leave him. All that time he wouldn't let me go. I had restraining orders, but they weren't like they are now. He could basically stalk me as much as he wanted because there were no stalking laws. As long as he stayed fifty feet away from me, he was fine. So he would come up with a hammer in his hand and he'd say, "I'm fifty feet away from you and there's nothing you can do about it." I worked at the deli counter of a local food store, and once he went there and said, "I'm gonna put your face in the meat slicer." Oh my god, it was so awful. I attempted suicide several times.

The police kept saying that there was nothing that they could do about it until something happened. And then something happened that was so bad. Four years into our marriage, we had a fight one night and he broke a wooden broom over my back. When he thought I was going to kill myself over it, he drove me to my parents' at 3 a.m. and kicked me all the way to the door while I was holding my three-year-old daughter in my arms. I refused to go back to his house without a police escort. When the police finally went into his house, he had clippings on the wall of men who had killed their wives and kids.

I divorced my husband in 1992, when I was twenty-nine. I stayed single for a while and then I met Sam, who was three times more abusive than my first husband. I guess he felt like he hit the jackpot when he met me because I had really low self-esteem and was really overweight, and I would agree to a lot of weird sexual things. By the time my second husband got finished with me, I was wearing blaring red lipstick and

I was working in the go-go club, stripping every night and going home to put all the dollars on his desk. Eventually I got pregnant, and he got angry because I wouldn't be able to dance and make money. He beat me in the belly until I lost the baby. I laid in bed for about three days, and he wouldn't let me go to the hospital. Finally the baby passed in the toilet. It was horrible, and I knew at that point that he was just going to kill me, so I left. But by the time I got out, I was pregnant with my son. When I was pregnant with my daughter, I quit heroin cold turkey, and I didn't do it again for ten years. Then, at my six-week checkup after the birth of my son, I was diagnosed with cervical cancer. I had several scrapings of my cervix, and a cone biopsy to remove all the cancer cells. I was given Percocet for the pain, which eventually triggered my addiction. When my daughter was thirteen and my son was four, I went full-blown back into addiction, and I ended up in jail over it. I called my mother and asked her to bail me out, and my mother said, "If you sign the kids over to me, I will bail you out." I said, "Absolutely not. I will not sell my kids for bail money."

I found a friend to bail me out. I went to court, but the jail had given me the wrong courtroom number. I waited and asked around, and I guessed I must have been put on the docket for another day, so I went to my mom's house to pick up the kids. She told me I'd just lost custody of my kids, that the judge had signed them over to her that morning in court because I hadn't turned up. Even though there had never been any Division of Youth and Family Services cases against me before, and I had never really been in any serious trouble, they signed my kids over to my mother. It turned out I had been only two courtrooms away. I remember my brother yelling in my face, calling me a crackhead, and my mother yelling that I was not allowed to see my daughter alone. I felt so small and worthless. Every time I went to see my kids, I ended up crying and skulking, until I eventually didn't go back any more. I was convinced that they were better off without me.

Within three weeks after I lost custody of my kids, I got on a bus and went to New York City. I ended up living under the George Washington Bridge for two years. Without my kids, I had nothing.

I was eventually arrested again, in 1998, for stealing. I always had a petty theft problem. I always felt that if I went into a store and I didn't steal something, I was getting ripped off. I have to tell you that I come from stock like that. My father was a Teamster truck driver, and everything that we got came in boxes and crates, and everything was openly illegal. In my family, it wasn't wrong to steal. After getting arrested that time, I decided I wanted to go back to my kids, and I went and put myself through a rehab program. When I entered that program I tested positive for hepatitis C, but it was early so I didn't get treatment. That is also where I met my current husband, Michael. I got clean, but they put me in a halfway house that was like crack city. Michael was visiting someone else there, and he was still a stranger to me then, but he just saw something in me and said, "You don't want to stay here." He took me to his house, and we've been together since then. Around that time, I went to court and started legal proceedings to try and get my kids back. I did get my son back in 2000, after nearly two years of visitations, but my daughter was sixteen by then. She had emancipated herself and was living on her own. Social workers asked my son to choose between living with my mother or with me. At that point, I'd been clean for a long time, but the social workers told me, right in front of my son, that he had said he'd rather be with his grandmother. How could the social workers ever expect him to trust anyone ever in his whole life? They were tearing that kid apart. I know what I did was wrong, but what they were doing was more wrong. So I took myself out of the competition.

I was in a house with my husband and I had a normal life, but the pressure of doing without my son was breaking my heart. Soon after returning my son to his grandmother's house to live with my mother, I went off smoking, shooting, doing pills, and everything else for about two days. The cops found me sleeping in the car in a parking lot across the river after my husband reported me missing. I said to the cops, "Do I have to go home?" And they said no, and I said, "Okay, then I'm not gonna," and I went back out again. If I had just gone home at that point, I would not have ended up in prison.

I just wanted to run away from all my issues, to run forever. So I went back out onto the streets and started using, and after the third day I ran out of money. By the fifth day, after the morphine lollipops, the morphine patches, heroin, crack, the cocaine, and all of that, I was a mess. I was in my car and I pulled into a supermarket parking lot in perfect view. I don't remember much, other than saying to a lady in the parking lot that my husband was in the hospital and he was having a hard time and that I wanted money. She was probably so scared of me, but in my mind, I was thinking, *Why isn't this lady giving me $20 or $40?*

I said to her, "I'll mail it back to you. Please, give me money before someone gets hurt." She opened her wallet and I picked out two twenties. Then, twenty-four hours later, I went back to the same place and asked another lady for another $40. This time I had a knife in my hand, and it worked again. Another twenty-four hours and I was back again to the same place. Now, tell me this is not insanity. I mean, who goes back to the same place three times? But on the third night, the police were there, waiting for me.

I EVENTUALLY MADE FRIENDS WITH THE MICE

Never before had I been in the criminal justice system. My psychiatric evaluation came back and it said I had diminished capacity, but when I went to court, I realized they were going to try it as a criminal case. Even though I had gone into rehab from the street with a diagnosis of dissociative disorder and borderline personality, the judge looked at me and said, "You look fine to me."

I was sentenced to seven years for armed robbery. I had to serve 85 percent of the sentence before being eligible for parole, due to the violent nature of my offense.

When I first got to the county, I was immediately isolated and put on suicide watch because of my psych record. I had no clothes, just a paper suit. I was put in a room with glass windows all around so other inmates, everyone, can see you. I couldn't shower alone and I couldn't have a razor.

I could understand not having a razor, but I couldn't have a comb, a brush, or a blanket. And because they thought I might hang myself, I couldn't have a sheet either.

I had to hold my emotions in, because if you cry, they send you back to maximum security so that you don't hurt yourself. But then you lose all the status you may have earned by working up to minimum, and you have to start all over again. You can't get to the halfway house until you do this, so in many cases your time gets extended. If you get sent to the men's prison in Trenton for serious mental evaluation, then they stop the clock on your sentence while you're there. So I had to tighten up and act like everything was all right. I just had to lay there and pretend I was sleeping and curl up in a ball. It's so inhuman. I felt like I was trying to come out of my body.

After seven days, I was moved to a facility where anyone who is sentenced for murder or armed robbery or is in protective custody is housed together, but are not allowed out at the same time. I was in the cell for twenty-two hours a day and allowed out for two hours for rec and my phone call and shower, but I was never out with another human being. I never saw anyone or interacted with anyone, unless on a visit, for an entire year.

When I first came to jail, I was scared of the dark, so just going through the terror of wondering who or what was going to crawl out from under my bed to get me was torture enough. But I eventually made friends with the mice, and started naming them. When the officers set sticky traps, I would secretly remove them so my friends wouldn't get hurt.

Other girls in secure cells would scream out of the side of the door to each other, but I did my time alone. I read and did a lot of yoga. I also noticed I paced a lot. Animals in cages at the zoo have the same behavior, circling back and forth to the edges over and over again.

When I got released into general population, I begged them to put me back into isolation. It was overwhelming to hear all those noises all at once, and to interact with people. I was a bit paranoid, and it was too much stimulation for my senses. I had formed a whole new me in the sanctity of my cell, and I felt no connection to the outside world.

I WROTE AND I WROTE AND I WROTE
AND I STAYED IN MY HEAD

I was mute by choice for my first year and a half in prison. I didn't let anyone speak to me. I kept my head down, and it was like I wasn't there. They tried to give me jobs. First they had me watch the garbage bins to make sure that they didn't overflow, but I was such a mental wreck then, it was difficult for me to be anywhere but under my covers. I just cried all day. Then they put me to work in the sewing factory, but not on a machine, I wasn't stable enough for that; they had me cutting the white strings off the garments. But really that was too much for me, and I started crying then too. It was torture for eight hours a day. So I asked for solitary, and I told the officers, "There is no way you can torture me more than you are doing now."

Those first couple of years in the segregation unit there was nothing to do, so I took pills. In prison there is a high market for tranquilizers and barbituates, painkillers also. The girls with prescriptions do what we call "cheeking." You pretend to swallow your pill, stick it between your teeth and gum, show the officer your empty mouth, and then go somewhere and spit it out. You can get $1 to $3 a pill, which is payable in items bought from the commissary, since we couldn't use money. It's actually disgusting, because you're eating something someone had in their spit. A lot of diseases are spread this way. I took painkillers until August 2006, when I made a conscious decision to stop. It's the best decision I made.

Another common practice is to make a "punch." A group of girls will get together and all put their psych meds in a container of ice tea, sometimes up to thirty pills, let the "punch" brew, and everyone drinks a cup of it. This can knock you out for twenty-four to forty-eight hours. A girl on my wing got airlifted out because she overdosed this way.

I faced a lot of abuse in prison. I asked for protection a few times while I was there, from both inmates and officers. The first time I asked for protection was because I was being abused by another inmate. We were on the same wing, which is a long trailer with thirteen beds on one side, and I had to walk by her to get to the bathroom or to get anywhere. Every time I went by, she would say, "I smell white people," or something like that, and threaten to hurt me for going by her. She was part of a gang and had a lot of power behind her. The abuse was so bad I was just not making it. I thought, *I can't live under these conditions any more. I can't move, I can't breathe, I can't get to the bathroom, I can't take a shower.* It was the same as the abuse on the street. I asked for help from my regular officer, and he told me that there was nothing he could do for me. He told me to work it out myself and said, "There are no cameras on the wing." So after that I snapped, and I really started acting out. For the first time in my life, I told someone that I was really gonna bash their head in. I guess it represented things in my life where I just felt people weren't helping me and protecting me. It felt like it used to with my brother and sisters, and I never really had the nerve to stand up to them, like I was a coward.

And then the prison doctors took me off of my medications without any help. In 2007, I went for my regular psych meds: Klonopin twice a day, Vicodin three times a day, and Risperdal. They told me everything but the Risperdal was discontinued because inmates were selling it. Well, I wasn't selling mine, I needed it—I'd been on Klonopin and other psych meds since I was fifteen.

I suffer from extreme anxiety, and anyone can see that when they've been with me for a while. When they suddenly took me off, there were withdrawal symptoms; I had diarrhea for about four days until I couldn't take it any more. I was so distraught that my officer sent for emergency help. When the assistant administrator came to see me about it, he said, "Let me tell you something. I'm here to protect and serve. I'm not here for your convenience. I'm here to make sure you get food and wake up in the morning."

I got so mad that I started refusing Risperdal, which was my antipsychotic medicine. So they threatened me with the psych unit, which they would do on and off for the rest of my stay. It was like a noose around my neck. You always have it in the back of your head. If you don't act right, if you don't get out of bed, if you don't do this, then you're going to the psych unit.

I had a lot of mental illness problems in my past, but in prison, you're not allowed to have them. It's not acceptable and they threaten you. So you have to internalize. So what I did was, I wrote letters every day, sometimes three times a day. I wrote my daughter and my son and my husband, and I wrote and I wrote and I wrote and I stayed in my head.

AS LONG AS NO ONE DIES ON MY SHIFT, I DON'T CARE WHAT YOU DO TO EACH OTHER

In 2008, I had to go to the lieutenant because this crazy lady was living across from me, and her crazy was running into my crazy. She told me she was going to cut people, and she was threatening violence and telling me who she was going to do violence to. At first I kept telling the prison staff, "You've got to get this lady away from me," but nobody would understand. I went to the psychiatrist, I went to the officer, I reported it to everybody. I can't tell you how many times I sat there and pictured myself dead. It's a miracle that I made it through alive then. Finally I made friends with the lieutenant, and went to him about the crazy lady. I said, "I can't do it, not one more day. I just can't live under these conditions," and he moved my room. But then the officers on my unit retaliated. They tried to sabotage his decision by calling the psych unit to have me moved there. It didn't work, but they tried. Another retaliation came when a new officer was put on the unit who was very disrespectful to women. He saw what my weaknesses were, so he used to jar me when I was sleeping. He would come in and wake me up out of my sleep and I would have nightmares. This officer obviously had issues with women, and he had to prove his manhood by demeaning them. Most women wouldn't allow that, but he preyed on the weak ones who'd been in abusive relationships all their lives. I fit that category.

Plus my PTSD[1] made me more fun to mess with, because loud noises or sudden movements caused me to jump and react. This officer would come right next to my bed when I was sleeping and scream my name really loud, just to enjoy my anxiety attacks. He was doing this for a while, and then he had me in the bathroom, telling me I couldn't go out on smoke break until I'd scrubbed all the rust out of the tub, but it was a stain that wouldn't come out. He would have me digging dirt out of drains, but I was still stupid and not standing up for my rights yet, so I was actually doing what he told me. But after about three or four months of this, I finally filed a grievance against him. That was the first time I'd ever written up an officer, and it was the first sign that I was getting better. I went to the prison administrator, who said, "You've been here for three years and I've never even heard your name. That's so unusual, for someone to be so under the radar, so it's got to be true." After that, the abuse from that officer lightened up a lot. But the rest of the officers, let me tell you. Half of them spend half their time in the bathroom texting, and the rest of the time, they're getting blowjobs in the bathroom, or they're calling you "crackhead," or "toothless," and that's when they are not high themselves. Several officers went to rehab while I was there. One married a pregnant inmate to avoid going to jail for sleeping with her, and some were dismissed for sexual assault.

There is such a thing as a "quiet storm." This is a pre-arranged fight by inmates that other inmates cover up. Most officers allowed this, and they'd say, "As long as no one dies on my shift, I don't care what you do to each other." That was the famous saying in there. Sometimes, just for fun, the officers would take a Blood and a Crip, who are usually held in separate wings, and have them switch their spots, just to watch them fight. I saw three girls get airlifted out. For them it was just pure entertainment. And again they'd just say, "As long as no one dies on my shift."

---

[1] Post-traumatic stress disorder. For a description and a list of symptoms, see the glossary.

MY TEETH ARE ALL GONE NOW

I have hepatitis C, but I was not really treated for it during my whole time in prison. When I went in I clearly told them I had it and I asked for treatment, but they refused to do more than give me a biopsy. They said that because my liver was only in stage one of damage, that it wasn't high enough to qualify for treatment. But my viral load is 10 million, which is high. Also they used my mental state against me and said I was not a candidate for treatment because of my past depression and suicide attempts. They just took bloodwork every couple of months, and not even that much, because due to my IV use, I'm a really hard stick, and they didn't want to be bothered.

I eventually forced them to do a biopsy, because I had started learning my legal rights. During the biopsy, I was handcuffed and shackled while they put a foot-long needle into my side to get a piece of liver out. Not only was this shackling demeaning, but it made the whole experience even more painful and stressful.

I still haven't been treated since my release. I'm still trying to find a hepatitis clinic that will accept my dismal insurance.

On top of this, my teeth are all gone now. When I first got into the halfway house, I asked the dentist for oral surgery for gum disease because I was in so much pain and my teeth were coming out of the gums. He replied, "Come back in six months and see how they feel." I told him I was being released in five months, and he said, "Oh well."

I didn't want to get treatment in the halfway house anyway, because the dental office was in the sex offender unit in a men's prison, and the male inmates used to jerk off while you waited for your appointment. The waiting area was surrounded by glass walls, and the men would expose themselves and pleasure themselves. I thought, *I'd rather lose all my teeth*, and I did.

HOW DO YOU GET FROM HERE TO COLLEGE?

When I got to the halfway house, I saw an African American lady who was carrying a book-bag, the kind with the wheels attached. Everyone else at the halfway house was wearing t-shirts and talking about drugs. That lady was close to fifty, and she had done more than twenty years inside. She wasn't trying to fit in, and she wasn't ashamed of her book-bag; she held her head high. She walked like she deserved to carry that book-bag, like she had every right to get a college education.

I wanted to be like her, free of shame, so I asked her where she was going with that bag, and she told me, "College." I said, "College? How do you get from here to college?" She told me about the program at the local community college that helps students in the halfway houses enroll in school during the day, with a set of academic, social, and financial support.

The administrators at the halfway house told me it was too late for me, that registration was already over, but I just kept calling and calling. I insisted. I kept fighting for my education.

Most of the inmates aren't educated enough or tenacious enough to keep up the fight. It is so hard, though. But I am so blessed, do you know what I'm saying? I've got an education now. The state pays for my bus fare, my books, and I get a check at the end. It is like God stepped out of the sky and shook my hand. When I'm done with school in December, I want to start a business to help people like me, who are coming out of prison with little idea of what to do. Even if I can just help navigate people to the right agency, I think that would make a huge difference. Now they just dump people out on the street without any support or idea what to do to survive. I want to help them.

Today I see a therapist and I'm on minimal medication. My belief in myself is what keeps me clean and sober. I'm not garbage. That was a hard lesson to learn. My own mother hasn't talked to me in years, and my children didn't accept me back when I came home, but I'd lived my entire life trying to make other people happy. Look what it got me. Now I live a quiet life with my husband, who waited seven years for me, and accepts me for my faults because he knows my heart is pure. I am not a criminal; I am a person led astray, who didn't have enough confidence to do the right thing. I am now a grown-up, and I take responsibility for my actions.

I entered prison at forty-one, but emotionally I was twelve. That girl doesn't exist any more.

MARILYN SANDERSON

43, currently imprisoned

Marilyn appears tired but optimistic as she talks with us in the sterile, claustrophobic visiting room at the Denver Women's Correctional Facilty, Colorado. She has blonde hair, bright, clear blue eyes, and a pale complexion that reflects a life spent largely confined indoors. After years of sexual abuse and violence, Marilyn had finally started to get her life on track, providing for herself and her young sons. Then, in 1996, she was involved in her boyfriend's death, and is now serving a seventy-year sentence for second-degree murder. During our meetings, Marilyn expressed regret over some of the decisions she's made in her life, and how she misses the life she'd created for herself and her children. She spoke to us of the events that led to her imprisonment, of changing conditions in prison, and of the degrading strip-searches she and her fellow inmates fought to put an end to.

MY HOME LIFE WAS NEVER
VERY STABLE OR CONSTANT

I was born in California. My parents divorced when I was about six, and I lived with my mom after that. I have lots of good memories of my father from when I was little and he was with my mom, and it was good after they first separated too.

I always liked school, and I did well in my classes. But I never really had many friends. It's hard to fit in when you move around so much and you're the new kid all the time.

I have one older full-blood sister and one younger half-brother, Samuel, and then there are some steps that I don't claim. My mom got married to her second husband, Frank, about two years after she and my dad divorced. Frank was sexually abusive toward me. I can say that now, finally. I remember, when I was about eight, him telling me to sit on his lap when no one else was home. He would rub my chest and fondle me— I didn't even have breasts. He would say it was "our little secret." One time we all tried to get away from him and he took a shotgun to us. My sister was holding my baby brother in the car, and I was in the front seat with my mom. I remember Frank with the shotgun, trying to bust through the window of the car. My mom took us to my aunt's house, and she and Frank divorced shortly after that.

My mom mostly bartended for a living, which is how she met her third husband, Sandy—his name was Jimmy Sanderson but everyone called him Sandy. Shortly after he and my mom got married, when I was about nine years old, he sent my sister to live with my dad in Kansas. She had snuck out of the house one night, and I was not allowed to let her back in. When I came home from school the next day, my sister was gone. I can never forgive Sandy for that. After my sister was out of the house, we moved as a family to Colorado. Sandy adopted my brother and me, so that's why I have his last name. My relationship with Sandy was stormy because he was an alcoholic and he was emotionally abusive to everyone. He was a control freak and wouldn't let me do anything. He was also physically abusive to my little brother, and he molested me a couple of times. When I was thirteen or fourteen, I was sleeping on the couch, and Sandy had been drinking. I woke up and he was sitting there. He stuck his hand in my shirt, and I asked him to please stop. He said, "Oh, I didn't realize." But then he did it again. A few weeks after that, I remember I was taking a shower and I looked up and he was just watching me. I was so afraid of him.

I left my mom and Sandy's house when I was sixteen and went to live with my dad and stepmom in Kansas. At first everyone got along. They gave me much more freedom than my mom and Sandy had, and I let it go to my head after being caged for so long. My dad and stepmom didn't check up on me, and I had no curfew. I could just do what I wanted; I was smoking marijuana, I was drinking. It was not a good time for me. The day after I graduated from high school, my dad took me to the Greyhound station to head back to Colorado. I was seventeen at the time, and it was another eighteen years before I had contact with my dad again.

NO ONE REALLY KNEW ABOUT THE VIOLENCE

I lived in Colorado for about a year after I came back from Kansas. That year, I got pregnant and had my first son, Nathan. I gave him up for adoption because I kind of flipped out after I had him. After that happened, I moved to California. I was eighteen, almost nineteen. I moved in with my aunt and uncle in the San Francisco Bay Area for a little while and worked at a health club they owned. Things start to get fuzzy around this time, because I started doing drugs. The first time I did it, I'd been out the night before and I was so tired, but I had to get going and go to work. Someone at work gave me some crank. She told me to try it, that it would help to get me going, so I did. It did get me going, and I was shaking and felt like my eyes were going to oscillate out of my head. That's how it started.

At the time I was dating this guy Armando, and I ended up moving in with him. He was the garage attendant at the building where I worked. He was also a drug dealer, so after that I started doing crank all the time. I was really, really addicted. I couldn't wake up in the morning unless I had it, and I couldn't even go to sleep at night unless I had it. It was a horrible thing.

During the four years we were together, Armando and I would get in fights all the time. I used to go to work with bruises and black eyes and who knows what else. I would try to leave, but he would always say he would kill me and leave me in a dumpster and no one would ever know. After one fight when I felt like I had to escape, I moved back to Colorado and started living with my family. A short time after that I found out I was pregnant, and Armando convinced me to move back to California.

I went back and forth for a while between Armando in California and my family in Colorado. During this time, I had my son Tom, in 1991, but I was still hanging out with Armando and doing drugs here and there. My mom gave me an ultimatum and said, "It's either your baby or your drugs," so I stopped. Whenever I would think about getting high, I would think about not having my baby. I'm in no way saying that it was easy. The *decision* was easy; it was the follow-through that was tough.

The other issue is that when I had Tom, it was very obvious he wasn't Armando's, because my son is half black, and Armando is Filipino. Armando hated black people, and I was worried he would do something to harm the baby or me, or both of us. I didn't want to take chances, so I finally decided to come back to Colorado for good.

MY BROTHER HAD EVERYTHING TAKEN FROM HIM BECAUSE OF ME

In Colorado I worked odd jobs, mostly fast food, and at a factory. I worked for temp agencies and when I got pregnant with my youngest, Timothy, I went on welfare. He was born in 1994. But by the middle of 1995, I got off all assistance except the food stamps. I was working a good job, and I bought us a new car, a Subaru wagon. It wasn't actually new, but it was nice and new to us. Then it all happened.

I met a man, Tony, and it went very quickly from start to finish. It was probably after two months that he ended up moving in with me and the kids. He took care of them while I went to work, which I was fine with.

Tony's death is why I'm in prison. On February 17, 1996, Tony and I got into an argument, and I put him out of the house. He kept calling and calling, but I wouldn't answer the phone. Later that night the phone rang and I thought it was a friend calling, but it was him. He convinced me to let him come over, but as soon as he walked in the door, he started yelling at me, beating me, raping me. I had been through this before with Armando, so I knew how to react and let it be as minimal as possible. Sunday, I woke up early, dressed myself and my baby Timothy—Tom was visiting his father—and I woke Tony up very lovingly. I didn't want him to touch me, but I was trying to wake him up in a good mood. Then I took Timothy to my sister's house.

I was really freaked out. When I was at my sister's, I had a conversation on the phone with my brother Samuel about Tony raping me and beating me. Later that day, I left Timothy at my sister's and went home. My plan was that if Tony wasn't there, I was going to hurry up and lock the doors. But when I walked in he was there, making dinner.

Then my brother came over with a friend of his. I went upstairs, and I heard my brother tell Tony to get up and get out. Tony refused, saying he wasn't going anywhere, and then I heard them start fighting. I don't remember much after that. I was taking a lot of Xanax[1] during that time, so my memory is fuzzy. I just know that Tony ended up dead. Later on I learned the cause of death was blunt-force trauma. My brother and his friend took Tony's body somewhere, and I went to the police and made up a story about some guy coming over. I don't even remember what I said exactly. Then somebody called the police and said that they thought my brother had been involved in Tony's death, so they called him in for questioning. At first he denied it, but two days later he turned himself in. He tried to say it was just him involved, but once I found out my brother had confessed, I told the truth and I got arrested. My brother's friend was also arrested, but he lied and cooperated. He did maybe eight years only.

After my arrest I was so distraught that for days I rocked and cried, rocked and cried. I was scared of everybody in jail. I was afraid I was going to get beat up. I never even really thought I would come to prison

---

[1] Alprazolam, a medication used to treat anxiety disorders and panic disorders. Side effects include memory impairment.

at all. Until the day I walked into prison in 1997, I was like, *This isn't real, this isn't real, this isn't real.*

I was charged with multiple counts, for first-degree murder, conspiracy to murder, and kidnapping. The prosecutors told me that if I went to trial the state would take my children and there was no chance I'd ever see them ever again. My attorneys, who were court-appointed, agreed with this, and I believed them. So I took a plea agreement for sixty to eighty years.

EVERYONE HAS BEEN AFFECTED

For the longest time I didn't take any responsibility for Tony's death. I thought, *I didn't physically kill him, so why was it my fault?* But now I have to accept responsibility. It is my fault that Tony is dead. It's my fault that my brother is in prison and my sister got charged with accessory after the fact. My brother had everything taken from him because of me. He got married in jail because his girlfriend was pregnant at the time. His son is going to be fifteen this year, and he's never been able to be a dad to him. I feel really horrible for what I've done to everyone else—not just Tony and my brother, but my sister, my kids, my mother. Also Tony's family, his friends—everyone's been affected.

My sons Tom and Timothy were bounced around between my mom, Sandy and my sister for about six to eight months. Some family friends also agreed to take them after I was in prison. My mom convinced me that it would be better for them to stay together and not be moved around so much. After I was sentenced, the family friends started talking about adopting them, and I was against it at first because I was still in denial about everything that had happened; I thought I was going home any time now. Finally, after two or three years in prison, I said okay to the family friends adopting my kids. I agreed because I wanted the kids to have stability, security, and parents who loved them. I didn't want to risk the state taking them away permanently. I felt so depressed to give them up, but I knew I was doing the right thing for them.

Today my sons are seventeen and twenty. I haven't seen them since they were about two and five. I don't see them because I think their adopted parents feel it's better for them this way. I have no relationship with them, and I've never heard from them directly. I have no idea what they think or feel about me, which is strange as a mother. A few months ago, I got a message from my youngest, Timothy, through my niece. All it was was "Hi." When my niece told me that, my heart bloomed with happiness. I was just so happy, I cried and cried. I was telling everyone, "My baby said hi." It was great. It still makes me smile.

THE MOST BEAUTIFUL THINGS I HAD SEEN

I've been incarcerated at three different facilities in the Colorado system. I arrived in the Denver Reception and Diagnostic Center (DRDC) in the middle of 1997. That was before they built the Denver Women's Correctional Facility, and everyone, men and women, had to go through DRDC. They're supposed to decide where you belong after that, but they just kept me there on permanent assignment for about a year. Then in July of 1998, I got sent to "Cañon," which is Colorado Women's Correctional Facility, in Cañon City. I spent six years there before they brought me to Denver Women's Correctional Facility (DWCF) in 2004.

Each facility is different. At DRDC, we were treated like humans. Officers would joke around with us and talk to us. If there was something wrong, they cared. They would say, "Hey, Marilyn, are you all right? Do you need to talk to someone? Do you want me to call Mental Health for you?" It wasn't, "Prisoner X, what's your problem?"

At Cañon, it was way more spacious. There were only about 200 women there. We had a yard, a tennis court, a baseball field, a volleyball court. It was expansive and it was nice. We got to go out into the yard, sit on the grass, look at the flowers, lean up against the trees, take nice pictures. There were chain-link fences, but you could see outside the facility. There were two horses on the land nearby, and every once in a while you could catch a glimpse of them. The first time I saw the horses,

I thought I was seeing things! After being caged up and not seeing any animals other than rats and snakes and spiders for so long, seeing the horses was just incredible. You could tell they were old and had been around a while, but I thought they were the most beautiful things I had seen in my whole life. I used to imagine they were mine, and that we were on a beach somewhere.

I WONDER IF THE STAFF
CONSIDER US HUMAN AT ALL

Some of the staff at Cañon, at least when I first got there, were similar to the staff at DRDC. They talked to you, and the inmates called them by their first names or their nicknames. But after a few years, prison administration was really cracking down on the staff being familiar with us. They had to call us by our last names, and we had to do the same. After a while they got new staff in, new captains, sergeants, and lieutenants, and it started turning into a real prison. The staff started being mean, and it just trickled down through the system.

Some of the staff would tell us that, in their training, they were taught that basically we are all animals and they shouldn't trust us with anything. They were taught to go the extra step to take our humanity away from us. It is so bad now that I seriously wonder if they consider us human at all. Women are affectionate creatures, and we need physical contact. But in prison, we can't ever touch anyone. We can't hug, hold hands, or pat each other on the shoulder to comfort each other, because you'll get a write-up for sexual abuse. I've created friends and families in prison, but I can't hug the women who I think of as my aunties.

Of course this is because of all the problems with rape and sexual assault in prison. But that happens more often between staff and inmates than between two inmates. Sexual assault between staff and inmates happens fairly frequently, but it is undercover. Sometimes it starts off being consensual, but then later it becomes an abusive situation.

A lot of women in prison are very vulnerable, and there are staff members who take full advantage of that. It used to be easy for women to be sexually assaulted here at DWCF, but now they have cameras everywhere, so it's not so easy. They started putting the cameras in a year or two ago, in the units, in the work areas, in the storm room, everywhere. But there are still areas where sexual assault can happen, like in closets that don't have cameras.

One time an officer came into my room during count. They aren't supposed to inspect while we're there; they're supposed to make us leave the room. But he came in, and he kept telling me to touch him—you know where. He said, "Come on, just do it, no one will know." I kept refusing, and he finally left. This sort of thing happens all the time.

There is a lot of verbal abuse by staff that goes on in prison, a lot of emotional abuse and screaming and yelling at us. Under the rules, you cannot have your head covered at night, because the staff have to be able to see that you are there. They count us at about 2 a.m. and they count us again at 5 a.m. If they don't see us or they don't think we're moving, they'll bang their flashlight on the bars. It's a loud cracking noise in the dead of night. A lot of us have PTSD,[2] and a lot of us have other emotional issues and problems with loud noises. When they bang the flashlight, I am up for hours with my heart pounding because they startled me so badly. So many of us are sleep deprived, because it's hard to get a deep sleep when you're in this environment.

There is little access to hygiene products unless your family sends money. We get one roll of toilet paper one week, then two rolls the next week, and if we need more we have to buy it. Soap, shampoo, tampons, toothpaste, toothbrush, lotion, etc. all have to be purchased from Canteen, which is sort of like a store that you order from. Things are expensive, and if you have no help from the outside, you're pretty much screwed. As far as earning money from our prison jobs, most people only get 60¢ a day for five days a week of work. Out of that, 20 percent

---

[2] Post-traumatic stress disorder. For a description and a list of symptoms, see the glossary.

is taken for restitution owed to the state. Generally speaking, most people only have about $10 a month to buy all their hygiene products, which isn't enough when you consider how much everything costs.

THE STRIP-SEARCHES WERE BEYOND HUMILIATING

One of the worst things the staff put us through was the strip-searches. Before when we got strip-searched, we'd give them our clothes and stand there in the room with nothing on. You'd run your fingers through your hair, show them the inside and the back of your ears, and run your fingers inside your mouth. If you have a belly, or boobs that hang, you'd lift them up. Then you'd raise your arms up, lift your feet up and wiggle your toes, bend over and cough, and that was it. That was bad enough, but after a while you got used to it.

Then after a while they started the "labia lifts" (that's what we called it). It wasn't just bending over and coughing. We had to spread our labia, and staff would make us cough while they were looking. They gave you an option: you could either lean forward, squat a little bit and spread your lips apart while they looked, or you could put your leg up onto a chair or a toilet and just cough, and you didn't have to touch yourself. Either way, it is invasive. If it's not to their satisfaction, they tell you to do it again. Then they tell you to turn around and face them and spread your most intimate parts apart so they can inspect. It is beyond humiliating. They were having us do it in a room that didn't have a sink, so we couldn't even wash our hands afterward. It was horrible.

Some staff would get right up on you and inspect in there with a flashlight. Now, if there's a legitimate concern with a particular inmate, with a history of smuggling contraband, that is one thing. But they were making all of us do this every single day. It was awful. Sometimes it was one officer at a time, sometimes two. When there were two officers, they would talk about you and what they were doing with you as if you weren't even there.

There is a captain who, when she stripped me out, said, "Now I want you to do this. I need you to bend over all the way, grab your butt cheeks, lift your butt up, and cough as you come up so I can see both of your holes." I said, "What? I have been here well over ten years, and no one has ever told me to do it like that." I felt extremely violated. I went back to my room and cried, I was so upset.

A lot of us talked about it and started filing grievances. Eventually the press found out about it and the facility was forced to realize how violating the labia lift really was.[3] At first the prison administration responded by making it discretionary, then they finally stopped the facility-wide strip-searches. Now, where I work, in the print shop, only one person a day gets stripped out at random. It is way better. But there are still some officers who think they're supposed to do the labia lift, so it still happens.

THERE IS NO REAL MEDICAL CARE IN PRISON

If you have an obvious emergency or an injury, the prison staff will deal with you immediately. Otherwise, you submit a "kite," which is a medical request form. You turn it in with your problem, and you may or may not hear back, and you may or may not get scheduled. You definitely won't hear for at least a couple of weeks; it's at the prison's discretion. You can do a self-declared emergency, where you say you need to see someone right now, but they charge you $5 for it.

I've had some medical problems. The prison has been slow to respond to a serious foot problem I had, and they failed to give me pain medicine after a biopsy and a hysterectomy. The worst was about two years ago, when I woke up one morning and the left side of my face was drooping.

---

[3] In a letter to the Colorado Department of Corrections before it had ended this practice, the American Civil Liberties Union (ACLU) wrote that "it is virtually inconceivable that the new requirement that prisoners hold open their labia contributes anything to prison security," and noted, "prisoners at the DWCF [Denver Women's Correctional Facility] have complained that the new breed of search exacerbates prior sexual trauma—an effect no doubt compounded by threats of being doused with pepper spray for noncompliance."

My tongue felt like it was ten times bigger than my mouth. My mouth wouldn't form words, even though my thoughts were working fine. At work that day, I was supposed to be the one answering the phone, but I told my boss I couldn't do it because I could barely talk. There was obviously a problem. It hadn't really occurred to me to go to medical at first, because I'd never had a good experience with medical since I'd been in prison. But a few days later I finally went. It took a few months for them to finally send me to an outside neurologist, who did a CT scan and an MRI. He found two white spots on my brain; one was the size of a silver dollar, and the other one was smaller. The neurologist expressed concern and said he needed to do some more tests. Next thing I know, they have me going to a Department of Corrections (DOC) neurologist, who could not figure out what was wrong with me. They did additional tests, but not the advanced tests the outside neurologist wanted. They did an eye test, a blood test, and a spinal tap. For the spinal tap, you're supposed to lay still for a few hours after it, but they put me back in the truck to come back to prison, which was a bumpy, hour-long ride, and then I waited for hours before I got back to my unit. I felt like I was dying, and my head hurt worse than it ever has in my life.

I never saw the outside neurologist again. The DOC neurologist told me they thought it might be white-matter disease, which means I have spots on my brain. They said there was no way of telling what caused it so they couldn't determine what it was for sure. I still have trouble getting the words from my brain to my mouth. And my face will still droop and I'll have trouble talking. It happens to me a lot. They won't let me see a neurologist any more, because they said no one can figure out a diagnosis so there's no point. Of course I am concerned that there are spots on my brain, but I'm already resigned to the fact that nothing is going to happen while I am in prison. I'll have to wait until I'm out to get real medical attention.

I STILL HAVE HOPE. I DON'T
ACCEPT THAT PRISON IS MY FATE

The governor's clemency board[4] is meeting in June. My mom talked to someone at the governor's office, and they told her that I'm first on the list of cases they're considering. I'm very nervous about it. My clemency is being sought on the basis of sentencing disparity, and the fact that my involvement in the crime was minimal.

I find strength because I still have hope that I'll get out. I don't accept that prison is my fate, and that's it. There are times when I just want to give up. I get overwhelmed with sadness and regret about everything; the knowledge that I was involved in a man's life being taken, everything he missed out on, everything I missed out on, my children growing up not knowing me and how much I love them, my brother missing out on his son's childhood. Those are things that can't be gotten back. But my mom helps to give me hope. And my biggest hope is that someday I'll have a relationship with my children. That keeps me going.

---

[4] A state-government board that meets to review clemency applications, with the power to commute sentences and grant reprieves and pardons for certain charges. People in prison may apply for clemency if their cases meet certain criteria defined by state law, and after all other judicial remedies have been exhausted.

TAISIE BALDWIN

34, formerly imprisoned

*The Jim Williams Motel Efficiencies sits along a busy four-lane industrial bou-
levard on the outskirts of Grand Rapids, Michigan. There's a McDonald's to its
right, a Wendy's across the street, and the parking lot for a laundromat and budget
supermarket to its left. Taisie likes her single-room unit here, just big enough for a
bed and a side table. When she was first released from prison, she tried living with
a roommate because it was cheaper, but she moved on when the roommate took Taisie's
money and spent it on crack. Taisie's voice is even and steady as she describes how she
ended up serving a multiple-year prison sentence for check and credit card forgery and
felonious assault. Her voice wavers only when she talks about Elaine, the daughter
she had in prison, who was taken from her just a few days after the birth.*

*Taisie's narrative has been edited from interviews conducted by Voice of
Witness and a previous testimony, in which she describes medicals runs to the
hospital and programs available to pregnant women in prison.*

FLASHES OF PLACES I'VE BEEN IN

My childhood, in my mind, is not chronological. It's flashy. My earliest
childhood memory is of being sexually abused by an uncle, in the bathroom of the trailer I lived in with my parents. I was seven then, and

I remember my sister being in a playpen in the next room. I don't think that was the first time, but I remember it because my mom found us. She cut my uncle up with a knife pretty badly, and then the cops came.

That's when the relationship between me and my mother went wrong. It was as if it was all my fault, and I'd ruined her relationship with the family. My mother would call me a slut. She'd tell me the sexual abuse was my fault, and there was nobody who could ever help me. She was angry at me, and I was angry with her, too.

My parents worked in migrant camps, picking fruit and working construction, and we moved a lot. I'd wake up one morning and the van would be packed up and we'd be on the road. They just didn't want to settle down in one place, I guess. By the time I was eighteen I'd been to about thirty-three different schools all over the United States. Sometimes I'd only be in school for a week and then I'd move to a different state. I remember being in certain places we lived in: Flagstaff, Milwaukee, Florida, South Fork, Butte, Cheyenne, San Antonio, Houston. There's no chronological order for me, just flashes of places I've been in.

Life was kind of an adventure. I remember times, like when we lived in Milwaukee, and my sister and I went to play hide-and-seek in the dumpsters in the back alleys with other kids in the neighborhood. There were other times where I camped out in the mountains, just seeing the beauty of the country and the earth and stuff like that.

In Milwaukee, I got accepted into a school for art and dance. I took the acceptance letter home, and my mom said no. She wouldn't let me do that. She wouldn't even come to my shows. When I was in Girl Scouts, she stole my Girl Scouts cookie money and I got kicked out.

As long as I can remember, my mom beat on me. She'd beat me with sticks and extension cords or anything she could get her hands on at the time. She'd punch me or grab me by the hair and throw me across the room. She'd go off because the dishes weren't done. She'd go off because I hadn't cooked or I hadn't done the laundry. It was always something I hadn't done. But I think that I was also really angry as a child. I back-talked her, I didn't respect her at all. I would do bad things, like break her stuff.

I was thirteen when my mom gave me to the state. At that time we were living in Three Rivers, Michigan. My caseworker from Children's Protective Services (CPS) was this woman named Eileen. She came and told me that my parents had given me away, and that CPS were taking me out of my home. My parents said I was unruly and out of control. My mom to this day says that she was forced to give me to the state, but if they were taking me away from her, they would have taken my sister too.

At first I was put into this place in Kalamazoo called the Ark. It was a place for kids who had nowhere to go. Then I went to live with a couple, also in Kalamazoo. They didn't really want to be foster parents; they were trying to adopt a newborn baby because they couldn't have kids. I stole money from them. I was having sex in my room. I was skipping school. At one point, when I was fourteen, I thought I was pregnant, and when I told the foster parents they called Eileen and said that I could no longer stay there.

I ended up going to Pine Rest Christian Hospital, a psychiatric hospital in Grand Rapids. CPS sent me there because I was so angry and depressed. I had a therapist there who tried to establish a relationship between my family and me. My dad would come visit me all the time and take me places, but if my mom came, I had to have supervised visits because our relationship was so messed up. We would just fight when we saw each other without supervision. Still, I wanted her to come. She kept saying she was gonna come to a therapy session, she was gonna come, she was gonna come, and then she never did. My therapist told me that my mom said she didn't want to see me if she had to have other people there. I was so upset that I ended up slitting my wrists. After that, they put me in what they called the "adolescent watch."

One night, I put my bag and my makeup Caboodle and all my stuff out the window. Then I went outside like I was going to smoke, and I left. When I got to the road, I saw this semi-truck driving my way, and I flagged it down. The driver was going to Arkansas and I said, "Can I ride?" I was fifteen. I guess at that age I realized what men wanted, and I slept with him all the way down to Arkansas in order to eat and shower. That's what I did until I got to California—I hitched rides with truck drivers in return for sex. I'd been gone a few months, and finally I called my mom. I hitched back to Michigan and she met me at a McDonald's.

After my mom came and got me, I remember us smoking marijuana together, drinking together. Then there was a knock on the door and my caseworker Eileen was there with my guardian *ad litem*—that's the person the court appointed to take care of me legally. They wanted me to go with them. Eileen was blocking my way to get to my stuff, so I threw her across the room. They called the cops after that, and I remember the cop coming toward me, but then I blacked out. When I woke up, I was in the back of a police car, hog-tied. I don't remember what happened, but my mom tells me I kicked the cop in the groin and took his gun. I don't know if that's true. Then the cops took me to a juvenile home, a lock-up. I was there for three years.

TWO DAYS AFTER I MET HIM, I MOVED IN WITH HIM

I got out of the juvenile home when I was eighteen, and I moved to Kalamazoo, where I met Billy. Two days after I met him, I moved in with him. We would have parties where we'd invite people over to gamble and get drunk and smoke. Mostly we were living in Kalamazoo, but we'd move around from room to room, wherever we could go and party. Billy was very abusive; he'd hit me and beat me up.

One night, he was acting real strange. It was the night he got his unemployment check, and I walked in on him smoking crack—that's where his money had gone. So that was really the beginning of me doing all the bad check-cashing and credit cards and anything for him to get high, anything to make him happy, because my happiness wasn't complete unless he was happy. At the time, I was working a lot at Denny's, mostly at night. I knew that Billy was doing bad stuff with the checks, but we still needed the money that I was making.

Billy got arrested first. I'd told him, "These checks are no good, you can't cash any more." But he went to the bank and gave them his ID. The bank employees told him that the computer wasn't working, have a seat. So the dummy sat and waited for the cops to show up, and then of course they came for me.

I was at the apartment when there was a knock on the door. It was a detective. He said, "I've got pictures of you, I know who you are. I know you've been using bad checks, so there's no use in telling us your fake name." I said, "Okay." But then he said, "I do know that you're working every night. So I'll tell you what. I'll come back here tomorrow, you'll come with me, we'll get you arraigned, and I'll get you a bond." So basically he was saying that I could stay out on bail and keep working, which I wanted to do.

Soon after that, I went to the landlord to pay the rent—we were two weeks behind. I had $110 from tips, but we owed $250 for rent. The landlord said I had to get out, that he wasn't waiting any more, he just wanted the money. I went back to my room, and there was a knock on the door. These two guys came in, saying, "You're getting out right now. We're packing your stuff." They tried to throw my dishes in garbage bags and I told them, "Get the fuck out!" I grabbed a knife and started swinging at them. I think I'd just had it with everything at that point.

The cops came and arrested me for assault. By then I had three felonies that I'd accumulated within seven months, all going on in court. I ended up taking a plea to take care of all my cases at the same time. I was given two to fourteen years for the bad checks, one to two years for the credit card, and one to four years for the assault, but it was all going to run concurrently. Basically, I had a two-year minimum with a fourteen-year maximum. I was sentenced on October 7, 1997, and I was sent to prison in Wayne County ten days later.

I ALWAYS HELD MY HEAD HIGH

When I got to the prison, I did twenty-eight days of quarantine and then they put me in a unit—the prison is divided into units, which are the different buildings. The next day, a doctor from healthcare called me and informed me that I was pregnant. I didn't believe her, because I'd never gotten pregnant before. I mean, I'd had plenty of unprotected sex, but I'd never gotten pregnant. I had always thought that maybe the guy who molested me when I was seven had done something to me so that I couldn't have kids, or something like that. It wasn't that I hadn't tried, because at the time I thought a baby could help all my loneliness. But I'd just never gotten pregnant.

I was told that I was about thirty-nine days pregnant, and that I had twenty-four hours to figure out what I was going to do. Was I going to keep the baby or get rid of it? I was only twenty years old, and I wasn't sure what to do. Billy was locked up, I was sitting in prison, and I didn't know how long I'd be there. And I wasn't talking to my family then, so I had nobody. But I knew I would never have an abortion, unless it was absolutely necessary. I knew I was going to keep the baby. I made contact with Billy, who was as excited as I was, and he promised to take care of our child until I got out.

I am a type 1 diabetic, and I have to take insulin shots. Because of the diabetes, the doctor said I was a "high-risk pregnancy," and that prison healthcare couldn't handle my prenatal care. So I had to have weekly doctor's appointments at a hospital outside the prison.

At times the medical runs were horrible experiences. At other times I looked forward to the escape, even though I went in chains. The guards put belly chains on me and kept my hands cuffed for the whole doctor's visit, unless the doctor said they had to take them off. It felt horrible to walk through the hospital in chains. One time, I remember I had two armed guards with me. They both had guns on their hips. We were in the regular elevator, and the guard pushed the button to go down. But then the doors opened on the wrong floor, and some guy was there. He looked at me, my belly chains, and the guards, and he said, "Oh, I must have the wrong elevator." Nobody wanted to be near me. It was embarrassing, but I always held my head high.

I was strip-searched completely each time I left and came back to the prison. That became hard at six or seven months of pregnancy. They made me squat and bend over, spread myself, and cough. I couldn't balance, so I had to hold on to something with one hand, and spread myself with the other hand. Then I couldn't get back up, but the guards wouldn't help me. It would take me about three minutes to get back up on my feet. The guards just stood there and looked at me.

Sometimes a guard would drive like a maniac to the hospital, and when I asked him to slow down, he'd refuse. Other times I began to get carsick, but the guard couldn't stop at the side of the road because I was a prisoner, and I was forced to vomit in the van.

MY PARENTS MADE BIG PROMISES

At the first ultrasound, maybe at eight or ten weeks, the technician looked at the monitor, got up, and ran out of the room. I panicked, because I figured there was something wrong with my baby. Then she came back with the doctor and she had a big grin on her face. The doctor looked at the monitor and told me I was pregnant with twins. I was so full of joy that first time I saw a picture of my babies on the monitor. I wanted so much to share it with someone, but the only person by my side was a prison guard, and I couldn't talk to her.

In prison, I was in a unit with women who were all pregnant. I remember being surprised that there were so many pregnant women in prison, some coming to prison just before their due dates. But it was good, because I talked to older women who had been through childbirth before. There was also a childbirth instructor who came from Children's Services. It was through the Wayne County Incarcerated Pregnant Women's Program. We had group therapy sessions in parenting, substance abuse, domestic violence, prenatal care, childbirth and postpartum. At times, the instructor tried to talk me out of allowing Billy to take care of our babies, but I insisted.

At seventeen weeks they did another ultrasound, and the technician got up and ran out of the room again. This time I knew that something was wrong. When the doctor came in, he said, "I'm sorry, but twin B's heart has stopped beating." I was devastated. I kept thinking, *How could my baby die?* The doctor said there was no reason, that "sometimes things happened like that." I was so worried for the other twin. Every week I panicked that they were going to tell me she had died too.

I told Billy about losing the twin, and it made me feel better to have someone to talk to. We'd been writing to each other before I found out I was pregnant. He was on jail work release, working at Burger King, and I could call him collect sometimes. He was there emotionally, and he had been happy for us when I found out I was pregnant. So I was hoping that he'd be there for our daughter, but it didn't happen. When I was about seven months pregnant, Billy had finished work release, and I called the house where he'd been renting a room. A guy there said that Billy had stolen all his money and disappeared.

Soon after, a woman from Children's Services told me that my baby would have to go into foster care. I was angry. I thought, *Here I am, pregnant, and they're telling me that they're going to take my baby.* I didn't want it to happen because I knew I would lose her. I figured I had a choice—foster care or my parents. It wasn't a hard decision because I had no other choice. I had memorized their last known address, so I wrote them a letter and told them that I had nobody to take my baby. I asked them to please help. My mom wrote back and said she'd talked to my dad and he'd said yes. So then they started coming to visit me.

We had our first visit when I was eight months pregnant. I was nervous, I didn't know what to expect. I hadn't seen my mom since February 1995, and by this time it was maybe March 1998. We'd been writing letters, but we hadn't spoken because the calls were so expensive. I was still worried that she couldn't be a good mother. During the visits, my parents made big promises. My mom said she'd changed, that she didn't get high any more. Part of me did believe it. But in the back of my mind I thought, *She's lying. She's the same person she's always been.* But I thought I had no choice, so I didn't listen. I just didn't want my daughter to go into foster care.

I FORGOT THAT I WAS A PRISONER.
I WAS A MOTHER

My perfect baby was born on June 25, 1998, after seventy-two hours of labor. After she came out the nurses wrapped her up and put her in my arms for a moment, but then they wanted to check her. They thought her arm might have been broken during delivery, so they took her for an X-ray. I was crying when they wheeled me out of the delivery room because I was so scared and worried about my baby girl and what I might have done to her. This whole time the guards had been waiting outside the door. One of them was nice. To take my mind off my baby, he tried to tease me a little about how loud I'd been when I was pushing.

Then they took me to a room on another floor. The guards were sitting next to my bed but they hadn't cuffed me yet. And then the nurse brought my baby back. She told me my pelvis bone had squeezed the nerves in the baby's arm, but that the bone wasn't broken and she would be fine. I was so relieved. The nurse had taken a few snapshots before the X-rays and she gave them to me. I was so happy that I had the pictures; I knew I couldn't take my baby with me, so it was the best I could have.

I held my daughter and started to breastfeed, but it was too emotional. I kept thinking that I was going to have to leave her, that I was going back to prison the next day. It felt like my whole body was breaking. I couldn't do it—the bonding was too much. Finally I asked for a bottle. I feel so horrible that I had to do that to her, but I just couldn't do it.

I named her Elaine, after my baby sister. Elaine means "light." She is the light of my life. She is my reason for living. Even though she couldn't understand the words I was saying, I wanted to comfort her with my voice. It made me feel better to know that she heard me.

Elaine slept in the bed with me. I needed her there. I wanted to touch her and feel her and look at her every second that I could. She had to be close to me. During that time, I forgot that I was a prisoner. I was a mother.

I think I stayed up the entire time I was there. I couldn't sleep, not even for a second. I didn't want to miss her. But the next morning the guards told me that I was going to be leaving that night, that it was prison policy that a woman can only spend twenty-four hours with her baby before she's brought back to prison. I stopped eating, because I wanted my blood sugar to be so low that they wouldn't be able to check me out of the hospital. I just wanted a few more minutes with my baby. I couldn't imagine how I was going to leave Elaine. I loved her so much.

Then on the morning of the third day, the guards came and told me that they were going to have the hospital take my baby out of my room if I didn't eat. And then a doctor came in and said the same thing. At that point I basically realized that I had to go back to prison, that I was done. By the afternoon my glucose was fine. I spent the last few hours of that afternoon with my beautiful daughter.

WHEN SHE TURNS EIGHTEEN I'LL BE THERE

The day I went back to prison, I held Elaine in my arms and promised her that I was always going to be there for her. I promised that I would be good, and that I would get out of prison so I could be with her. Then a guard came in and told me that I had to be strip-searched before I left. The nurse took the baby while I went to get searched, and after that she gave her back to me. By then I was sobbing and begging the guards, "Please give me another minute." But they kept saying, "We have to leave, Baldwin." I took a breath and gave the baby back to the nurse. Then they put belly chains on me again.

I was crying so hard I couldn't breathe. I felt empty, like I was leaving my soul at that hospital. For all I'd been through, leaving my baby was the most painful thing I'd ever felt in my life.

When I got in the van, one of the guards had to sit in back with me. She told me, "If you wanted to have children, you would have stayed out of prison." I wanted to hurt her so badly, but there was nothing I could do.

When we got back to prison I started fighting with other women and getting misconduct tickets. They called me a "management problem." I wasn't thinking about the consequences, I was just hurt and angry, and I wanted my Elaine back.

My parents came to see me about three months after the birth, and they brought Elaine with them. I could tell that she loved my father, that they had a bond; her eyes lit up when she looked at him. Two weeks after the visit, I got a phone call while I was in segregation,[1] after one of my fights. I called home, and my mom told me that my dad had died of lung cancer. Then, fifteen days later, I got a phone call from my attorney telling me that my mother had given my baby to the state, and that I had to be in court in the next three days.

I went to court and tried to fight it. My attorney told me to do well in prison, go to school, take parenting classes, basically to do whatever I could. Michigan law states that if a parent is incarcerated for two years, their parental rights can be terminated. I fought for two years, and I went to court every three months. I saw the parole board, but they gave me eighteen more months. When I went to court in September of 2000, my mother testified that she didn't think I could take care of a baby. A couple of days later I got a letter telling me that my parental rights had been terminated.[2] According to the law, I had "neglected" my child because I was in prison. I sat down right there in the prison yard, reading the letter, and I couldn't get up. I felt so lost.

I appealed, but by that time Elaine was with a foster family. She'd been placed with them in 2001. My attorney told me that Elaine's foster parents wanted to adopt her, and that they would let me have contact with her only if I gave up the appeal. If I didn't, the Family Independence Agency would place Elaine with a different family, who would adopt her immediately and seal the file. So I called the foster parents and I asked them if I did stop the appeal, if I would be able to have contact with

---

[1] People in prison can be moved to segregated housing, away from the general prison population, for protection or for disciplinary reasons. For more details, see the glossary.

[2] For details about how parental rights are terminated, see Appendix V.

Elaine, and maybe sometimes get pictures. They said yes, so I gave up the appeal.

Elaine's foster parents adopted her. I thought they were a good family, so I mostly felt lucky. They were allowing me to stay in contact through phone calls once a month. Elaine wrote me a letter when she was eleven, and she knows that I'm her birth mother.

Her adoptive parents haven't let me talk to her since I got out of prison in spring 2010, when she was twelve. She's thirteen now. When I asked about their promise, they said that they didn't think that I was ever going to get out. They're a very religious family, and they said that she was getting rebellious and so they wanted to take everything out of her life except God. I asked them if they had talked to her, or asked her what was going on. They said no, that they just were waiting for God to take care of it.

I worry about Elaine. They might have raised her, but she's got my blood in her. She's going to question everything, she's going to have an open mind. I just want to talk to her, to let her know that I'm checking on her. But now they aren't telling her that I'm calling and writing letters. They promised me that I could see her, that I could be there, but they lied to me.

When Elaine turns eighteen, I'm showing up. I just want her to know that I love her, and that I've tried to be there for her. I know I can't do it until then, but when she turns eighteen I'll be there.

VICTORIA SANCHEZ

36, currently imprisoned

*In 1995, Victoria was arrested for a murder she was involved in three years ear-
lier, when she was sixteen years old. Although she was a minor at the time of the
murder, she was tried as an adult, and was subsequently sentenced to life without
parole. Victoria talks about her painful separation from her four-month old son
Ethan upon her arrest, and how she tried to cope with this in prison by adopting
several of the cottontail rabbits that roam the prison grounds. "I raised one for
three years, potty trained and all. I became its mom." Victoria also describes her
relationship with a member of staff, which resulted in an extension of six years on
her sentence, and how she overcame her battle with heroin to become an advocate
for juvenile offenders.*

ARE WE GOING TO TRY HER AS AN ADULT?

I was born in 1975 in Harbor City, which is near Los Angeles. Both of my
parents are from Mexico, and they met here when they were teenagers. In
Mexico, my mom started working when she was five years old at a place
where they make tortillas, so she never really got to be a kid. If she didn't
iron my uncles' clothes right, they would literally throw her on the floor
and kick her. All she knew was, if something didn't go right, there were

beatings. That's the way my mom was raised, so that's how she raised me and my five brothers.

When I was around seven years old, I was molested by my uncle. He'd been living with us for a while, and anything I wanted he would get for me, so I loved him. But one Christmas Eve, he climbed into my top bunk and forced me to do it. I didn't know about sex then. I was so naïve that I didn't know what a virgin meant. All I knew was the Virgin Mary. I felt so ashamed, and I didn't want to be around my uncle. I wanted to tell my mom, but I knew I wouldn't be his favorite niece any more. Finally I just told her, and my uncle ended up leaving.

When I got to high school in 1990, I started rebelling and getting involved with gangs. At the time, my mom said, "One apple has gone bad, the rest are not going to spoil," and she moved down to Mexico with my five younger brothers. My dad and I stayed so he could work and send money to them.

In ninth grade, I dropped out of school and I ended up meeting this guy who was in my cousins' gang. I was sixteen, he was eighteen. He became my boyfriend and I ended up getting pregnant by him, but I had a miscarriage.

And then, in 1992, the incident that brought me here happened. I got involved in a murder. I don't want to talk about what happened out of respect for the victim and her family. But I will say this: I was sixteen at the time. I personally did not use a firearm. I did not take a life. But my boyfriend did.

When it happened, my dad said, "You're going to get killed yourself," and he sent me to Guadalajara. I fell in love with the ranch life there. People are so different, so polite, and you don't have to worry about going outside and being robbed.

Eventually I met a man. He played guitar in a band and he was very handsome. He was a very good man. We were in love, and then I got pregnant. I was eighteen at the time, and he was a little older. We lived in Guadalajara together, but when I was six months pregnant, I said, "I'd better go back to the States and have the baby over there, just to make sure everything is okay," and he agreed.

I went first, and my parents paid for a coyote[1] to bring my boyfriend over to the States, and we got married in 1994. My husband worked construction with my dad, and I ended up getting a job at Price Club; I was one of those people who demonstrates the food at lunchtime. My son Ethan was only four months old when I got arrested in 1995. It was for the murder my old boyfriend had committed three years before.

I went to Juvenile Hall. The people there were very, very nice, but I was so traumatized being separated from Ethan, who was still breast-feeding at the time. I was suicidal. I wouldn't eat. The staff there were really watching me because they were scared I would hurt myself. They don't give the girls visiting hours with their children, but the watch commander set up contact visits for me with my son. My mom came back to help me raise Ethan, and she would bring him whenever visits were allowed on the weekend.

It was very emotional to see my son. Every time, I would see him growing up and changing. This was my boy. I was his mom, and I was supposed to be there with him, changing his diaper, feeding him. It was hard. Every time he'd come to see me, I'd take off his little shoes because I wanted to see his little feet and see how much they'd grown. It got to where he was one or two years old and he knew I was going to ask him that, so he'd take off his little shoe and show me his foot.

My mother raised Ethan to know me as his mother, and every time he comes to visit me, I can feel that connection and that bond with him. I know a lot of women who are in the same situation and don't have that bond with their children. I am so lucky.

The watch commander never asked for anything in return. The people who worked in Juvenile Hall genuinely cared about the girls and formed genuine relationships with them. They knew we were lost souls. But I was only there for thirty days.

---

[1] A person who takes money to help others illegally cross the U.S./Mexico border.

At my hearing, the judge asked my attorney, "Are we going to try her as a juvenile because she was sixteen when it happened, or are we going to try her as an adult?" My attorney didn't tell me that it was better to be tried as a juvenile. He told me, "If you get tried as a juvenile, you're just going to have one judge deciding—guilty or not guilty. If you're tried as an adult, you'll have twelve jurors decide your fate. If I were you, I would go as an adult." So I went with what the attorney said, and then they cuffed me and took me to a tank, which is a holding cell, with adults. I shouldn't have listened to what the attorney said. That was a terrible mistake.

YOU WOULDN'T TREAT AN ANIMAL LIKE THAT

It was an ugly and drastic change when I went to that adult county jail in LA. When I was booked in, I had the ugliest feeling. All these women were there, talking about their drug use, prostitution, and other things that I really didn't know about. I was terrified.

When I went to court, I had to be completely shackled with arm and leg restraints, and I had to wear a bright red outfit. I did my county time like that. I was there from March '95 all the way to June '96. I fought my case there, if that's what you want to call it. My attorney didn't actually fight for me. He came and saw me two or three times at the most.

County was an ugly time because of more than just my attorney. There was this bailiff from Pasadena. This other inmate told me, "He likes to talk to girls, and he'll feed you. I'm gonna have him pull you." The bailiff wrote court papers saying my presence was requested, and then they put me and the other girl on a bus to Pasadena. When I got there, I understood what was going on: the bailiff was having sex with the other inmate.

I didn't have sex with him at first. But then he pulled me again when the other girl was not there. He wanted to have sex, he wanted nude pictures of me. Finally I let him, and we end up having sex in an office.

He kept giving me things so that I wouldn't say anything. He would give me shampoo, lotion with perfume in it, good toothpaste, stuff that you don't get in jail. I also knew that if I ever did say anything, he knew where to get me. He had other deputies that would get me, and I knew what deputies did. Everyone knew about the elevator rides. If a deputy had something against you, or if they didn't like you, they would take you in the elevator and beat you up. The way that those deputies treated the women—we weren't even like animals to them, because you wouldn't treat an animal like that.

In October 1996, when my trial in LA County was over, they brought me up here to Central California Women's Facility (CCWF) in Chowchilla, Madera County. I was given a sentence of life without parole. My old boyfriend, who I had the case with, got life too.

YOU GET LONELY

When I got to prison I had to learn how to survive, how to live, how to not do something that was going to get me beat up, stabbed, or hurt in any kind of way. You have to learn and you have to be quick to learn.

You get lonely. Women who haven't been with other women before, they do it in prison out of loneliness. Affection, you know? You just want to be with someone. I ended up getting a girlfriend—something I swore I wouldn't do. Everything I swore I wouldn't do, I ended up doing!

Laurie was a prison guard. She met me the very first day that I came, and she asked me a question that I was tired of being asked: "So what are you here for?" I didn't want to talk about it, so I just looked at her and I replied, "Overdue library books." That was our first encounter.

Laurie would make it a point to come around where I was. One lady walked up to me one day and straight out told me that Laurie liked me. I couldn't believe it. I'd never been with a woman before, and I thought, *Are you serious? Is this happening?* One time I was sitting on top of a fire hydrant in the yard, and Laurie came over and told me that she thought I was pretty and that she wanted to get to know me. That was the beginning of the relationship.

She would make it a point to trade places with my housing staff so she could be close to me. It went on for a while this way, and I did start feeling attracted to her. She made me feel good. We never had sex, but we did kiss. Laurie and I were together for four years. She was a beautiful person. She made this not feel like prison, because of the treatment, the respect, the hope that she brought me. She was different. She didn't belong working here.

Laurie ended up quitting the job in 1999. We never got caught. The staff were never sure, but they kind of suspected it, and they thought it was my fault. If you ever get involved with staff, it's always your fault. You did it, you manipulated. After Laurie quit, she was close with my family. She would go and stay with my mom down south. She was also good to my son, and would help him out. She took him to Disneyland, bought him bikes and toys and clothes.

I was doing okay for a while after Laurie left. Then a few months later, I started hooking up with a new girl, and she used heroin. I had never seen it before, and I remembered I used to put down the dope fiends, I would talk really bad about them. Then my time hit me. First my grandpa passed away, and I was trying to deal with it as best as I could, but I started getting suicidal again. I thought, *I can't live like this. I can't take being separated from my family.* I thought about all the things that I had gone through.

A few weeks later, a cousin I was really close to passed away too. That just sent me over. I knew my girlfriend still had some heroin, so I took it, and it felt so good. I thought about my son growing up without me, my grandfather passing away; everything my family was going through because of me being here. I didn't feel anything, and none of it hurt as badly as before. After that, my life revolved around drugs. Heroin numbed my sentence. Heroin became like my wife, my husband, whatever you want to call it. That was my life.

You can get it any way you want. If you have money on your books, you shop for other women. You give them hygiene, stamps, whatever they want, and they give you heroin in exchange. With me, it came easy.

I found ways to get it, and people just loved to get me high for free. It's just how I am, I guess. I'm talkative, a good listener, I sit around and have a conversation. Some gave me it because they wanted to have sex with me. Rarely was a time I would have to buy it. It would just come to me. Here, free high! Come, free high!

You could also get it from the staff. After a while I became involved with a medical technical assistant (MTA). I was really, really sick at that point. My knee hurt. My kidneys hurt. I'd pee and blood would come out. I would get these fevers out of the blue. Even on heroin, I knew I was sick.

One time, I was getting delirious. My roommates called the staff and got a wheelchair for me and took me to medical. This is when I met the MTA. Staff were not allowed to be in the room when medical checks you, so I was in there by myself with him. He checked my temperature. He touched my forehead and said, "You do feel clammy and hot." Then he moved his hands to feel my neck, and then he put his hands down my shirt.

I looked at him. I couldn't believe it. He said, "I've seen you before and I've checked you out. I think you're so beautiful and I really want to get to know you and talk to you." I told him I wasn't feeling good, so he gave me medication—someone else's medication—and then he said, "Come to the medical unit tomorrow and I'll help you get some more."

I saw him a couple more times after that. He would give me medication, and even nice lotions. I told one of my friends that this guy liked me, and she said, "Work him! Work him! You know you can get whatever you want. I'll help you." And then she told me to ask for a P.O. box on the outside.

He got it for me, and then we began to have sex and see each other a lot. He was bringing drugs in from the P.O. box he got me. After that first time when he touched me, I would numb myself with heroin every time I went to see him.

When I look back on it now, I see that the trade we had going on was wrong. We were humping, he was bringing me drugs in exchange. What the heck was I doing? That was just the same as prostitution.

I WAS HIGH EVERY DAY FOR SIX YEARS

I was high every day for six years total. During the time I was with the MTA, from 1999 to 2000, he would bring me bottles of vodka. So for two days I would use heroin and then on the third day I'd drink vodka. I was high for two days, drunk the third day.

I did end up having feelings for him, and we shared a lot of personal things. I wanted to believe he really cared for me. But we were just humping. And this time people noticed.

Laurie was the one who told on us. Since she was close with my family, she read a letter that I'd written to my brother. I'd told my brother, "There's someone in my life. He got me a P.O. box on the outside, if you ever wanted to write me directly." It was dumb because my brother never wrote anything that was wrong, so he could have just written me here in prison.

Laurie called up here and told on us. She didn't give my name, but she gave his. An investigation went down, and the officers went to the P.O. box and found heroin, weed, and pictures of me and the MTA together.

In early 2000 I had to go to court again. I was taken out of CCWF and taken to Fresno County jail because the case was in Fresno court. I was there for nine months. The investigation unit here wanted me to testify against the MTA about the sex and the drugs. They said, "What he did was wrong. He should never have stepped out of those boundaries with you. He used you." They made sense, but I felt so wrong about everything I had done. I felt so wrong telling them we'd had sex, so I refused to talk.

In the end I got six years added to my sentence. I never saw the MTA again or talked to him, but I was told he got a ninety-day observation. I'd already ruined my life, and now I'd helped ruin someone else's. People have told me, "Victoria, he's probably done it before! You're not his first time." In fact, I knew he was seeing another girl at CCWF. But I still felt so guilty.

I STARTED HATING THE DRUG

After that trial, I was brought back to CCWF and put in lockup. I was watched 24/7. My mail was monitored and my food was brought to me; I couldn't go anywhere. The COs[2] began to randomly search my room, and they started verbally abusing me. The rumor was that I'd gotten ten members of staff walked off. They'd say things like, "Don't look at Sanchez, she'll hypnotize you!" They called me the Black Widow. But even to this day, even though they say that about me, staff try to get with me. They say things like, "We could go for a quickie here!"

The women staff were also much harder on me. When I hooked up with a man, they reacted so differently from when I was with Laurie. Today everyone says I manipulated the MTA. If they only knew the truth. He started it!

When I got back to prison after the case in Fresno, I went back to my old routine. Twice I almost OD'd. The first time my friends threw me in the shower, slapped me, walked me around, and kept me from nodding out. They put me in cold water and just kept walking me around. My friends brought me back. They saved me.

In 2004 I started using less because something inside of me was being fixed, spiritually, mentally, emotionally. My woman at the time, Sarah, she was a big-time drug addict. She always wanted to be high. It hurt me to see how she had to be high to numb herself from her reality, and it brought me back to the reason why I started using. I started hating the drug, and I began weaning myself off of it. I got to the point that if I did it, it was a recreational-type thing. And then it got to where it started to make me ill, not good.

In January of 2005, I ended up getting really sick. The doctors didn't know what was wrong with me. They kept giving me the runaround, doing X-rays on my lungs, until finally I was hospitalized here at CCWF. They isolated me because I had lupus and they didn't want me to catch

---

[2] Correctional officers.

anything from anyone else. Being sick was like a spiritual awakening. I felt so much pain in my body, my lungs hurting.

I told God, "Just kill me, take me so I don't feel me any more, so I don't do this life sentence. Just take me away. And if I have a purpose in this prison, then show me and lead me to something. I'm sick of having to be high to live life, having to numb myself, so I ask You to give me the strength to live and show me my purpose. And at the same time, I'll give You this addiction. Give me the strength to not want or crave this addiction, not to need that drug to make it every day in here."

After that, I never used it again.

EVEN THOUGH WE'RE HERE, WE CAN HAVE A PURPOSE

In 2005, I felt this force to bring hope to these women in here, and show them that there is something out there. So many of them come in here like me, and become lost souls in addiction. Even though we're here, we can live and have a purpose. Even though we're here, we have to fight for our freedom. Who's going to do it if we don't? That year I also heard that finally a change had happened. The Supreme Court decided that there would be no more death penalty for juvenile offenders. As an advocate, it raised my hope and faith much higher.

I kept seeing battered women coming in to CCWF. I'd see youth who'd been arrested at sixteen years old. If you're affiliated with a gang, you're brainwashed, you're manipulated, you're a battered human. I kept thinking, *How come we're not looking at these cases? How come we're not fighting these cases?* It wasn't just for me, but for future generations that are just being thrown away.

I didn't know how to go about it, so all I could do was tell them about the injustices that happen in here. So I started helping women write 602s, which are complaints against prison or medical staff, and I started helping them find their way around the prison, to get real help. If you get arrested at sixteen, you're stuck there, at the age of that child inside you. Your mentality and your ways are different from the other people who are here in prison. And even if your case happened at that time and you're arrested later, you're still traumatized, and it's the same thing. The child is inside. The fear is inside.

I kept thinking, *There are so many youths in here, and nothing is being done about it.* They have Narcotics Anonymous, Alcoholics Anonymous, and battered women groups here, but never one for young offenders. So a few of us got together and said, "We need a group." We worked on it for a long time. Different inmates, different staff were telling us there was no money for it. We fought from May 2008 until June 2009, when the group finally got approved.

The group is called the Juvenile Offenders Committee (JOC). Many staff support us. We get to meet once a month, we get to have visitors come in from the free world to talk to the girls. It's costing the state no money.

The six co-founders of the group, we became the executive body of the group and we run it right now. JOC is my heart. There are 120 women in the group, and I try to keep a connection with all of them because it helps me also to remember, *Victoria, you're not the only one serving such a harsh sentence. Go to one of them and give them a hug, just talk to them, and they'll understand. They'll know they're not alone.*

I believe that one day I'll leave this place. I'll see my son again. Ethan is sixteen now, and he still lives with my mom in Southern California, near where I grew up. He has a new baby brother and sister from his father. His brother and sister live in Mexico, but he sees them a lot and goes there for summers. I get to see him once a quarter; I don't want my mom to make the trip up here too much. He'll be eighteen soon though, and then he can come up by himself.

MY SON IS AN ACTIVIST LIKE ME

Because of my case, my son advocates for the youth. Ethan's gone to Sacramento and spoken to senators and assembly members on behalf of youth getting a second chance. When they ask him why he's there, he tells them he's not only there for his mother, who was sixteen years old at the time of her crime, but for all the youth and future generations that are being thrown away. All the attorneys and organizations tell me how articulate he is. He has a demeanor about himself; he's only sixteen going on seventeen, but he's so grown up. He always tells me, "Mom, don't worry about me. I would not give you more pain while you're in this place by me doing something stupid. You do not have to worry about me."

He's just amazing. He is in ROTC right now. He wants to be in the army. He's an A student. He wants to become an attorney, his dream since he was five.

And now I've shared my life with him. Me and my son, we're working together to change things.

CHARLIE
MORNINGSTAR

66, currently imprisoned

Charlie is a Native American who was born biologically female but has identi-fied as a male for as long as he can remember. At five-foot-two, Charlie cuts a slight figure, but his voice is deep, and bounces off the glass windows of the private visiting room where we sit and talk. His long ponytail, once jet-black, bears a growing number of gray hairs. His walking stick hangs on his wheelchair, which sits outside in the common room with the guards (who relentlessly refer to Charlie as "her"). In 1984 Charlie was convicted of the first-degree murder of his girl-friend and sentenced to twenty-seven years to life in prison. He contends that he is innocent of this crime. For his narrative, he prefers not to discuss his conviction in detail. Instead, he describes the societal and institutional pressures to conform to conventional gender identities that he has felt during his life. He speaks about the discrimination he has experienced as a transgender male during the past twenty-five years in the prison system, and his efforts to maintain his dignity and strength throughout. In the last few years, Charlie has started a group in prison to help people with gender-identity issues, a project which helps him stay motivated as he awaits parole.

MY MOM SHOWED HER LOVE BY
ALWAYS BEING THERE FOR US

I always knew that my spirit was masculine, that it wasn't simply homosexuality. My grandmother knew it too, but I think my mom's whole perspective on it was worry. Considering the world and the human beings in it, it put me in danger. And that's all she could think of. She said that other people weren't going to understand, and that she didn't want to see me hurt. She tried to prepare me for the world the way it was. She said, "You will find that people do not understand you as you are, no matter how good a person you are."

On October 10, 1945, I was born on a reservation in the Northwest. My two younger sisters and I are real close in age—we were born one, two, three—but it was as if I was a lot older. I was the boss. My mother had polio and she walked with crutches, so when we went places I was kind of the herder to keep my sisters together—hold their hands, make sure they didn't take off.

When I was a kid, my mom was strict. We were really poor, and she raised us all by herself. She was determined. Some people like to think love means hugging you and kissing you on the cheek all the time. My mom showed her love by always being there for us, by making our clothes, by always being busy doing stuff for us.

My mother was twenty-three when she had me. We left my dad when I was four. He drank a lot, and he was abusive. At first my mom thought that we needed a father, so she was going to put up with him. But when he hit her and knocked her down in front of us, she decided that no, we didn't need to see all that.

I recall jumping on his back to make him stop. I remember telling him, "You're not my daddy any more." One time, he came back and my mom locked herself and us kids in the bedroom. We pushed the dresser drawers up against the door because he was trying to break down the door. We were all pushing and scared to death and he was hollering and yelling that he was going to kill her. So my mom dropped me out of the window and I ran down the road and called the police. As soon as they took my dad, we left.

I FELT THEY WERE TRYING
TO TAKE AWAY WHO I AM

I was raised on a reservation, and then I went to a boarding school that was run by Jesuit nuns. It was up on a hill, and was primarily surrounded by wheat fields. It had crab apple trees in the playground and benches built around the trees. We ate a lot of canned crab apples!

The boarding school was really strict. It was almost military-like. We had to make our beds a certain way and have everything all lined up in our drawers. We were required to wear dresses, but other than when I was in school, I only wore jeans, and my shoe choice was always brown Oxfords. I was pretty mischievous and inquisitive, so I used to get in trouble. My friend said a nun told her I was a gifted student they didn't know what to do with. Back then the only kids who went to schools for gifted students were those whose parents had money. I was pretty much alone, mostly set off by the fact that I was really shy. Other than that, not many kids like a teacher's pet.

In the seventh grade, my family moved to the nearest city and I went to school there. There was no high school on the reservation, so either you did that or you went to boarding school. I didn't want to go to eighth grade. I just told the teachers, "I know how to do the work." And they tested me and they found out that I did, so I skipped the eighth grade and went to public high school when I was eleven, in 1957.

I don't believe that I felt any kind of prejudice until just before I started high school. When the school district tested me, did I.Q. tests and all that bunch of stuff, they told my mom that she needed to do something. They said she needed to discourage my masculinity, because otherwise I might become homosexual. So my mom tried to discourage me from what I call being myself—dressing the way I dressed. She said that it would only lead to problems for myself. Her assumption was that I would become homosexual, and she was worried about the discrimination that would occur toward me. Before entering high school, I didn't even know the word *homosexual*. Growing up, people on the reservation and at boarding school would talk about males being more girl-like, or females being boyish. There wasn't really a stigma. Mostly, the reservation kids just accepted that I was once a little girl who became a little boy—without any surgery or anything, but just because of the way I was. They kind of took it like, "Okay."

When I started going to public high school it became more apparent that people treated other people differently. I felt as if the students thought I was different because I was Indian. It was a predominately white school, and the other students there didn't have anything to do with me, didn't include me. It wasn't really any blatant acts, though.

In my first year, I did well academically and I made honor roll. But I didn't participate in afterschool sports and activities because I had a paper route to do, and I did odd jobs for people. I took care of canaries for this lady, and I used to help this man cut and stack wood. With that money I could go buy a loaf of bread, some milk, rice, whatever, something that we might run out of. At home we were always running out of stuff like that. I would work, and it gave me satisfaction to be able to help out, so I just kept on doing it. Sometimes my mother laments that I always wanted to do those things to help. She says, "Well, you never really had a childhood as a result." But for me, challenges and learning new things were fun.

In my second year, I joined the band. That was my only extra thing that I did. I played the trumpet and then I played the drums. That was one of my outlets, and one of the few activities that I had with other kids. One thing I liked about the band was the band uniform—you wore pants. Even then, at the public school, girls were required to wear dresses. I hated wearing those dresses. I just felt they were trying to take away who I am. Because of that, toward the end of my second year in high school, I didn't want to go any more. Then, when I was a junior, I wouldn't go to school. You could consider that trouble, truancy, whatever. I think that it may have started with missing one or two days. Then I saw how far I'd gotten behind in school, and finally, when I was fifteen, I just said, "Heck with it," and stopped going.

I DIDN'T LET ANYBODY KNOW
I WAS PHYSICALLY FEMALE

On the reservation there weren't any jobs, because it's rural, it's not a city. Some people might work construction, highway-building and stuff, that was near the reservation, because there wasn't that much construction going on in the reservation. A few people might work at the Indian Agency.[1] There was farming, but the farming was done by a white farmer who leased your land to farm it. And some Indians might work for the farmer, but not very many.

In the city next to the reservation, I observed that the good jobs were not done by Indians. I never saw any minorities working at a bank, or in the big clothing stores, like JC Penney's. So that wasn't an option for me. You could be a laborer as an Indian, but it seemed you could never aspire to be anything else.

After working for a while in a grocery store, I heard from some people that there were so many minorities in California, and that it would be easier to get a job there. My mom had gotten me a car, and one night, I just decided to go. I was almost nineteen.

When I reached LA, I had run out of money and I was sleeping in my car. I found work as a dishwasher for four days, for three meals a day and $1 an hour. I saved that money, rented a room and then went on daily pay, where you go and work different places, different jobs.

One of my jobs was at a gas station. When I worked there, I found out about prejudice against gays and lesbians. There was a gay bar across

---

[1] The Bureau of Indian Affairs is an agency within the U.S. Department of the Interior. It is responsible for providing services to American Indians and Alaska Natives and implementing federal programs within reservations.

the street and some of the male patrons of the bar were dressed kind of feminine. I heard the things my coworkers had to say, some things the other patrons had to say. They called them freaks, weirdos. They said anyone who could act like that was not normal. When I heard those comments, it scared me.

During that period I did not suffer the kind of discrimination that I might have suffered. I was passing as a male, and I didn't let anybody, except for my partners, know that I was physically female. My circle of associations weren't gay; I didn't go to gay bars and stuff like that. I knew I was better off not letting anyone know about my biological sex, because I didn't know who I could trust. I felt that people would not accept me for myself.

I KNEW MORE EDUCATION
WOULD GET ME A BETTER JOB

After several years, I met some Indians in the Los Angeles area, and so I did not feel as homesick. I found other people who talked the same, had gone to Indian boarding schools. Everyone had the same perspective, and it was comforting. One day I saw an advertisement for a Native American scholarship event. I went to the event because I wanted positive associations with other Native Americans.

There, I met another Indian who was an upperclassman at UCLA. We became friends and he encouraged me. This was back in 1972, when I was twenty-seven. Financial aid was available to Native Americans at that time, and he told me, "Now's the time to go to college. Have you ever thought about it?" He even helped me fill out the application. In the current market, I wasn't marketable because I didn't have a college education, and I knew that more education would get me a better job. So I started participating in this college-prep program at UCLA that was meant to bring minorities with academic deficiencies up to college level.

I started singing with a group at UCLA, made up of mostly reservation Indians. I also started going to powwows at least twice a month—they didn't call them powwows where I'm from, they called them celebrations. A powwow is a gathering of Indians with games, dancing, singing. For the most part, it's a positive setting. People come together to have fun, to celebrate.

I spent the next ten years studying and working. After going through the college-prep program over five years at UCLA, I went to school for two years in Whittier, working a succession of jobs at the same time. Then I decided to transfer to Cal Poly for a pre-veterinarian program. I'd completed three and a half years of the program, and had been taking care of two of my nephews for several years, before my arrest in 1983, when I was thirty-seven.

During my fourth year of college, I was arrested and charged with first-degree murder. While the charge and the sentence impact my life, I feel that the discrimination I received during arrest, trial, and commitment to prison is the greatest injustice I have experienced.

IT'S LIKE MY GENDER WAS WHAT
I WAS REALLY ON TRIAL FOR

I was arrested in Los Angeles County and then brought to San Bernardino County, where I went to trial. They put me in the women's county jail and my case was sensationalized in the newspapers with headlines like, "Woman who lives as a man murders girlfriend." When I first arrived, news reporters drove up into the back of the jail and tried taking pictures. I think every time I went to court they tried taking pictures. Every day, for a period of time, there was something in the news.

From leaving high school to my arrest when I was thirty-seven, I was exclusively male. I was able to be me, and to be accepted as me. That period ended a month before my arrest, when the police were investigating my house. One of the officers said, "We're kind of wondering, if we took you to jail, would you go to a men's jail or a women's jail?" I just looked at him. He said, "I'm asking you if you are biologically female or biologically male." I told him, "Biologically female."

Throughout the whole eighteen months that I was in county jail during the trial, I was in segregation. At that particular time, guards were isolating females who were masculine, butches, dykes, whatever they called them in those days, in the segregation tanks, away from the rest of the female population.

They had four isolation cells, two on one side of the jail, two on the other side. And the guards would move me all the time between all of those isolation cells. Sometimes in the middle of the night they would come and move me to another isolation cell. I never knew why, but one of the trustees[2] later told me that she had overheard the guards talking about how moving me might make my psychological state break down in some way, so that they could have me confess.

Whenever gender-identity was discussed at the trial, I would be on the verge of shock, to the point where it was early September in Southern California—and that's the hottest time of the year—and I was freezing to death. It was kind of like, *Everything's a nightmare, I want to wake up soon.* And every day was like that.

One of the jurors said that he had a problem with my gender-identity, something like that. He said he had a problem with my gender, since some people called me "she"—mostly the district attorney—and some people called me "he." He was getting confused. Afterward the district attorney said, "If you are really thinking about it, most of us, almost everybody, has a problem with that." I felt it was obvious that this juror was partial, but the judge allowed him to stay. He just asked the juror, "You could still make a fair, impartial decision, right?"

The district attorney brought up my gender-identity repeatedly. She filed for the judge to admonish the jury that I was to be called "she." My attorney tried to file a motion to drop any "also known as," or "aka," since I had previously legally changed my first name from "Charlene," to "Charles." The judge ordered that on the record my name appear as "Charlene" because "Charles" was a masculine name.

---

[2] A prisoner who is allowed to work inside or outside jail.

In one way or another, the D.A. made sure that my gender was always in the air before the jury, as if that was what was I really on trial for. In the opening statements, the D.A. referred to my appearance and talked about the way I walked, to give the picture that I was aggressive and danger-ous. She portrayed me as someone who would fly off the handle and not tolerate anything. The D.A. asked every witness the question, "Did you know Morningstar was born female?" and she referred to me as someone who was "masquerading as a male" to infer dishonesty. The jury were not really paying attention to what the actual evidence was, or whether the actual evidence that they say they had was credible. The judge also seemed to favor the prosecution, because most of the defense's objections were overruled. My attorney was dumbfounded about how to fight the whole gender identity issue. He was frustrated, he wanted to confront it—he even asked to educate the jury on homosexuality, but the judge denied it. In 1984 I was convicted of first-degree murder and received twenty-seven years to life.

I CAME HERE AND I THOUGHT I HAD RIGHTS

When I initially came to state prison, the guards took me to the captain of the receiving center. There, he notified me that in prison it's illegal to have sex, whether mutually consented or not. That's the first thing he said to me. This is before I had been completely processed, because then they give you a shower and debug you and all of that. What was significant about it was that none of the other people that came in on that bus were taken to the captain. I thought, *I smell prejudice.* The guards had read about my trial and perceived me as a sexual deviant, and considered segregating me from general population. Also, at the receiving center, a group of staff had turned up to see what I looked like, as if I was some kind of animal at the zoo.

Sex wasn't on my mind. I was still in shock, scared to death, but in fight mode. By fight mode I don't mean physically striking back, but being aware that an attack was imminent. So I had already pretty much decided that I was going to stick to myself and do whatever was necessary. Because, really, I didn't think that I was going to be in prison that long. I thought, *This is going to get fixed.*

Mostly the male guards, and also some of the women guards, acted as if I was going to be a predator against the other women. The guards have a word that they coined: "homosecting," which means engaging in homosexual activity, as in sexual activity. It isn't a real word. They also call homosecting acts that might lead to illicit sexual behavior. They won't look at two very feminine-looking prisoners walking holding hands; they hardly pay attention to them. But if someone who looks more masculine is holding hands with someone who looks feminine, the guards will say something to them like, "Hey stop that homosecting!" Well, that's gone on since I came to prison. If I hug someone in an affectionate manner to say hello, the guards read into it.

At first, I withdrew within myself. I just didn't talk to anybody. First of all, there was the "she/her" thing that's like scratching on a blackboard—when you've lived all this time being called by masculine pronouns. Since the staff knew about the newspaper articles about "the woman who lived as a man," they would talk about putting a dress on me in an attempt to humiliate me.

It hurt—deep-gut pain. Some of the prisoners are looking at you like you're a freak, and then the other ones are looking at you like you're sirloin steak, thinking, wouldn't it be nice to get it on with you.

When I moved to my first housing unit, there was this one attractive young woman. She would say things like, "I'll show you where the dining hall is," or, "I'll find some clothes for you." She would come over to my cell and talk and stuff like that. I just thought she was being friendly and nice. So one day we were sitting there on the lower bunk and we were talking, and a guard threw the door open and told her to get out of there. Then he slammed the door and locked me in. Well, it wasn't until much later that I found out that this particular woman had been having an affair with this guard. And then I found out about a year later, after she paroled, that he had written in a log that he'd found us in a sexual position.

When I found that out, I wrote him up—I 602-ed it. A 602 is an inmate grievance form. I took a proactive stand against someone who was discriminating against me. The cost of getting a homosexual write-up for most people is that they lose sixty to ninety days, get extra duty, etc. Losing those days means they are added onto your sentence. If you are not a lifer, you can earn those days back with good behavior, and parole on your original date. But for a lifer the parole board will see the offense for which you were already punished and potentially deny you a parole date, which, under Proposition 9,[3] means no more parole hearings for another three to five years. Thus, rather than sixty to ninety days, at a minimum, it will cost a lifer three to five years.

The 602 was not effective at getting the write-up removed from my file, but it didn't bother me any more. Unlike a lot of the women in prison, I came here and I thought that I had rights. I continued to write-up officers about discrimination. At the time it wasn't even a law not to discriminate based on sexual orientation. People here are harassed for having short hair and get in trouble for possession of boxer shorts. The guards claim you're not properly dressed if you don't have a bra and panties on, and this makes you subject to disciplinary action.

Being able to wear certain clothing, like boxer shorts, is important to me, but I'm denied this in prison. Other transgenders are denied this too. People can get boxers illegally through contraband by special vendors or when family members send them in. But I choose not to go about it illegally. So I started writing, and pretty soon they stopped saying things to me, because they knew I was going to write them up. That helped, and it gave me more fortitude. It heightened my belief in myself and my ability to take care of myself. I thought, *Now I know some of the tools to take care of myself in prison.*

---

[3] Also known as the Victims' Bill of Rights Act of 2008, California's Proposition 9 legislated strict parole reforms. This included restrictions on early release from prison, additional time between parole hearings, and notification of the crime victims of all related criminal proceedings (including parole and sentencing hearings). Proposition 9 has been subsequently challenged by criminal-defense groups.

LOSING SOMEBODY TO A LIFE SENTENCE
IS ALMOST LIKE THEM DYING

My mom couldn't visit me for several years because of her financial situation. The reservation is 995 miles from the prison. If you go by bus, it costs $192 for a one way ticket and takes over thirty hours each way. Later she developed health problems, which made it even harder for her to come. I had been in for five years when she was first able to visit, I believe it was 1988. I had not seen her since early 1983, and I didn't think I was going to see her again. My friend Barb made all the arrangements for my mom—a place to stay, airline arrangements, made sure she got there, and everything like that.

I met Barb in 1987, through a really complicated series of events. My lawyer's secretary stole some personal property from my storage unit. Eventually, the secretary got evicted from her house, and Barb, her landlady, ended up in possession of some of the contents of the house. This included a lot of my photographs, my Indian regalia, things that had belonged to my great-great-grandmother, and also some court-related motions and documents. She started reading the court documents, found out I was in prison, and decided to try to find out how she could get this valuable stuff back to me. She got visiting forms for her and her husband, got in contact with me, and asked if she could come to the prison.

At first I was a little bit leery. It took me probably two years to fully embrace her. Growing up on or near a reservation, and being socially among only Indians, it was real hard for me to trust people from other groups as much as I trusted Indians.

With Barb, it was the first time that some white person had done something for me and was so genuinely concerned for me. She told me, "From everything that I've read, I don't believe you did this crime, and I think the conviction occurred because of discrimination and prejudice. I'm one of the people of the state of California who should have been watching, and I wasn't."

For me, it was kind of like, *Wow, I guess the whole human race isn't so bad.* It was as if Barb and her husband took the weight of the whole state, and they tried to make my life in prison easier. I didn't have a television, so they bought me a television. My family didn't have enough money to send me quarterly boxes in which you can get food, clothing, that sort of thing, so Barb started doing that for me too.

Even when Barb couldn't come to see me, she made sure that her husband or her son came, even if it was just for an hour or so, just to get me something out of the vending machine. Most notable to me about Barb's family was the fact that they would take time and come on Christmas Day. To this day, Barb and I are real good friends. I saw her the whole period I was at my first prison. But I haven't seen her since I came to this, new, prison ten years ago. She's in her seventies now, so she can't get away to travel up here. I just talk to her on the phone once a week.

My mom's visit in 1988 was a birthday gift from Barb. She wanted to surprise me, but in prison there's no such thing as surprise. You have to submit the paperwork and everything, so I knew about it four months ahead of time. My mother came on a Family Living Unit (FLU) visit,[4] where you can stay overnight with your family for three days. She looked like she had aged. Losing somebody to a life sentence is almost like them dying. It had aged her a lot.

I enjoyed FLU visits a lot. You're not under the eye of officers and cameras watching you while you visit. You're in a relaxed, home-like atmosphere where you can sit back and talk. We talked about family, ancestry, reality. We talked about the possibility that she might not be living when I get out, and how that bothered me.

At that time, people could bring food in from the outside for FLU visits, like pre-packed food to cook. So we would get a small turkey and make a holiday dinner type of thing, and we would sit down and eat

---

[4] An extended, overnight visit by a family or spouse to a person in prison, which takes place in a designated, semi-private area of the prison designed for this type of visit. For more details, see the glossary.

and talk. They don't let visitors bring in outside food any more, I think, because they began considering it a security risk.

The last time I saw my mom was in 1994. I was still at my first prison. Then, in 1996, they stopped lifers from having those kind of FLU visits. It was real hard because my mother was getting older. I didn't like her going to the regular visiting room because she has lupus, an auto-immune disease, and you can catch cold, flu, all of that really easily.

My mom didn't have a phone for a long time. Once a week I wrote her letters until about 2001, when I finally talked her into getting a telephone. Her physical condition was getting worse, so I convinced her to get one of those lifeline telephones. Then in 2003 I told her, "I'm going to call once a week." It's kind of expensive but it's important to both of us. Since then I've been calling her once a week. I still talk to her. You get fifteen minutes, but it actually works out that you have ten minutes talk time because of the interruptions[5] and the bad connection.

I haven't seen either of my sisters for twenty years. They live on the reservation and they can't afford to travel. But I talk to them occasionally.

AS LONG AS YOU FEEL INADEQUATE, YOU WILL NOT BECOME ALL YOU CAN BE

I am taking hormones now. I started about a year and a half ago in mid-2009, when I was sixty-four. I get them through the medical department. If you are designated as having gender-identity disorder, then it can be prescribed. Previously, you could only get hormones if you were taking them before you came to prison. Now, if the prison psychologist diagnoses you with gender-identity disorder they are required, as per a recent lawsuit,[6] to give you hormones. In 2008 I found out that I

---

[5] Calls from prison are often interrupted with automated reminders stating how much time is left on the call. For more details on telephone communication from prison, see Appendix VIII.

[6] *South v. Gomez*, 129 F3d 127, 1997 WL 683661 (9th Cir. 1997).

could request hormones through an attorney for the Transgender, Gender Variant, and Intersex (TGI) Justice Project,[7] who let me know about the ruling.

I was excited to start a process that would align what I look like more with my spiritual self. And now, after doing it for a year and a half, I feel positive about taking hormones. It's the start of a change that can be legal. I would like to be legally male.

While in prison, I had noticed over the years the discrimination, and that people didn't have anybody else they could talk to about gender-identity issues. There was no kind of advocacy. So in 2008 I started the Two Spirits Wellness Group. In Native American culture, there aren't just two genders, and the term "two spirits" is recognition that those people who are gay/lesbian/transgender are actually two spirit people, in their psychological self, their spiritual self. And that maybe the one spirit—male or female—is more dominant than the other, but always recognizing the other. This is a relatively new term in a lot of Indian languages. They used to have a word that meant "boy like girl." People would say that you were born with female biology, but they usually knew early on in your life that you were more boy-like, or just the opposite for a male child. So in most Native American cultures, they recognize this as another natural form.

When the Two Spirits Wellness Group first started, there were about six people. There are about fifteen people on our docket list now. At the meetings, first of all, we identify. We'll go around the circle and say "My name is... and I'm transgender, or I'm lesbian, or I'm bi." Like that. And we'll say what name we like to go by and what pronoun we'd like to go by to each other. We talk about first recognizing. We do that to reaffirm identity to everyone else, and to encourage other people within our group to say who they are.

---

[7] A California-based organization that works with transgender, gender variant/gender-queer, and intersex people in California prisons and elsewhere, largely on alternative sentencing, access to hormones, legal assistance, and community organizing.

Two Spirits is one of the only places in prison where we discuss sex and the risks of having sex. We do have peer helper educators who talk about health concerns, including AIDS/HIV and hepatitis C. But to openly discuss sex the topic, we don't have that.

Sex is against the law in the prison system. But the fact is that it's still going to go on. There's no way to get protection, so if you do it, since hep C is so rampant, there is a risk that you'll get it. I think most of the Two Spirits group express an appreciation just to talk openly about these issues, how they feel, how they're treated, with people who understand their perspective.

Most of the people who have started taking hormones in this prison are doing so after I let them know about it in the Two Spirits group. There are some people who did not really know who they were, they hadn't explored that they were transgender males. They had just considered themselves gay, or masculine lesbians, and because of the stigma they couldn't admit it to themselves that they really were males.

In Two Spirits meetings, I relate my own experiences to others in the group, and it helps them identify. I started it mostly for people to be able to get a stake in their spiritual identity. We believe that you are what your spirit dictates. In my case, my spirit dictates that I am masculine. We try to help you become strong in your spirit and identity, and to help you be able to function without feeling humiliation, feeling that you are a bad person. As long as you feel inadequate, you will not become all you can be. So you need to be in a better spiritual state.

Some of the members are Native American, but I open it to everybody. In Native American tradition, there's no separation between your heritage, your religion, your anything. All of it really entails your spiritual self. The whole thing is that all living things created have a spiritual entity. My whole thing is to let people have a space to be themselves.

I go before the parole board again for consideration in July. I'm ready to get out of prison. I feel physically, psychologically, and spiritually strong.

IRMA RODRIQUEZ

45, currently imprisoned

Irma spoke with us while still in prison. A woman who looks much younger than her age, Irma had her dark brown hair pulled back in a braid, and she wore a prison-issue white baseball jersey and blue denim pants. The prison garb did not hide all of Irma's tattoos, which mark significant experiences in her life: her past loves, her gang affiliation, the daughter she had at fifteen. Irma has spent much of her life in and out of prison, mostly on drug-related offenses. During that time, she went through several rounds of rehab for her drug abuse, and has now been clean for over three years. In 1990, while in prison, Irma was misdiagnosed with HIV, and for the next seventeen years was treated with extremely toxic drugs that were contraindicated for her other illnesses. She spoke to us of the discrimination she experienced as an HIV patient, the effects of the HIV medication on her health, and the prison's refusal to accept responsibility for her misdiagnosis.

USING DRUGS SEEMED NORMAL TO ME

One of the first things I remember was when I was five years old. This big blue car pulled up to the trailer where I lived with my mom in LA, and a lady with a big old hat came and put me in the car. She was from Child Protective Services, and she took me away with her. Later I found out that someone had called Child Protective Services because of my stepfather, Luis. He never molested me, never touched me. But he was a heroin addict. I remember smelling burnt matches all the time as a kid. I still hate that smell.

That day, Luis had gone out to cop some dope and left me alone in the trailer with the outside of the trailer door tied shut. A lady in another trailer saw that and called the police. Luis was just getting home when the police arrived, and I'll never forget that feeling. I was so scared that they were going to arrest him, and that they were going to take me away. And of course they did. Child Protective Services took me to court, and the judge didn't let any of my immediate family members have me. I remember screaming, but it didn't matter. I went back and forth between my grandparents and my godparents for a while, but finally the court agreed to let me live permanently with my grandparents.

My mom would try to get me back, but she was an active heroin addict—Luis had turned her on to the drug—and the court wouldn't give her custody. She tried hard, even getting herself on a methadone program. And she was doing good, she always kept jobs. I remember her going in for her methadone treatments. They'd give her a lockbox for her take-home medication, and it looked just like a lunch box to me; I remember I wanted one like that for school. But all her efforts made no difference to the court, and they wouldn't give me back to her. In the end, my mom got hooked on pharmaceutical meds—Valium, codeine, anything that was a downer.[1]

My grandparents tried their best with me. My grandma was a cafeteria dietician and my grandfather was a janitor. He did floors, she cooked, and they supported me to the best of their abilities. But even so, I didn't have too much of an affectionate childhood. I wasn't hugged a lot, I wasn't nurtured I think the way I should have been. My family just didn't know how to do that.

---

[1] Valium and codeine are both prescription medications that can be used, and are often abused, to affect mood and relieve pain. Because of their sedative affect, they are also referred to as "downers."

My grandfather couldn't read or write, but still he expected respect. When the social workers visited, he thought that it was the most disrespectful thing for the government to come knock on his door and expect to just come in. I remember after the social workers left he would be so angry and offended. But he was scared, too, of the courts and of Child Protective Services. His guard was up, and he treated me like a princess because he was afraid they'd take me away. He'd say to my grandma, "Don't touch her, don't yell at her. You just give her what she wants." In the end, though, I think I would have been better off disciplined instead of enabled with toys and candy and ice cream.

My grandmother tried to teach me that to be the best person you can be in society, you just have to do what's right. But my grandfather had no education; he just rolled with the punches, ditching and dodging. So I had two different kinds of nurturing, good and bad. In my case it just happened that the bad nurturing outweighed the good nurturing. Soon enough, I started learning how to manipulate. If I didn't get what I wanted, I knew that all I had to do was scream, and I got it.

In second grade I started having visitations with my mom on the weekend. At the beginning I never really wanted to go with her. I didn't trust her. But in sixth grade, when I started developing, things began happening. I started wanting to smoke, I wanted to pluck my eyebrows, I wanted to do all sorts of stuff my grandparents wouldn't allow. And at my mom's house I could do anything I wanted because she was hardly there. I'd have boys over, I could leave and not come back until the next day, and she wouldn't question it. She'd yell, but all it took was a pill and a glass of Kool-Aid to keep her quiet.

In seventh grade I ran away for four days. My grandparents finally gave up on me. They couldn't control me any more, so they gave me to my mom for good. By that time, the courts were already out of our lives, and the only person we had to worry about was the welfare social worker. That was nothing; we just had to go in, dress nice, and show that I was in school. That was it, and we got our checks.

Once I was back with my mother, it all started: the cigarettes, the drinking, the hanging out with gangs and going out with boys. I even became a prostitute, and I started using drugs. With my mother already living the life of an addict, it seemed normal to me. My mother did it and my stepfather did it and everyone else out here was doing it. I'd walk outside my mom's apartment and there were gang members drinking and smoking and whatever.

IT'S LIKE THE CYCLE WAS NEVER BROKEN

I was locked up at the age of twelve for truancy, being a runaway and a delinquent, and for using PCP. My grandparents were devastated. They just couldn't understand how it had gone wrong. But they were loyal, and when I was in juvenile hall my grandmother would not miss a visit. That lady was the first one there and the last one to leave. I remember the counselors there would give her lists of things I was allowed to have, half of which I didn't even need, and she would bring every single thing on the list. My grandma even started bringing things for the other girls, too. It was like she was the grandma of the whole unit. All the girls knew that when she was coming, everybody was getting something.

I was in for three months, and then they let me out. But I was only out for a couple months and then it began all over again. It was like a cycle. I would be out for a little while, and the probation would come and pick me up again, out of nowhere.

I wrecked my teenage life. To me, life was hanging out and going to parties and going to the drive-in with the guys.

Once, when I was fifteen, I was sent to a juvenile probation camp instead of juvenile hall. When they began letting me go out on passes to go home for the weekend, I just left. That's when I got pregnant. By then I was drinking alcohol and smoking PCP on a daily basis. When my baby daughter was born she was taken into custody and I was sent back to juvenile hall. My grandparents were too old to take care of the baby. By that time, though, my mom had gotten off the methadone and was able to get custody of her.

I was so glad my little daughter didn't end up in foster care. I hear a lot of stories about sexual abuse here in prison. I've seen women crying on the phone because they've just heard that somebody had touched their little girl in the wrong areas; I don't think I could endure hearing that about my baby. And it breaks my heart to hear these girls talking about having sex with their fathers, of being abused. I might have had a harsh childhood, but not like the stories that I've heard from the women in here. There are some really hurt individuals in here, and I'm not talking just mentally, but physically—scarred and damaged so they can't have kids. So it makes me so grateful that my mom was able to rebound and care for my daughter. At least she avoided being abused in foster care. But of course, in the end, she had a baby at fifteen too. It's like the cycle was never broken. My mom wasn't married and had me young. I wasn't married, and I had my daughter young. I only hope my granddaughter will be able to break the cycle.

YOU CAN GET ACCUSTOMED
TO THE LOSS OF DIGNITY

The first time I was sent to prison, I was eighteen. I was convicted of possession, transportation, and sale of PCP.[2] I had large quantities, apple juice bottles of that stuff. My first trip to prison was for six years, and I've pretty much been in and out since then. Now I'm in my mid-forties. In the first institution I was taken under the wing of lifers who knew I was a baby and couldn't take care of myself. A lot of them played mom and a lot of them played sister, and they taught me the morals and principles of how to carry yourself, and the dos and the don'ts of surviving in prison. I learned that you have to carry yourself right, carry yourself with respect.

It's hard to explain how degrading prison is to someone who's never experienced it. You are told when to wake up, when you can bathe, when

---

[2] Phencyclidine, a synthetic drug also known as angel dust. Users experience distorted perceptions of sight and sound, and symptoms resembling those of schizophrenia, including hallucinations and extreme anxiety.

you can brush your teeth. You stand for twenty minutes waiting for a door to open just so you can walk in a line and go eat. You're given three minutes to shovel down your food and then you're right back in that line, waiting for the door to open up again so you can go put your stuff away. Through all this you have constant yelling over an intercom.

There's a lot of heartache, a lot of crime, and a lot of violence and chaos. Crammed into a building with 200 women you've got 200 different kinds of cultural backgrounds, ethics, beliefs, attitudes, and emotions. You've got 200 different ways of processing emotions. There are some women who can't read, some who weren't even taught how to shower. They come in here and they are stripped of their dignity. They can't even go to the bathroom without male staff watching. You can get so accustomed to the loss of dignity that your standards just disappear.

But some women come in who have never even taken off their clothes in front of their own husbands. They get so upset and so embarrassed, they cry. What makes me the saddest is that I find myself hardening up, saying things to them like, "What are you crying about?" I have to remind myself to have compassion. Just because I'm used to it doesn't mean someone else is. It's so sad to see women coming here who really don't know how to deal with prison. They've never been out of their homes. They're in here for ridiculous stuff: making bad decisions, helping someone out. They were just so naïve and gullible that another person was able to reel them in. And they're incarcerated with people who've committed murder. It's like one pit. Everyone's thrown in one pit.

YOU'RE CONSTANTLY LIVING ON THE EDGE

It's two o'clock in the morning, how did this door get open? Even now, when things are supposed to be better, COs routinely come into our rooms and take our things. A lot of us have arts and crafts supplies to make cards with, like cardstock and markers. We might also have books or other small things. Routinely the COs will come with their gloves and bags, and they take everything. You've got three blankets? Trust me, they will take them away. You have a homemade pillow sewn up, they'll take that. You're constantly living on edge. Sometimes I feel like they set some women up. They know who's going to blow her stack about having her things taken, and they purposely target her, just so that she will lose it and they can bust her.

I WENT IN FOR ANGEL DUST BUT
I CAME OUT USING HEROIN

There is an abundance of drugs in prison, more than on the streets. It's the currency of the place. You buy it, get it for free, do whatever. You become a runner, do a favor for an inmate, she'll give you half of the drugs. Even your tray of food—hamburger night, pork chop night—you take the pork chop back, you get dope in return. I went in for angel dust, but I came out actively using heroin. I had tried heroin in the free world, but I wasn't an active heroin addict because of my mother. I knew I didn't want to follow her example, so instead I'd used PCP. But when I got to prison I started using heroin, and by the time I got out I was hooked.

After that I was just in and out of jail and prison. Out for sixty days, back in again. In for four years, out again, violate parole, back in again. It was the same thing over and over again, for years. The only thing that changed was that in the early 1990's I switched from heroin to crack cocaine. Every time I went into prison, I came out with a worse addiction. Crack cocaine is just overpowering, I can't even express what it's like. I'm clean and sober now, and I look back and say to myself, "God! What the hell was I thinking?" I look at my arms, at the scars and tattoos, and I see how girls without them can wear pretty shirts and stuff, and it just makes me so sad. I just had no sense of worth. It just didn't matter.

It took me a long time to get clean. I've been in and out of programs. I've worked with sponsors, I've gotten therapy, I've done outpatient, I've had intensive family therapy counseling. It seems that when I did the intensive family therapy, that's what caused me to reuse drugs even more. A lot of the help I got was court ordered; it was nothing that I ever chose to get. I wasn't ready for it, and I was scared. Fear turns into anger and anger turns into resentment and resentment causes you to use, because if you don't know how to deal with the resentment in a healthy way, you have to numb it. So I'd use more. It was only when I was really ready to face all that stuff, when I came to it on my own, that I got clean.

The first time I got clean was for nine months. It was in 2004, and I had just been paroled. Rehab worked that time because I was ready, and because I had extensive care and a structured program. Through the program, I got a maintenance job, and so I went from rehab straight into work. They helped me get financial aid, I picked a college, got into it. They helped me all the way through. But I relapsed and ended up back in prison. I went back in in 2006, and I'm due to be released very soon. This last time I went in, I got clean again, and I've stayed clean for two and a half years.

But I used for a long time, and my body is a mess. I bruise easily; I just tap myself and I end up with a raised, painful lump. I've wrecked my body so much that even just having a menstrual period, I'm doubled over in pain. I haven't been able to get pregnant since I had my daughter. My periods are so bad that the prison doctors are monitoring them now. But that doesn't mean anything. They're not trying to fix the problem, or even diagnose it.

IN PRISON, YOU HAVE NO INFORMATION. YOU DON'T KNOW THE TRUTH

In the middle of 1990 I was diagnosed with HIV. While I was in jail, I was seen by officers from the public health department, interviewed and counseled, and given a blood test. It came back positive, and I have to say I wasn't surprised. With my history of drug use and the prostitution, it made sense. But you can imagine this diagnosis was devastating to me. I even tried to commit suicide.

I was sent to the prison's Chronic Care Program (CCP), where they kept people with chronic illnesses. In the CCP I had restrictions galore. I couldn't go to any other prison, I wasn't eligible for transfer to less restrictive institutions, and I was medicated. For almost ten years I was on three combinations of HIV therapy. They'd test my white blood cell count and it would come back really low. They'd screen my blood for my viral load, and the results would be terrible.

The side effects of the medication were awful: vomiting, diarrhea. Every day I had to stand in the med line, sometimes for hours in the heat. I was also regularly sent for chest X-rays with the other HIV women. And of course, because of the open treatment and the marked bags of medication, everyone knew I was HIV positive. People would harass me, the COs would discriminate against me. The whole system discriminated against HIV patients. For example, in 1999, I wanted to transfer to Valley State Prison for Women. They had just opened a dry cleaning vocational training program, and I was a perfect candidate for it. The prison agreed that I fit all the criteria and should be sent to the program. Then they decided they weren't going to house HIV inmates at VSPW; they were going to keep them in one place so they could be treated together.

Then, in 2007, after more than a decade and a half of aggressive treatment, the prison finally decide to retest me. The test came back negative. Negative! It turned out that I was not HIV positive, that I never had been. This negative result was confirmed in 2008. The first HIV test they did back in 1990 was wrong.

I'll never know what happened to the original lab reports, whether they were falsified or whether it was just due to incompetence. They've retested me a few times, as recently as last year, and I'm still testing negative. But at the same time, I worry that maybe I have a special strain of HIV that's just not showing now. Am I gonna pop up with full blown AIDS a few years from now? I can't stop thinking, *How could I have had so many lab tests that showed high viral loads in my blood?* I'm scared. As it is there are so many diseases, like with the hepatitis they've got the whole alphabet now. How do they know that I don't have a silent strain of HIV that's just hiding? I have no access in prison to medical information beyond what they tell me. That's what it's like to have a disease in prison. You have no information, you don't know the truth. In fact, I don't even know if I can trust this last test. Am I really negative? I don't know what to believe right now. I don't know what to do. I wish I could go see a doctor out in the free world who could screen my blood and see once and for all if I'm really HIV negative.

After all this happened, I petitioned for a hearing with the Chief Medical Officer. Before prisoners can bring a law suit against the Department of Corrections, they first have to file an in-house grievance. It took me exactly nine months from the time I filed the grievance for the Chief Medical Officer to hear it and interview me. When I walked into the hearing room, there was a whole panel of people— medical officers, public health officials, nurses. They were ready for me. The public health nurse who initially sent me to be tested claimed that she'd never interviewed me. But how else would I have been referred for treatment? She insisted that she had no record of that, that she didn't recall it. It was ridiculous. We all knew that I'd been treated for HIV, but she kept insisting that she'd never given me the diagnosis.

The people on the panel claimed that it wasn't their fault, that they simply treated me for a disease they were told I had. They refused to acknowledge that they were the ones who told me that I had the disease.

IT'S LIKE YOU'VE BEEN PUT IN A LITTLE BOX

Out in the world, when you get a diagnosis of a serious disease like this, you would go get a second opinion, just to be sure. But in prison, that isn't an option, so you have to rely on their diagnosis. You have to trust them. That's what I did, and look what happened. My advice, even to people in the free world, is to be your own best advocate. Do your research, get on the computer if you have access to one. Try to find out as much as you can, and make sure you get a second opinion.

My liver has gone through the stress of processing HIV medications, which can cause damage. But I don't even know if there has been any damage, because they won't test me. So I'm trying to monitor my own body to see what the effects of the drugs have been. I've had a series of problems which may be related to the HIV treatment, and may be related to my many years of drug abuse. For example, I've had my gall bladder out. I also have neuropathy in my legs, which causes terrible pain. I don't know the cause, but many other HIV-positive patients I know experience the same kind of pins and needles in the bottom of your foot where you can't even step on your foot. I wake up at night sometimes because my whole leg feels like it's going to crack off.

It took nine months for the decision from the hearing to come through, during which time they kept sending my forms back to me, telling me the wording was incorrect or the filing dates were incorrect. Because I had to go through this process before even considering a lawsuit, I resubmitted three times, but each time they'd send it back, claiming there were clerical errors. But during the process I had a public interest attorney from the prisoners' rights group Justice Now with me, so I was sure that the forms had been in perfect order.

In the end, the prison refused to accept responsibility. They blamed the mistaken diagnosis on the lab, and told me to go ahead and take it up with them. I tried to do that, but the lab was closed down by then. It turns out it had been shut down by the government because it was falsifying tests.

I also have, for years, been testing positive for tuberculosis. Each time they say it's a false positive. When I had the HIV diagnosis they would say that a false positive was a side effect of the disease. But now, I don't know why I keep testing positive.

I also have these ongoing gynecological problems that won't clear up on their own. I keep testing positive for vaginal bacterial infections. I've had Pap smears that showed abnormal cells, which they diagnosed as a bacterial or fungal infection. They've given me a variety of medications for these vaginal problems, including medications for herpes, despite the fact that I did not test positive for the disease.

Even when I catch a simple cold, I can't shake it off like my roommate does in three, four days. I carry it for about ten days.

I've also tested positive for hepatitis C, and for many years was considered a dual-diagnosis patient. Since the HIV diagnosis has been disproved, sometimes I wonder whether the hep C diagnosis is accurate. But according to the prison, I'm positive. They won't treat me, however, because interferon[3] is not available for women like me, who have less than a year left on their terms.

More than anything I've gone through in my life and in prison, this medical stuff has messed me up. If you live in the free world, I don't think you can really understand. When you're in prison, it's like you've been put in this little box, and little slips of paper are put in the box with you, with pieces of information. You can't verify it, you don't know if it's true, you don't know what to do or how to act. And worst of all, there's no way of you getting out of this box. You just have to keep breathing.

---

[3] An antiviral medication used to treat hepatitis C.

APPENDICES

APPENDICES CONTENTS

A NOTE ON THE APPENDICES

Appendices I–VI and parts of this introductory note have been selected from *Women in Detention in the United States*, a report submitted to Rashida Manjoo, the UN Special Rapporteur on Violence Against Women, in preparation for her return visit to the United States in January 2011. The Special Rapporteur visited the United States to follow up on her 1998 visit, where she visited eight U.S. prisons to investigate violence against women in custody and in other contexts, including women in the military and domestic violence. Her report on the most recent visit, which includes descriptions of abuses in women's prisons and recommendations to address such abuses, was released in June 2011. *Women in Detention in the United States* was prepared by attorney Deborah LaBelle; Robin Levi (of Justice Now); Brenda V. Smith (of American University Washington College of Law); and Danielle Lang, Caitlin Mitchell, and Hope Metcalf (of the Detention and Human Rights Project of the Lowenstein International Human Rights Clinic at Yale Law School); with support from Virginia Taylor, Ashley Prather, and Jaime M. Yarussi. Selections have been adapted for length and fit. *Women in Detention in the United States* is based on extensive research into case law, academic publications, and qualitative and quantitative studies relating to incarceration in the United States. The report is guided and informed by interviews with nearly twenty experts on women in prison in the United States, including women prisoners, attorneys, academics, legal practitioners, and activists.[1]

Appendix VII was written by Jessie Hawk, a 2011 graduate of UC Hastings Law School. It is based on two reports published by the Legal Action Center, "After Prison: Barriers Facing People with Criminal

Records" and "After Prison: Roadblocks to Reentry." Appendix VIII is based on a memo by Jessie Hawk.

Appendix IX is selected from a series of essays and one blog post written by David Kaiser and Lovina Stannow for the *New York Review of Books*. "The Rape of American Prisoners" appeared in the *Review*'s March, 11, 2010 issue; "The Way to Stop Prison Rape" appeared on March 25, 2010; and "Prison Rape and the Government" appeared on March 24, 2011. "Prison Rape: Eric Holder's Unfinished Business" appeared on the *Review*'s NYRBlog on August 26, 2010. Selections have been adapted for length.

GLOSSARY

602—The formal process to file internal grievances and complaints against prison personnel, policies, or practices within the California Department of Corrections (CDC).

Accessory—A person who intentionally assists another in committing a crime. An accessory is not necessarily present during the crime, but may be involved in planning, driving a getaway car, or concealing evidence.

Assaultive Offender Program/Violence Prevention Program—A group therapy program in Michigan prisons designed to change violent attitudes and behaviors.

Association of Black Women Lawyers—State and regional groups organized through state bar associations, whose chapters focus their work on legal issues involving women and children, as well as black female participation and representation in the field of law.

Battered Woman Syndrome—A pattern of symptoms, including fear, a perceived inability to escape, and learned helplessness—as well as an accurate assessment of the likelihood of reprisal—that appear in women who are physically and mentally abused by a husband or partner over an extended period of time. Since 1987, some states have allowed this as a defense in criminal trials.

C.O.—Correctional officer. Responsible for overseeing individuals who have been arrested and are awaiting trial or who have been convicted of a crime and sentenced to serve time in a jail, reformatory, or prison. Also known as prison officer and prison guard.

Corrections—The agencies or facilities concerned with the custody, confinement, supervision, or treatment of alleged or convicted criminal offenders.

D.A.—District attorney. An elected official of a county or a designated district with the responsibility for prosecuting crimes.

Family Living Unit (FLU) visit/Extended Family Visit—An overnight visit by spouse or family to a person in prison, which takes place in a relatively private area designated for this purpose. These are only allowed in some states, and can be denied to people serving life sentences. The exact length and limitations of the visit is governed by state law.

Hysterectomy—An operation to remove all or part of a women's uterus, usually considered after less-invasive treatments for a medical condition have been found unsuccessful.

Justice Now—A nonprofit organization based in Oakland, California, that is focused on the needs of people in women's prisons. The organization provides legal services and works with people in prison, their families, and their communities on issues involving education and prisoners' rights.

Labia lift—A method of strip-searching used by corrections officers at the Denver Women's Correctional Facility (DWCF). In September 2010, in the face of public outcry after this practice was reported in local newspapers and by the ACLU, the DWCF implemented a new strip-search policy ending this practice. For a description of the impact of this practice, see Marilyn Sanderson's chapter.

Legal mail—Mail to a person in prison from an attorney, officer of the court, or a legal service organization, which is separated from general correspondence and allowed a greater degree of privacy. For specific details, see Appendix VIII.

Oophorectomy—The surgical removal of one or both of a woman's ovaries. Also known as ovariectomy.

Parole—The release of a prisoner before his or her full sentence has been served. Release is granted for good behavior on the condition that the parolee must regularly report to a supervising parole officer for a specified period.

Parole board—A governmental body that decides whether prisoners may be released from prison before completing their sentences.

Petition—A formal written request made to a court.

Post-traumatic stress disorder (PTSD)—A mental health condition than can occur after witnessing or experiencing a traumatic event that involved the threat of injury or death. Symptoms can be disruptive to the sufferer's everyday life, and may include nightmares, flashbacks, uncomfortable reactions to certain situations, detachment, anger, and severe anxiety.

Prison vs. jail—Jails are mostly used to hold individuals awaiting sentencing or serving short sentences, and are run by local governments (such as a county). Prisons hold individuals serving long sentences, and are organized and staffed by state or federal systems.

Probation—A court-imposed sentence that allows a convicted individual to remain in the community instead of being incarcerated. During probation the individual must abide by conditions, such as drug testing, a curfew, or staying within a particular county or state, and is subject to the supervision of a proba¬tion officer.

Protective custody—A restrictive form of confinement akin to solitary confinement imposed on inmates for their own security or well-being. Protective custody is frequently employed for inmates convicted of sexual crimes against children, or whose position or physical characteristics leaves them especially vul¬nerable to harm from the general prison or jail population.

Segregated Housing Unit/Administrative segregation (adseg)—An isolated living area within a prison used to separate an individual from the general prison population for punitive or security purposes. Also known as solitary confinement, and colloquially referred to as "the hole."

Shackling/belly chains—The practice of restraining prisoners with various types of chains and shackles, especially during transport. A belly chain is a constricting chain around the waist, to which arm and/ or leg shackles can be connected. For details on the practice of shackling imprisoned mothers during labor and while giving birth, see Appendix IV.

Statute of limitations—A time limit for prosecuting a crime, based on the date when the offense occurred. The purpose of such a statute is to require diligent prosecution of known claims, and to make sure that claims will be resolved while evidence is still available and witnesses' recollections are still fresh.

Transgender, Gender Variant, and Intersex (TGI) Justice Project—A California-based organization that works with transgender, gender variant/gender queer, and intersex people in California prisons and elsewhere, largely on alternative sentencing, access to hormones, legal assistance, and community organizing.

Warden—The head official in charge of a prison.

TIMELINE

While the struggles of women in prison in the United States have many common threads, their lives are largely shaped by state-specific legislation and culture, rarely by federal legislation. This timeline attempts to capture that reality by highlighting state legislation that led to nationwide trends, as well as relevant federal legislation.

1835—The Mount Pleasant Female Prison, the first prison in the United States to house only women, opens in New York.

1869—A bill for a "Female Prison and Reformatory Institution for Girls and Women," pushed by Quaker reformers concerned about sexual abuse of prisoners, passes the Indiana state legislature.

1873—Indiana Women's Prison opens. It is the country's first adult female maximum-security correctional facility,

1927—The first federal women's prison, the Federal Industrial Institution for Women, opens in West Virginia.

1956—The U.S. Congress passes the Narcotics Control Act of 1956, beginning a trend of increasing penalties for drug use and possession.

1970—The Comprehensive Drug Abuse Prevention and Control Act introduces an extensive classification system for drug offenses, increasing federal control over identified substances. This allows for the federal prosecution of drug sellers and users.

1971—President Richard Nixon popularizes the phrase "war on drugs."

1973—New York passes the Rockefeller Drug Laws, establishing more severe sentencing standards for drug offenses. The rigidity of the sentencing rules sweeps many women into the prison system who might otherwise have been sentenced to either jail or probation. The sentencing laws are soon replicated by other states.

1977—The Washington State Supreme Court establishes the "reasonable woman standard" in *State v. Wanrow*, laying the groundwork for the battered woman syndrome defense.

1987—The Missouri legislature becomes the first in the country to vote to allow evidence of battered woman syndrome as a defense in a criminal trial. Other states soon follow suit.

1992—The Federal Highway Apportionment Act provides financial incentives to states to suspend the driver's licenses of those convicted of minor drug offenses.

1993—Washington State passes the country's first "three strikes" law, starting a nation-wide trend of mandated long sentences for minor crimes.

1996—Congress passes the Prison Litigation Reform Act, which limits the ability of people in prison to access federal courts.

—The Federal Personal Responsibility and Work Opportunity Reconciliation Act bans those convicted of drug offenses from receiving federal food stamps and Temporary Assistance for Needy Families. At a time when upwards of 80 percent of women in prison and jail are mothers, this ban has a dramatic effect on their ability to care for their dependent children.

1997—President Bill Clinton signs the Adoption and Safe Families Act, requiring early termination of parental rights for women in prison.

1998—The Aid Elimination Provision of the Higher Education Act prohibits students who have been convicted of drug offenses from receiving federal financial aid toward their tuition.

—The U.N. Special Rapporteur on Violence against Women visits the United States to investigate conditions in U.S. women's prisons. Her subsequent report, published in 1999, highlights the appalling conditions around health and sexual abuse that she found in women's prisons, as well as abuses around family unity. The report also notes the over-representation of women of color in prison as evidence of deep-rooted discrimination within the criminal justice system.

2000—The U.S. Supreme Court, in *Apprendi v. New Jersey* (530 U.S. 466 [2000]), rules that the Sixth Amendment right to a jury trial prohibits judges from enhancing criminal sentences beyond statutory maximums based on facts other than those decided by a jury beyond a reasonable doubt. Prior to *Apprendi*, judges could sentence defendants for counts of which they had been acquitted, which had resulted in substantially increased sentences for many female defendants.

2005—The Higher Education Act is reformed to allow aid for students found guilty of drug offenses before their enrollment. However, their financial assistance will be cut if they are convicted of such an offense during their time as a student.

—In the Supreme Court cases *United States v. Booker* and *United States v. Fanfan*, the Court rules that the Sixth Amendment right to a jury trial requires that current federal sentencing guidelines be advisory, not mandatory. This permits lower court judges to deviate from previous sentencing rules if they feel it would serve the interests of justice.

2009—The U.S. Court of Appeals for the 8th Circuit rules that shackling pregnant prisoners violates the Eighth Amendment.

2011—The U.N. Special Rapporteur on Violence Against Women returns to the United States to examine violence in the United States and includes visits to U.S. prisons to look for changes since her visit in 1998. In June 2011 she releases her report on this visit, detailing changes and ongoing violations, as well as recommendations.

APPENDIX I: THE LEGAL FRAMEWORK OF INCARCERATION AND ACCESS TO REMEDIES

To understand the challenges facing imprisoned women in the United States, it is crucial to first examine the access that these women have to remedy and redress. This is a right recognized in most international humanitarian and human-rights treaties, including the Universal Declaration of Human Rights,[2] the Convention on the Elimination of all Forms of Discrimination against Women, and the Declaration on the Elimination of Violence Against Women.[3] Without access to courts and fair, impartial judicial and administrative proceedings, the rights of a person in prison cannot be protected. This lack of remedies creates a climate of impunity in which further violations are likely to occur.

In the United States, the substantive rights provided by the U.S. Constitution to people in prison have been significantly eroded over the past few decades. Since the passage of the Prisoner Litigation Reform Act (PLRA) in 1996, there have been significant procedural barriers to litigation. Women in prison are thus forced to rely on what are often inadequate internal prison-grievance systems.

The difficulties of pursuing litigation, combined with further barriers relating to evidence and credibility, means that sexual abuse in prison is rarely prosecuted. The most substantial efforts at reform have been attempts to amend the PLRA through legislation and to combat unconstitutional conditions of confinement through oversight mechanisms, such as the Special Litigation Section of the Civil Rights Division of the U.S. Department of Justice.

The Promises of the Constitution

The Eighth Amendment to the United States Constitution bars the infliction of punishment that is "cruel or unusual,"[4] but the provisions of the Constitution that provide a degree of protection for people in prison have been interpreted by U.S. courts in ways that severely limit their reach. The Supreme Court has held that because the Eighth Amendment concerns "punishment" rather than "conditions," inhumane conditions of confinement can only constitute a violation under certain circumstances.[5] "Punishment" is the official sentence given at the time of conviction, while "conditions of confinement" is a broad term used to describe the qualitative elements of a person's experience while she is imprisoned. These elements include food, medical care, safety from physical harm, and placement in solitary confinement or in an overcrowded cell.

To prevail in an Eighth Amendment claim alleging unconstitutional conditions of confinement, a petitioner must satisfy both an objective and a subjective requirement: first, she must show that the conditions are objectively "serious."[6] Second, she must show that the prison official in question had a "sufficiently culpable state of mind."[7]

The Supreme Court has found that when prison conditions fail to provide the "minimal civilized measure of life's necessities"—including the basic physical requirements of food, clothing, shelter, medical care, and personal safety[8]—they are "sufficiently serious" to meet the objective requirement of the Eighth Amendment test.[9] In practice, however, courts have set an extremely high bar, emphasizing that the purpose of confinement is to punish, and thus uncomfortable and even harsh conditions are neither unusual nor cruel.[10] In addition, the Supreme Court has found that multiple forms of abuse and deprivation cannot cumulatively constitute cruel and unusual punishment.[11] Instead, each abuse must be evaluated individually on the basis of the test articulated above.[12]

Even if the conditions of confinement meet the objective threshold of being "sufficiently serious," a petitioner must also prove that the officials overseeing the incarceration were "deliberately" or "recklessly indifferent" before the conditions can be considered unconstitutional.[13] This standard leaves petitioners vulnerable to continued incarceration under conditions that are found to be objectively "cruel and unusual" solely because they cannot prove that the prison officials knew of and disregarded those conditions. Moreover, because this standard is subjective, a court ruling that particular policies are barred by the Eighth Amendment in one prison, or in relation to one person in prison, will not guarantee that other petitioners can successfully bring a suit challenging the same policies carried out in another context.

Even when conditions of confinement are found to be unconstitutional, courts may be reluctant to intervene based on a general practice of judicial deference to prison administrators.[14] In the area of First Amendment rights, for example, the Supreme Court has found that a regulation that impinges on a prisoner's right of expression may be valid "if it is reasonably related to legitimate penological interests"[15]—a standard giving a tremendous amount of leeway to prison administrators and correctional officers.

Limited Access to Courts: The Prison Litigation Reform Act (PLRA)

While people in prison are afforded some protections under the Eighth Amendment, successfully overturning violations of these protections requires access to the court system. The Prisoner Litigation Reform Act (PLRA), enacted in 1996, prevents many claims from reaching the federal courts in the first place.[16]

The legislative purpose of the PLRA was to keep frivolous lawsuits brought from prison out of federal court, and to shift the burden of adjudicating claims to the prisons' internal grievance systems.[17] The breadth of the PLRA, however, combined with the fact that courts can apply the PLRA regardless of whether a prison's grievance system provides an adequate or fair alternative, has the effect of limiting access to remedies.

The provisions of the PLRA that have most significantly affected claims from people in prison are: the requirement of administrative exhaustion, the requirement that plaintiffs must have suffered physical harm in order to collect damages, the limitation on attorney's fees, and the application to juvenile prisoners. Additionally, the PLRA limits the scope of consent decrees and imposes a more restrictive time limit on these kinds of agreements.

The PLRA compels administrative exhaustion by mandating that "no action shall be brought with respect to prison conditions... by a prisoner... until such administrative remedies as are available are exhausted."[18] The Supreme Court interpreted this provision (in *Woodford v. Ngo*) to require people in prison to take their claims through the entire applicable prison grievance process, complying with all technicalities, in order to gain access to the federal courts.[19] As a result, claims can be barred if prisoners misfile a complaint, report to the wrong authority, or make any other minor, technical error that results in a dismissal of their grievance.[20] Claims have been barred despite the fact that special circumstances—such as illiteracy, physical illness, and mental illness—would have made compliance with standard grievance procedures impossible.[21] In one particularly notorious case,[22] it took a court almost five years to determine that a group of women filing a class action suit alleging sexual assault had not properly exhausted their administrative remedies.

This "exhaustion" requirement has created two particularly powerful barriers to prisoners seeking judicial review. First, it compels women in prison to report up the chain of command as specified in a prison's grievance procedures, even when this would require reporting to the very individual who is responsible for the abuse. Second, in order to follow the internal regulations of the prison, claimants must file grievances within what is often an extremely small window of time following an injury. On average, prison regulations require filing within a few weeks; in some prisons the time frame is as short as two days.[23] These barriers are especially formidable in cases of sexual assault and abuse.[24]

Another problematic set of policies within prison grievance systems are those based on the premise that people in prison are non-credible and should not be believed when their stories conflict with reports by correctional officers.[25] For example, in New York State, women seeking redress for sexual abuse by prison guards are required to produce physical proof, an extremely difficult task.[26] Prison administrators often fail to keep grievances confidential, with the result that retaliation for complaining—by other prisoners, and particularly by the abuser—is commonplace.[27]

The PLRA's physical injury requirement is a second major barrier to litigation. The Act provides that "no Federal civil action may be brought by a prisoner... for mental or emotional injury suffered while in custody without a prior showing of physical injury."[28] Under this provision, some courts have found that prisoners have no judicial remedy for violations of non-physical constitutional rights, including religious, speech, and due process rights.[29] Courts have banned awards of compensatory damages for any non-physical injuries, no matter how intentional the act and no matter how damaging the effect.

The physical injury requirement has also been interpreted to bar claims from prison based on incidents of non-physically-injurious sexual abuse, such as sexual harassment, threats of assault, or groping.[30] Some courts have found that sexual assault itself does not constitute a physical injury within the meaning of the PLRA.[31]

Additionally, the PLRA caps the fees an attorney may recover from defendants in prison reform litigation,[32] which makes competent representation more difficult to find, and results in many women in prison—who have no automatic right to appointed counsel—filing claims pro se (on their own behalf).

A final area of concern is the application of the PLRA to juveniles incarcerated in juvenile institutions. Most lawsuits concerning juveniles are filed on their behalf by parents or guardians, yet compliance with internal grievance procedures by parents or guardians has been deemed legally insufficient under the PLRA.[33] This element of the law has effectively reduced the number of juvenile lawsuits able to reach federal court.

Effects of the PLRA and Efforts at Reform

The consequences of the PLRA have become quite clear. By 2006 the number of prisoner claims brought in federal courts had dropped by 60 percent, despite a massive increase in the imprisoned population since the PLRA was enacted ten years earlier.[34] Advocates have found that the PLRA's procedural barriers ultimately bar meritorious claims as well as frivolous ones, create incentives for prisons to make their grievance procedures complex and opaque, and result in a climate of impunity within prisons and jails.[35]

Courts across the country have chosen to apply and interpret the PLRA in widely differing ways. While some have taken an extremely literal approach,[36] others have created safeguards, refusing to apply the exhaustion requirement when administrative remedies do not exist or when special circumstances excluded access to remedies that are available.[37] Whether and how the Supreme Court will interpret the PLRA remains unknown; this suggests that amendment through statute may be the most effective way of addressing the problems the PLRA has raised.

While numerous efforts have been made to reform the PLRA, as of today none have been successful. Congress's 2003 passage of the Prison Rape Elimination Act (PREA) created the National Prison Rape Elimination Commission (NPREC),[38] a group tasked with studying the causes and consequences of prison sexual abuse and developing national standards to eliminate prison rape. NPREC recommended that Congress modify the PLRA's exhaustion requirement by allowing people claiming sexual abuse from prison to automatically exhaust their remedies after ninety days of reporting, regardless of when the incident allegedly occurred. (For more details on the NPREC report, see Appendix IX.) In 2007, Congress responded to the commission's early findings with the proposed bill H.R. 4109, The Prison Abuse Remedies Act, which would have (1) eliminated the physical injury requirement; (2) provided a ninety-day stay of non-frivolous claims relating to prison conditions, so as to give prison officials adequate time to consider such claims through the administrative process; (3) made the PLRA inapplicable to prisoners under the age of eighteen; and (4) eliminated certain restrictions on awarding attorney fees in civil actions brought by prisoners. Human Rights Watch praised the proposed bill as an appropriate response to the PLRA, one which would put the United States in compliance with international human-rights agreements relating to the treatment of prisoners.[39] Unfortunately, the bill never reached a vote by either legislative body of Congress.

Beyond the creation of NPREC,[40] the Prison Rape Elimination Act functions on several levels: it requires an extensive yearly survey on the incidents and effects of sexual assault in correctional settings nationwide;[41] it has created a national clearinghouse with information and assistance to authorities about prevention, investigation, and prosecution;[42] and it provides $40 million yearly for state grants to fund policy improvements.[43] The statute requires the U.S. attorney general to adopt a final rule creating national standards based on these recommendations; the rule will be automatically binding on the Federal Bureau of Prisons, and each state will be required to comply with the rule or risk losing 5 percent of federal funding designated for criminal justice activities.[44]

The statute's reporting requirements have generated a great deal of data in a field previously short of empirical research, and policy advocates as well as practitioners agree that changing institutional culture is key to affecting change in correctional settings. Some experts believe that the passage of PREA and the continued reporting of the Bureau of Justice Statistics may reorient culture and improve conditions.[45]

Additionally, there is evidence that states and correctional facilities are taking PREA seriously. In at least seven states, correctional authorities have implemented and publicly shared written correctional policies in response to the goals and requirements of PREA.[46] California and Texas have both passed laws to implement the Prison Rape Elimination Act, and both have created, in addition to other reforms, independent ombudsman positions in charge of impartial resolution of complaints.[47] The American Correctional Association has created new standards, and revised old ones, to better combat sexual abuse in correctional settings.[48] Further, the passage of PREA, and the subsequent hearings and debates within NPREC, bring important policy questions to the forefront of the public debate. These include: how the PLRA blocks remedies for sexual assault victims, whether the ban on providing funding through the Violence Against Women Act to certain incarcerated persons should be lifted, and whether conjugal and family visiting programs could ease the problem of sexual abuse.[49]

But even reforms that have successfully been signed into law face a number of obstacles in practice. One significant barrier to prison oversight is the restriction on media access to prisons and prisoners. The Supreme Court has given state and federal prison administrators wide latitude in limiting prisoners' ability to communicate with persons on the outside, and with members of the media in particular.[50] Further, the Court has held that the press has "no constitutional right of access to prisons or their inmates beyond that afforded the general public."[51] (Details about the limits on communication from prison can be found in Appendix VIII.) Additionally, the majority of cases of sexual abuse in prison are not prosecuted,[52] often because of inadequate grievance-reporting systems, fear of retaliation, or delays that compromise evidence. In the instances when reports of sexual abuse do reach prosecutors' offices, prosecutors have reported that they are reluctant to pursue these cases because of the relatively modest penalties involved.[53]

APPENDIX II: FORMS OF VIOLENCE AGAINST INCARCERATED WOMEN, PART I— SEXUAL ABUSE AND MISCONDUCT

Custodial sexual assault in the prison system, dubbed by a number of legal scholars as "America's most 'open' secret,"[54] is a well-known, if not always publicly recognized, problem in U.S. prisons. Women in prison, as well as men, are too often left unprotected and without redress for sexual abuse by both custodial staff and other imprisoned women.

Until recently, however, there was little to no available data on the prevalence of sexual assault in prisons, especially among women prisoners.[55] Reports by the Bureau of Justice Statistics (BJS) are the first to systematically analyze national data on the problem. The reports—compiled to meet the requirements of the Prison Rape Elimination Act, passed in 2003—confirm the above finding of highly variable but persistent prevalence. The 2008–2009 BJS report, released in August 2010, indicated that 4.7 percent of women in prison had experienced inmate-on-inmate sexual victimization within only the past twelve months, and 2.1 percent had experienced staff sexual misconduct in the same time period.[56] These aggregate numbers, however, hide the significant variance among the institutions. Several women's institutions had much higher rates of abuse; in one institution, nearly 12 percent of women experienced abuse.[57] Earlier regional studies had found rates of in-prison sexual victimization as high as 17.2 percent, in a large Southern prison system;[58] and a rate of sexual coercion of 27 percent in one Midwestern facility. [59] While data on the problem has improved, advocates suspect that under-reporting likely still exists, due to prisoners' lack of trust in confidentiality and fear of retaliation.[60]

Sexual abuse in women's prisons takes many forms. Women may be sexually assaulted by other prisoners or by correctional staff and volunteers. The conduct might involve forced non-consensual sexual penetration, but might also be limited to unwanted sexual contact and touching.[61] In the case of staff sexual misconduct, advocates report that while forced non-consensual sex does occur, more often staff members exert their position of power to coerce sexual activity. As a result, women often exchange sex to protect their rights to phone calls, visits, or basic supplies such as food, shampoo, and soap.[62]

Women in prison—most of whom have been previously traumatized by sexual or physical abuse, often as children—are particularly vulnerable to sexual abuse.[63] Victims of sexual abuse often suffer from lifelong physical and mental repercussions, such as post-traumatic stress disorder, anxiety, depression, and thoughts of suicide.[64] Additionally, the stress of abuse in prison might be magnified by the inability to escape one's perpetrators and the fear of retaliation if abuse is reported.

Cross-Gender Supervision and Searches

The United States is, as noted by legal scholar Brenda V. Smith, "one of the few developed countries that permits cross-gender supervision of male or female prisoners in sensitive areas such as living quarters, showers, and bathrooms."[65] International standards, in fact, require that only female officials supervise imprisoned women[66] (although anecdotal evidence of abuse by female staff does exist). The 2007 Bureau of Justice Statistics report, which showed that staff sexual misconduct against women was overwhelmingly perpetrated by male staff, lends empirical support to advocates' long-held belief that cross-gender supervision in private quarters exacerbates the problem of custodial sexual assault.[67]

Male correctional officers can often view imprisoned women in their most intimate moments—while they are changing, in the shower, and in the bathroom[68]—and the problem of cross-gender supervision is particularly acute during physical searches. Many advocates argue that state correctional policies requiring cross-gender invasive body cavity searches may, in and of themselves, constitute state-sponsored sexual abuse. In addition to violating international standards, invasive cross-gender searches may violate the remaining Fourth Amendment right to privacy and may "exacerbate traumatic experiences and constitute cruel and unusual punishment."[69] In 2010, the Colorado ACLU discovered that the Denver Women's Correctional Facility (DWCF) had instituted a new, randomized strip search that required women to hold open their labia for inspection by officers.[70] Following significant press coverage, the Colorado Department of Corrections ended the practice, but the incident demonstrates the ongoing concern surrounding such invasive searches: their necessity, their legality, and their connection to sexual assault and sexually degrading behavior. At minimum, these policies create additional opportunities for sexual abuse.[71]

Legal Framework and Responses to Sexual Abuse and Misconduct

International human rights standards very clearly protect prisoners from custodial sexual abuse. The International Covenant on Civil and Political Rights (ICCPR) and the Convention against Torture (CAT), both of which the United States has ratified, require states to protect individuals from torture or cruel, inhuman, or degrading punishment and treatment. As Human Rights Watch has reported, both of "these treaties and the Standard Minimum Rules for the Treatment of Prisoners... require states to ensure that those who engage in such abuse are appropriately punished, and that individuals seeking to complain about such ill-treatment are provided with an effective remedy."[72] Further, "Article 17 of the ICCPR protects all individuals against arbitrary interference with their privacy, and the Standard Minimum Rules specify that the privacy of female prisoners should be respected by male corrections staff."[73]

In *Farmer v. Brennan*, the U.S. Supreme Court found that deliberate indifference to the substantial risk of sexual assault and abuse is a violation of the Eighth Amendment.[74] However, as discussed in Appendix I, meeting the subjective standards of Eighth Amendment jurisprudence is often very difficult.[75] Courts have also been somewhat unwilling to recognize conduct that does not include physical penetration as a constitutional violation.[76]

Since the mid-1990s, there has been significant domestic and international advocacy and legal work around the issue of custodial sexual abuse in the United States. In 1996, the National Institute of Corrections began an investigation into the problem of staff sexual misconduct;[77] in 1999, the investigative arm of the U.S. Congress, the Government

Accountability Office, issued a report on staff sexual misconduct;[78] and early litigation on the issue was initiated both by advocates and the Department of Justice.[79]

International organizations such as Human Rights Watch and Amnesty International have issued reports on the sexual abuse of women in U.S. prisons, in 1996 and 1999 respectively.[80] Finally, the U.N. Special Rapporteur on Violence Against Women commented on the problem of sexual abuse of women in prison in her 1999 report on violence against women in U.S. state and federal prisons.[81] Most advocates agree that this work, both domestic and international, has spurred a national conversation and at least some changes in policies and practices within prison systems.[82]

Its progress can be seen in contributions to both state and federal legislative changes. Since the majority of people in the U.S. prison population fall under the jurisdiction of the states, and federal constitutional claims are difficult to sustain, state criminal laws are arguably the most important mechanisms for addressing sexual misconduct in prisons.[83] The advocacy movement spurred the passage of state laws criminalizing all sexual conduct between custodial officials and prisoners. In 1990, fewer than twenty states had criminal laws specifically prohibiting the sexual abuse of prisoners. Now, according to a national survey conducted by Brenda V. Smith, "each of the fifty states [has] enacted laws protecting offenders from sexual abuse by staff."[84] Federally, there have been numerous attempts to amend the PLRA, although none have been successful.[85] As mentioned above, Congress unanimously passed the Prison Rape Elimination Act (PREA) in 2003, which seeks to establish a "zero-tolerance" standard for the incidence of sexual abuse in U.S. correctional settings—including adult prisons and jails, community correctional supervision and juvenile justice agencies, as well as immigration detention facilities.[86]

The standards recommended by the National Prison Rape Elimination Committee (NPREC), a product of the PREA, propose reform of the current legal "exhaustion requirement," which has limited access to courts. They also prohibit cross-gender strip and visual body cavity searches, as well as cross-gender pat downs, and they ban non-medical staff from viewing opposite-gender prisoners while nude or performing bodily functions.[87] If implemented, these recommendations would bring the United States closer to the accepted international standards on cross-gender staffing of detention facilities.[88] The NPREC report also recommended that the Victims of Crime Act guidelines and the Violence Against Women Act—which prohibit the use of funding for any person in prison, and to imprisoned victims convicted of certain crimes, respectively—be amended to provide more equitable funding to all victims of sexual violence.[89] (Details of the PREA, NPREC, and other attempts to amend the PLRA are described in Appendix I, above.)

APPENDIX III: FORMS OF VIOLENCE AGAINST INCARCERATED WOMEN, PART II— LACK OF ADEQUATE HEALTHCARE

According to advocates and researchers, lack of adequate healthcare is the most pressing concern for most women in prison.[90] Inadequate access to proper healthcare services— characterized by delays, neglect, and outright mistreatment—is a pervasive problem affecting men and women alike in prisons across the United States.[91] However, women in prison in the United States generally present "far more serious and longstanding health problems when they first enter the system."[92] Further, women in prison also have distinct biological and acquired medical risks and needs that require customized attention.[93] Prison healthcare systems, designed around the needs of men, have proven systematically unable to respond to these gender-specific needs.[94]

The Requirements of Domestic and International Law

The Eighth Amendment of the U.S. Constitution, which forbids "cruel and unusual punishment,"[95] requires the state to provide adequate medical care to those individuals it incarcerates.[96] In order to bring a successful claim under the Eighth Amendment, the person in prison must show that a prison official was "deliberately indifferent" to a "serious medical need."[97] This standard requires a claimant to prove both an objective element and subjective element: first, that a "serious medical need"[98] went untreated or was inadequately treated, and then that the prison official subjectively knew about and disregarded the substantial risk of harm.[99] As discussed in Appendix I, the "deliberate indifference" standard's subjective element makes it very difficult for prisoners to succeed even where there are demonstrated violations.

International law standards require the provision of adequate and qualified medical, dental, and mental healthcare.[100] The Standard Minimum Rules require that medical officials see prisoners complaining of illness without delay, and that people in need of specialized treatment be transferred to appropriate facilities to receive adequate care.[101] On October 14, 2010, the Third Committee of the United Nations recommended to the General Assembly new rules for the treatment of women in prison (known as the Bangkok Rules). In addition to the requirements of the Standard Minimum Rules, the Bangkok Rules recognize that prison systems are often designed to meet men's needs, and require the provision of adequate gender-specific and gender-sensitive healthcare.[102]

Delays in Access and Mistreatment of Women in the Prison Healthcare System

In a 2001 legislative hearing on women's medical problems in the Valley State Prison for Women in California, Assemblyman Carl Washington commented that "from what I've heard, cats and dogs are treated better than some of these people."[103] Anecdotal and empirical evidence, from advocates and in published literature on the subject, indicates that women often experience extreme delays in access to healthcare, and sometimes outright mistreatment, despite serious medical needs.[104] In interviews, advocates reported numerous instances of delay and grossly inept care, including a woman who waited three months to have her broken arm cast, a woman with hepatitis C who repeatedly requested medical attention to no avail,[105] and a woman who was misdiagnosed with cancer, given chemotherapy, and sent to hospice care, only to be told months later she did not in fact have cancer.[106]

Prisons are often understaffed with unlicensed or otherwise under-qualified physicians and medical personnel. The physician/inmate and nurse/inmate ratios almost always greatly exceed the national recommendations of the National Commission on Correction Healthcare.[107] Staffing shortages lead to the types of delays in care and neglect discussed above.

To fill the gap, prisons routinely use non-medical staff, dubbed "medical technical assistants" or "gatekeepers." Although these individuals ordinarily have little or no medical training, and often have no written protocols, they have the power to determine whether a prisoner can see a physician.[108] Women in prison report similar difficulties and delays in access to medication. Simple requests for Tylenol or cold medication are often ignored or only filled days after the need has passed.[109] Women requesting pain medications are often labeled as "drug seekers" and routinely denied.[110]

Even if a woman manages to reach a prison doctor, there is no assurance of quality of care. Prisons and jails routinely hire doctors who, according to experts in correctional medicine, "would not be acceptable to practice in the free-world civilian sector": doctors with limited licenses, sexual abuse convictions, or significant substance-abuse problems.[111] Further, indigent women in prison may be reluctant to request care; increasingly, correctional facilities charge fees for medical services provided to prisoners, dissuading people in serious need of medical attention from seeking it.[112] In one study, women reported that they had never had a Pap smear because they could not afford the $5 co-pay.[113]

Access to obstetrical and gynecological care, a key element of comprehensive healthcare for all women, is at best inconsistent in U.S. women's prisons. Since prison healthcare is designed on a male-centered approach, gynecological care, essential to women's healthcare, is labeled a "specialty service." Lack of access to ob-gyn care can cause delays in the diagnosis of serious diseases such as breast cancer, ovarian cancer, and sexually transmitted diseases. Although doctors recommend that young to middle-aged women[114] in the general population have annual pelvic examinations, Pap smears, and access to reproductive health information, these services are not regularly offered in prisons.[115] Women consistently report the lack of regular checkups, Pap smears, and follow-ups for irregular Pap smears.[116] One study showed that only 53 percent of jails provided gynecological and obstetrical services.[117]

Women in prison often report shortages of everyday hygienic products, including soap, toilet paper, and sanitary pads. Without access to soap, hot water, and laundry facilities, the spread of disease—already a significant problem in such crowded conditions—can run rampant.[118] A woman in a Texas prison wrote, "We only get six tampons a month... and a roll of toilet paper a week. The rest of the time we are using rags as toilet paper."[119] Advocates confirm that women are not always provided with sanitary pads. One advocate discussed the palpable discomfort in a meeting of correctional facility leaders, almost all men, when advocates raised the question of access to hygiene products.[120] The lack of access to tampons and pads once again highlights the ways in which the system is not designed to respond to gender-specific concerns.

Increased Rate of Disease

Women in prison have higher rates of HIV and other diseases than men in prison because chronic and/or serious diseases such as AIDS, tuberculosis, and hepatitis C require special attention that often is not provided in women's facilities. In 2004, approximately 2.4 percent of women in prison were diagnosed as HIV positive, compared to 1.7 percent of men.[121] Women entering prison "are at greater risk than men of entering prison with sexually transmitted disease and HIV/AIDS because of their greater participation in prostitution and the likelihood of sexual abuse,"[122] according to Stephanie Covington, the co-director of the Center for Gender and Justice. While this rate is on the decline—3.5 percent of women in prison were HIV positive in 1998[123]—people in prison are still eight or nine times more likely to be infected with HIV than the general population.[124]

While many prisons do offer HIV testing,[125] comprehensive HIV treatment is rare in prison facilities,[126] and quality treatment and educational and support groups are often not available. Further, people living in prison with HIV may be subject to stigmatizing behavior by prison officials, and often suffer from the same delays in healthcare access and neglect as the general prison population, which can be deadly for women suffering from AIDS.[127]

Men and women in prison are also nine to ten times more likely to have hepatitis C (HCV) than the general population.[128] While some prison administrators have put policies in place to address what some experts refer to as a silent epidemic, advocates argue that "too little is being done… too late."[129] Ultimately, many prisons do not provide adequate treatment, and every year 1.4 million female and male prisoners carry HCV back to their communities after their release.[130] Women's prisons have also experienced serious epidemics of tuberculosis and MRSA (a highly contagious and dangerous mutation of staph). The overcrowding in women's prisons, combined with the lack of sanitary supplies and conditions, aggravate the spread of such highly contagious diseases.[131]

Drug Treatment and Mental Healthcare

Reports estimate that between 60 and 80 percent of women in prison face substance-abuse problems.[132] Women are more likely than men to report using drugs at the time of their offense, and nearly a third of women reported committing their offense to obtain money to buy drugs.[133] Women are increasingly arrested for drug crimes. The Institute on Women and Criminal Justice found that "between 1997 and 2006, women's arrests for drug abuse violations rose by 29.9 percent, while men's arrests for the same type of crimes rose by 15.7 percent. Over 200,000 adult women were arrested for drug abuse violations in 2006, an increase of nearly 23 percent from 2002."[134]

Despite the increasing problem of drug dependence among people in prison, in 2006 only 11.2 percent of prisoners who met clinical criteria for a substance abuse disorder received any sort of professional treatment.[135] An analysis of survey data conducted by

Columbia University's National Center on Addiction and Substance Abuse found that women are actually slightly more likely to receive treatment than men, but only by a small margin.[136] Although methadone maintenance therapy is a known effective treatment for heroin addiction and other opiate dependence, a 2009 nationwide study revealed that only about half of prison systems offer methadone treatment.[137] Of those facilities, half only offered methadone to pregnant women or for chronic pain management.[138]

Women use drugs in different ways and for different reasons than men. The Columbia University study showed women are more likely to use drugs to relieve emotional or psychological issues, often related to a history of abuse.[139] However, the study reveals that women's treatment options are often modeled after male programs and are not tailored to these differences.[140] It suggests that in order to effectively treat women in prison and reduce recidivism, prisons should adopt programs built for women's needs, such as trauma-informed approaches to drug treatment.[141]

Women in prison also tend to have much higher rates of mental health problems and dual diagnoses (the co-occurrence of a mental health disorder and substance abuse problem). Data from The Sentencing Project showed that women in prison are highly likely to have histories of physical or sexual abuse. Over half of all women in prison reported experiencing sexual or physical abuse before entering prison.[142] In a 2005 mental health study, nearly all the women inmates interviewed had been exposed to a traumatic event, with 90 percent reporting one interpersonal trauma, and 71 percent reporting exposure to domestic violence.[143] Medical research has widely demonstrated that histories of violence and trauma significantly affect an individual's physical and mental health.[144] In 2005, according to data collected by the Bureau of Justice Statistics, nearly three quarters of all women in state prisons had a mental health problem.[145]

Researchers and advocates report that few women in prison receive mental health services, and when they do, the care is inconsistent and does not meet medical standards.[146] Of the 12 percent of women in jails diagnosed with severe psychiatric disorders, only 25 percent of them receive mental healthcare.[147] Meanwhile, many women are heavily medicated with psychotropic drugs without corresponding mental healthcare services or therapy. Women in prison are significantly more likely to be medicated than men: 22 percent of women are given psychotropic medications compared with 9 percent of men.[148] Numerous advocates report overmedication of women, causing stupors, drooling, and a generalized inability to function.[149] Some advocates posit that the overmedication of women is a result of gender roles: women are not expected to engage in criminal behavior, and therefore when they do, their problems are "psychiatrized" and "controlled" via medication.[150] Whether the explanation is explicitly gendered or merely a result of negligent or absent medical services, most researchers agree that many women in prison are often overmedicated and undertreated.

Many women suffering from mental health disorders in prison experience a self-perpetuating downward spiral in their mental health. When they act out as a result of untreated mental health issues, they are often punished by being sent to administrative segregation. Isolation conditions in most segregation units are extreme, and their detrimental effects on prisoners' mental health are well-documented.[151] Many advocates and experts argue that isolation is particularly harmful to women.[152] Because their mental health is so poor, they are unable to "earn" their way out of segregation, and their mental health continues to deteriorate in isolation.[153]

Additionally, in many prisons, "suicide watch" is experienced as punishment rather than treatment. One prisoner writes, "I had to strip in front of male and female guards. For the first fourteen days [under suicide watch], I lay naked in a cell by myself, in a room with a broken window."[154] Another writes, "They take you and put you in a holding cell that's smaller than this. There's a bunk in there and they chain you to it. They take away your clothes and your blanket, everything. You have nothing... If I wasn't suicidal, that'll drive you to it."[155] Therefore, rather than seeking treatment, women report hiding suicidal or self-harm tendencies to avoid segregation.[156]

Legal Challenges to Women's Medical Conditions: Flynn v. Doyle

In May 2006, the ACLU sued on behalf of women prisoners in Wisconsin's Taycheedah Correctional Institution, alleging serious deficiencies in the provision of medical care at the facility. The court records document the inadequacy of treatment, including (1) nurses acting as improper "gatekeepers" to access to treatment; (2) delays in treatment reaching several months; (3) unreliable and dangerous provision of medications by untrained officials; (4) lack of an on-site infirmary; and (5) lack of follow-up from off-site care.[157] The ACLU demonstrated that while seriously mentally ill men in Wisconsin have access to the Wisconsin Resource Center, a facility with extensive mental health services, women have no comparable option.[158]

The court issued a preliminary injunction as to the dispensation of medications by untrained officials and denied the defendants' motion to dismiss, finding that the ACLU had alleged facts sufficient to demonstrate Eighth Amendment violations. The ACLU reached a settlement with the defendants in June 2010.[159] The Wisconsin Department of Corrections agreed to improve its medical facilities and policies to meet the National Commission on Correctional Healthcare's accreditation standards. They are also constructing a Women's Resource Center to provide adequate mental healthcare equal to the treatment provided to men.

APPENDIX IV: PREGNANCY, ABORTION, STERILIZATION, AND SHACKLING

Between 6 and 10 percent of women in United States prisons become pregnant each year.[160] Although little reliable data exists, one advocacy group estimates that approximately two thousand incarcerated women give birth annually.[161] Pregnancies in correctional institutions are usually unplanned and high risk, due to psychiatric illness, alcohol and substance abuse, and poor nutrition.[162] Access to appropriate medical services, therefore, is even more important to preserve the health of the mother, and her child, if she chooses to continue the pregnancy.

Access to Abortion

There is now a significant body of U.S. case law holding that a woman does not lose her Fourteenth Amendment right to choose to terminate her pregnancy[163] as a result of her imprisonment.[164] Upon legal challenge, courts have struck down corrections policies that either flatly prohibit transportation of prisoners to obtain elective abortions[165] or require women to petition for a court order to authorize transport or temporary release to obtain an abortion.[166] Only one court has held that refusing women access to elective abortions is a violation of a woman's Eighth Amendment right to adequate care for "serious medical needs," and that therefore correctional facilities must provide funding if it is not otherwise available.[167]

Since most women in prison are indigent, and are paid only 12¢ to 40¢ per hour for work done while imprisoned, many are effectively unable to obtain abortions. Many advocates argue that while the state can attempt to recover costs, it must provide access for indigent women. One court recently agreed, at least as to the costs of transportation and security, when the Arizona district court held that Sheriff Joe Arpaio's policy of charging prisoners upfront for security and transportation for the procedure was unconstitutional.[168] At a constitutional minimum, facilities must provide timely access to abortion, but not necessarily funding.

Studies show that the realities of correctional facilities do not live up to constitutional standards. A recent survey concluded that policies are "highly variable" across the states and inconsistent in practice.[169] Only 68 percent of correctional health providers answered affirmatively when asked whether women at their facility are allowed to obtain an elective abortion.[170] 88 percent of that group replied that their facility arranges transportation for women seeking abortions.[171] These findings are consistent with the experience of advocates, who report that while the law in this area has improved, the realities have not kept pace. The number of calls from women whose access is being impeded has not decreased.[172]

A recent ACLU review of available prison standards found that twenty-two states had passed standards for abortion access for women in prison.[173] Likewise, a thorough 2004 review of state policies by scholar Rachel Roth found that fourteen states had no written policy at all on abortion access.[174] The dominant policy in states appears to be to

"permit prisoners to obtain abortions on the same basis as other 'elective' medical care...
paying for transportation and security to an outside medical provider as well as paying
for the abortion itself."[175] The author of the study found that as of 2004, four states—
Alabama, Indiana, Mississippi, and Wyoming—still prohibited access to abortions unless
they are to save the life of the mother. Further, general restrictions on abortion access,
such as waiting periods and two-trip requirements, may increase the price of an abortion
for incarcerated woman to between $2,000 and $3,000 for a first-trimester abortion.[176]

The problem appears to be particularly acute in county jails. Since jails are typically
only used for shorter-term detention—pre-trial or short sentences—officials there often
try to avoid addressing the situation. Because access to legal abortion is restricted to
the first weeks of pregnancy, and the risks of the procedure increase with time, such
an attitude is harmful to women seeking abortions. A recent New York Civil Liberties
Union (NYCLU) report confirms this trend. A study of the New York county jail system,
which houses three thousand women at any given time, indicated that less than half of the
counties had any policy specifically addressing prisoners' access to abortion, and only 23
percent provided for unimpeded access.[177]

Under international law standards, governments have a general responsibility
to ensure access to safe abortion when it is legal. At least six treaty-monitoring
bodies—CEDAW, CRC, ICCPR, ICESCR, ICERD, and CAT[178]—have discussed the
importance of access to abortion to women's rights to life, health, privacy, and non-
discrimination.[179] State responsibility is arguably strengthened in prisons, where the
government monopolizes prisoners' access to care, and is required to provide adequate
care.[180] While U.S. courts have repeatedly held that a woman retains a right to abortion
in prison, access to the courts is limited, and courts often fail to address the fiscal
realities of women in prison.

Sterilization and Denial of Reproductive Capacity

In addition to the lack of access to abortion across the country, advocates are concerned
that women are being denied their reproductive freedom in other systematic ways. Justice
Now has begun to research and document incidents of sterilization occurring after delivery
or during other medical procedures, which may take place without informed consent or
under coercion.[181] In the course of this research, Justice Now has found that the California
Department of Corrections has performed 116 tubal ligations since 2006, making it the
only voluntary procedure besides tooth extraction that the department performs.[182]

The result of many of the mandatory minimum sentence laws, indeterminate
sentencing procedures, and other harsh incarceration policies that have increasingly led to
longer sentences for people in United States prisons—and which have disproportionately
affected women there—deprive many women of all reproductive capacity. Many of these
policies apply primarily to drug offenses, and women are increasingly, and at higher rates,
imprisoned for drug-related crimes.[183] As a result, women enter prison at a young age and
remain there during all their childbearing years. Incarcerated women have voiced serious
concern about their effective inability to ever have children, and advocates are increasingly
concerned about this less visible, but severe, reproductive injustice.[184]

Prenatal Care

Inadequate access to medical care in prison extends to prenatal care. Pregnant women regularly report that "they do not receive regular pelvic exams or sonograms, that they receive little to no education about prenatal care and nutrition, and that they are unable to maintain an appropriate diet to suit their changing caloric needs."[185] Two recent studies demonstrate how unprepared prisons are to respond to the distinct needs of pregnant women. A review of state policies by the ACLU revealed that only thirty-five jurisdictions (thirty-four states and the District of Columbia) have any correctional policies relevant to pregnancy-related care.[186] Comparing those policies to the national standards provided by the National Commission on Correctional Healthcare (NCCHC) and the American Public Health Association (APHA), the ACLU found nearly all the policies seriously lacking.[187]

In one particularly egregious case filed in 2009, the ACLU represented a woman in Montana who was five months pregnant when she voluntarily reported to the detention facility to serve a short term for traffic violations.[188] While in detention, she was refused access to essential medication for her ongoing participation in a treatment program for a diagnosed opiate addiction. As a result, she "suffered complete and abrupt withdrawal, experienced constant vomiting, diarrhea, rapid weight loss, dehydration, and other withdrawal symptoms, all extremely dangerous during pregnancy."[189] Only after nine days and the intervention of a public defender was she able to continue her treatment. Advocates indicate that many prisons force pregnant women to go without any drug treatment ("cold turkey"), even though withdrawal symptoms can put serious stress on the pregnancy.

In October 2010, the Rebecca Project for Human Rights and the National Women's Law Center released a state-by-state report card on conditions of confinement for pregnant and parenting women. The report based its "grade" for prenatal care provision on whether the state met the following basic standards: (1) provides for medical exams as part of prenatal care; (2) screens and provides treatment for high-risk pregnancies; (3) addresses the nutritional needs of pregnant women; (4) offers HIV testing; (5) provides a preexisting arrangement for deliveries; (6) provides advice on activity levels and safety; and (7) requires prisons to report all pregnancies and their outcomes.[190] Twenty-seven states received an F, indicating that they have none of these policies. Eleven states received a D, indicating that they have one or in some cases two of these policies but generally do not provide adequate prenatal care. No state received an A, which would indicate compliance with all of the standards indicated above. The two reports demonstrate that, while some states have begun to recognize the importance of prenatal care and to institutionalize policies on it, most are still unprepared and unresponsive to the needs of pregnant women in prison.

Shackling in Labor

In many U.S. jails and prisons, the Center for Reproductive Rights has reported, "pregnant women are routinely restrained by their ankles or their wrists when transported for prenatal medical appointments or to go the hospital." Often they "remain shackled during labor, delivery, and the post-delivery recovery period."[191]

During transportation, a shackled woman is put at a greater risk of falling, and if she does, she will be unable to catch herself.[192] During labor, shackling restricts a woman's ability to move freely to alleviate pain,[193] and the resulting stress may reduce the flow of oxygen to the baby during delivery.[194] If complications result, doctors' ability to quickly respond with an emergency cesarean may be hampered.[195] In 2007, the American College of Obstetricians and Gynecologists (ACOG) wrote: "Physical restraints have interfered with the ability of physicians to safely practice medicine by reducing their ability to assess and evaluate the physical condition of the mother and the fetus, and have similarly made the labor and delivery process more difficult than it needs to be; thus, overall putting the health and lives of women and unborn children at risk." [196]

Additionally, shackling incarcerated pregnant women violates international human rights standards. Rule 33 of the U.N. Standard Minimum Rules for the Treatment of Prisoners prohibits the use of restraints except when necessary to prevent the prisoner from causing injury to herself, others, or property, or when the prisoner is a flight risk. Most incarcerated women in the United States are not imprisoned for violent crimes, and a pregnant woman's flight risk, especially during and directly after labor, is questionable. In 2006, both the U.N. Committee against Torture and the Human Rights Committee expressed concern regarding the U.S. practice of shackling women during childbirth.[197] Likewise, during the Special Rapporteur's 1998 visit, she noted that the shackling of pregnant women in the United States "may be said to constitute cruel and unusual practices."[198]

There have been a number of improvements in U.S. practice in recent years. Ruling in *Nelson v. Correctional Medical Services* in October 2009, the Eighth Circuit held that women have a "clearly established" right not to be shackled during the "final stages of labor... absent clear evidence that she is a security or flight risk."[199] In 2008, only two states had laws prohibiting shackling of pregnant women, but as of October 2010, the number had increased to ten.[200] Also in 2008, the Federal Bureau of Prisons issued a new policy mandating that restraints will not be used during labor, delivery, or post-delivery unless there is an "immediate and credible risk of escape that cannot be reasonably contained through other methods."[201]

However, this progress is limited. Forty states and the District of Columbia still have no such laws; seven correctional departments have no formal written policy governing the use of restraints on pregnant women; and twenty-three state departments of corrections allow the use of restraints during labor.[202] The laws that exist typically do not create private rights of action (which allow a private party to bring a lawsuit), and there is significant evidence that these policies and laws often are not enforced or followed in practice.[203]

Further, *Nelson* and a number of the protective policies and laws are limited only to shackling during delivery—they do not address the larger problem of shackling incarcerated women throughout pregnancy. (Recently, California's Governor Schwarzenegger vetoed a unanimously passed bill prohibiting the use of shackles on pregnant women during transport, labor and delivery, and recovery, absent a safety concern.[204]) While the movement to end shackling in labor is growing, advocates argue the "current patchwork system of laws, regulations, and written and unwritten policies has created an atmosphere of noncompliance among correction officials."[205]

APPENDIX V: ACCESS TO CHILDREN, LOVED ONES, AND INTIMATE RELATIONS

In the United States, part of the meaning and purpose of incarceration is removal from social and familial relationships. Standard prison rules severely restrict the ability of people in prison to visit with friends and family, or to engage in physical or sexual contact with people outside the prison. Logistical and financial barriers make it difficult to take advantage of even the limited possibilities for contact and communication through authorized visits, telephone calls,[206] and mail. Relationships and intimacy are restricted within prisons as well: consensual sexual activity between people in prison is generally prohibited, and social deprivation—in the form of administrative segregation or solitary confinement—is one of the most severe punishments inflicted there.

For many imprisoned parents, regardless of gender, one of the most devastating aspects of imprisonment is forcible separation from their children. Women in prison face particular challenges relating to infants and children, in part because they are more likely than male prisoners to be primary caretakers.[207] Women may lose custody of their children while they are imprisoned, and even if custody is maintained, prisons make it difficult for women to visit with their children and infants. For all of these reasons, maternal incarceration is very destabilizing to a family's health and stability.[208]

The Legal Framework of Maternal Incarceration

The U.S. Supreme Court has recognized certain rights relating to children, family, and consensual sexual activity. Specifically, it has found that a parent's right to raise his or her own children is fundamental,[209] and that a parent's interest in the care and custody of his or her children does not "evaporate simply because they have not been model parents or have lost temporary custody of their child to the State."[210] The Supreme Court has also found that consensual sexual intimacy is a form of liberty that receives special protection under the Constitution.[211] These constitutional protections, however, are precarious in the context of the prison, where the "rights" and "liberties" that exist in the outside world are necessarily compromised.

The Adoption and Safe Families Act (ASFA), passed by Congress in 1997, was designed to move children from the foster-care system into permanent homes and to prioritize children's health and safety over biological family reunification.[212] Referred to as "the most sweeping change to the nation's adoption and foster-care system in nearly two decades,"[213] ASFA has made it easier for states to terminate the parental rights of imprisoned mothers whose children have been placed in foster care. Most significantly, ASFA requires states to file a petition terminating parental rights when a child has been in foster care for fifteen of the most recent twenty-two months, unless a relative is caring for the child or there is a compelling reason why termination would not be in the child's best interests.[214] AFSA does, however, also allow states to bypass the duty to make a "reasonable effort" to reunite children with their biological parents in certain situations.[215]

Additionally, ASFA provides cash bonuses to states that increase their adoption rates—sums of $4,000 for each child adopted above the previous year's number, and $6,000 for the adoption of a child who has a physical or emotional disability. Because custody issues are handled through state courts and as a civil matter, mothers facing the termination of their parental rights have no automatic right to counsel.

There is considerable variation in how ASFA is applied across the states. While ASFA requires the initiation of termination proceedings, the law of a given individual state specifies how the actual termination of rights is to be determined and carried out, and how the state's interest in the child's welfare is to be balanced with the parental rights of incarcerated mothers. While some state laws consider a variety of factors when deciding whether to terminate parental rights, other states authorize termination based on single, bright-line rules, such as whether the mother is serving a sentence of a particular length, whether she has had a certain number of contact visits with her child, or by the type of conviction she received.[216]

While ASFA has increased the nationwide adoption rate, it has also resulted in incarcerated women losing their parental rights, not because they were abusive or neglectful, but because the placement of their children into foster care made them unable to maintain contact over the required fifteen months. Data from the Bureau of Justice Statistics suggests that ASFA may have a disparate impact on women, since women in prison are more likely than men to have children in foster care[217]—since they are more likely than their male counterparts to have been primary caregivers of young children prior to imprisonment,[218] they are less able to rely on their children's other parent to take on the caregiving role for the duration of their sentence.[219]

Even when able to retain custody, most women in prison have few opportunities to see their children. There are fewer correctional facilities for women, and most of these are located in remote, rural areas, far from many of the women's homes and communities. This distance creates a major logistical and financial barrier to visitation.[220] More than half of imprisoned mothers never receive visits from their children during their time inside.[221]

Considering that a large percentage of women in prison are there serving sentences for nonviolent, drug-related crimes, and that separating mothers and children is detrimental to mothers, children, and communities alike,[222] many advocates support sentencing alternatives that would allow mothers and children to stay together. The Rebecca Project for Human Rights, an organization that is one of the foremost experts on incarcerated mothers, strongly supports family-based programs that provide services such as therapy, parenting classes, and substance-abuse treatment.[223] Thirty-four states already make alternative-sentencing programs of some kind available to women, although they may have limited capacity. Prison nurseries are available in thirteen states, and, though inferior to family-based alternative sentencing, they offer some opportunity for mother-child bonding. Seventeen states do not offer family-based treatment programs of any kind.[224]

APPENDIX VI: DISCRIMINATORY PRACTICES AND SPECIAL POPULATIONS

Women of Color

The racial disparities of the recent prison boom of the past few decades, dubbed by experts the "race to incarcerate,"[225] have been profound. Nearly 60 percent of the current U.S. prison population is black or Hispanic.[226] It is now a well-known fact that, if the trends persist, about one in three black males born today can expect to go to prison in his lifetime.[227] Although rates of incarceration are higher for men in general, racial disparities persist across gender lines. Rates of incarceration for women of color have rapidly increased in recent years; black women are incarcerated at a rate three times higher, and Hispanic women at a rate one-and-a-half times higher, than that of white women.[228] Black women are the fastest-growing population in prisons.[229]

The possible causes for the racial disparity are complex and varied. Social and economic inequality along racial lines likely contributes to racial differences in some crime rates.[230] However, the black/white racial disparity in prison, overall eight to one, significantly outstrips racial disparities in "unemployment (two to one), non-marital child-bearing (three to one), infant mortality (two to one), and wealth (one to five)."[231] After close analysis of the available data, scholar Michael Tonry found that only 61 percent of the black incarceration rate can be explained by disproportionate crime rates.[232]

Rates of incarceration for drug offenses illustrate the point. While over half of persons sentenced to prison for drug offenses are black,[233] national data shows that rates of illegal drug use are fairly consistent across all races.[234] These disparities between incarceration for drug charges and actual drug use are consistent among women as well as men.[235]

There is a large body of literature demonstrating racial bias and/or discrimination at all stages of the law-enforcement process: police enforcement, prosecution, conviction, and sentencing.[236] Furthermore, many experts have criticized the numerous "race-neutral" criminal laws that have foreseeable disparate impacts by race. Most notoriously, the federal crack-cocaine law, which until recently inflicted a one-hundred-to-one penalty for the possession of crack cocaine (a drug associated closely with African American use) over possession of powder cocaine, a more expensive but pharmaceutically similar drug.[237] State and federal "school zone" drug laws, which penalize drug offenses within designated school zones more harshly, also have a racially disparate impact. Since blacks are more likely to live in dense urban areas where residences are generally closer to schools, black individuals convicted of drug offenses are often subject to harsher penalties than white people convicted of the same offense.[238] Most recently, states have begun to criminally prosecute women who use drugs while pregnant. Although studies show that the number of white women who use drugs while pregnant is higher than the number of black or Hispanic women who do, women of color are "increasingly the focus of drug tests, arrests, prosecution, and incarceration for drug use during pregnancy."[239] Despite the stark racial disparities created by discriminatory policies and practices, a series of Supreme Court verdicts have made racial discrimination cases practically impossible to bring successfully.[240]

Because they are overrepresented in the prison system, women of color disproportionately suffer the long-term effects of sexual abuse, inadequate healthcare,[241] and other human rights abuses prevalent inside the system. Further, scholar Kim Buchanan, among others, argues that the widely held racialized image of prisoners contributes to the pervasive indifference to their treatment, thus preventing effective change and reform within the institutions.[242] In other words, the very same racial biases that place people of color in prison in high numbers also exacerbate the poor conditions of their confinement. Women of color, because of their disproportionate rate of incarceration, also bear the stigma of past imprisonment unequally; women who have spent time in prison will have a more difficult time obtaining a job, are more likely to be homeless, and, if they are convicted of a drug felony, will be barred from federally funded public assistance.[243] Felony disenfranchisement laws disproportionately deprive women of color, as well as men of color, of the right to vote. Currently ten states permanently disenfranchise some or all persons convicted of felonies, and only two states do not disenfranchise persons with criminal convictions at all.[244] One in fifty black women cannot currently vote—four times the rate of disenfranchisement for non-black women, and an increase of 14 percent since 2000.[245] These disenfranchisement laws not only deeply affect the individual women who are deprived of this fundamental right, but also have ripple effects on the political power of black communities.

As discussed above, as more women are incarcerated, more mothers are incarcerated and lose access to their children, sometimes permanently.[246] Unsurprisingly, given the racial disparities in imprisonment, children of color are overwhelmingly more likely to have a parent in jail: one in fifteen black children, one in forty-two Latino children, and one in 111 white children have at least one imprisoned parent.[247] Imprisoned mothers are more likely to be living with their children at the time preceding their sentence, making their imprisonment likely to be more disruptive to their home. If no other family member is available in these situations, children are generally sent into foster care. Studies have found that black children are overrepresented in the foster-care system in practically every state.[248] Ultimately the data shows that, in the words of sociologists Bruce Western and Christopher Wildeman, "the prison boom has been massively corrosive for family structure and family life" in African American communities.[249]

Native American Women

There is little documentation of the treatment of Native American women[250] in United States prisons. NPREC (hereinafter referred to as "the PREA Commission") did not investigate sexual abuse in tribal detention facilities, nor did it mention Native Americans in its section on "Special Populations" or its discussion of the relationship between sexual abuse and race.[251] Yet Native Americans are overrepresented in United States prisons, with a rate of incarceration that is about 21 percent higher than the national average.[252] The rate of incarceration for Native American women, along with black women, has increased more rapidly than the rate for women belonging to other racial or ethnic groups, with Native American women twice as likely as white women to be incarcerated.[253] Advocates argue that Native American women are disproportionately represented because of deep-seated prejudice,[254] and because their communities struggle with some of the most extreme poverty, unemployment, and alcoholism in the country.[255]

Within prisons, needs specific to Native American women, particularly those related to religion and spiritual practices, are overlooked. The Supreme Court has found that state prisons cannot deny individuals of minority religions the right to practice their religious faiths.[256] Native American women in prison have not, however, been able to exercise these rights.[257] Like imprisoned women generally, Native American women are often housed far from their communities, where chaplains of their faiths are unable to provide culturally appropriate services. States have been unwilling to provide the necessary funding to hire Native American spiritual leaders.[258]

While mental health is a major concern for all women in prison, advocates argue that Native American women's mental health needs may be overlooked, due to the fact that, for this population, mental health and spiritual practice are often intertwined.[259] Native American women are also likely to enter into prison with high rates of past trauma, based on the fact that this population contends with a rate of violent victimizations outside of prisons that is more than double the general rate.[260] Native Americans are two and a half times more likely to experience rape or sexual assault than members of other races,[261] and they experience the highest rates of domestic violence of any group in the United States.[262]

One reason for high rates of violence against Native American women is that the U.S. criminal justice system involves additional complexity when applied to tribal areas, making it difficult for victims of crime to seek redress. While most people living in the United States have to contend with the dual state-federal systems, Native American peoples living on Indian lands exist in three overlapping jurisdictions: federal, state, and tribal.[263] Tribal courts have jurisdiction over crimes committed by Native Americans on tribal land; until recently, however, tribal courts could only sentence offenders to one year of imprisonment in a tribal jail, a fine of $5,000, or both.[264] Pursuant to the recently passed Tribal Law and Order Act, tribal courts can now sentence certain offenders to up to three years of imprisonment, a fine of up to $15,000, or both.[265] Federal courts have jurisdiction over all crimes specified by the Major Crimes Act of 1885 (which include murder, manslaughter, rape, assault with intent to murder, arson, burglary, and larceny),[266] while state courts have jurisdiction over specific crimes on tribal lands that are specified under Public Law 280, a law that clarifies conflicted jurisdictions.[267] Law-enforcement officials and attorneys are often not prepared to handle the overlap between the jurisdictions or to determine how cases should be tried, creating a climate of impunity in which violent crimes against Native American women go unpunished.[268]

Lesbian, Bisexual, Transsexual, and Queer Women in Detention

Lesbian, bisexual, transsexual, queer, or otherwise non-gender-conforming individuals in women's prisons—as well as female-identified individuals who are sentenced to men's prisons—face particular challenges to their safety and well-being. Studies have consistently shown that those with a non-heterosexual orientation, or whose gender expression does not fall neatly into categories of male and female, are vulnerable to being targeted and abused both by staff and by other prisoners.[269] While most available documentation focuses on the treatment of these individuals in men's prisons and jails, it appears that abuse is prevalent in women's prisons as well.[270] As with hate crimes that occur outside of prison, these individuals are targeted and victimized specifically because of their perceived or actual sexual/gender identities.[271]

Within women's prisons, there is often an underlying assumption that prisoners should be passive, emotional, and submissive—and that since, in the analysis of the phenomenon by Justice Now, "obviously non-feminine behavior landed them in prison, incarceration should 'restore them to it.'"[272] Prisoners who appear as masculine or "butch" are routinely subjected to threats, harassment, and physical abuse by correctional officers.[273] The PREA Commission found male corrections officers to be the perpetrators of most of the violence directed at LBTQ women.[274] Male guards may perceive prisoner masculinity as a form of insubordination and a challenge to their authority, and may respond with confrontation and retaliation. Guards may engage these individuals in power struggles, informing them that if they act "like men" that is how they will be treated, and single them out for particularly forceful disciplinary action. Prisons also subject non-gender-conforming individuals to "forced feminization" through restrictive codes relating to dress, hair length and style, and other aspects of physical appearance.[275]

Male-to-female transgender individuals are one of the most vulnerable sub-groups of LBTQ women. While they may neither identify as male nor be perceived as male by others, they are often housed in men's prisons, and their gender nonconformity puts them at extremely high risk for abuse.[276] *Farmer v. Brennan*, the case in which the Supreme Court unanimously ruled that deliberate indifference to the substantial risk of sexual abuse violates an incarcerated individual's rights under the Eighth Amendment, concerned the failure of prison authorities to protect a transgender prisoner from rape,[277] and Congress relied upon this case in its findings supporting the Prison Rape Elimination Act.[278]

Juveniles

Though not a focus of this book, girls confined in juvenile detention facilities[279] face many of the same challenges of women in prison generally. These include the threat of sexual assault, lack of access to families, policing of sexuality, and inadequate physical and mental health services. Young people, however, are particularly vulnerable to abuse and mistreatment, and are less able than adults to follow grievance procedures and seek remedies for injuries. That girls suffer from a more acute version of the abuse that characterizes adult women's prisons reveals a central, underlying problem: juvenile facilities are too much like adult prisons. Many of the abuses stem from the fact that these facilities are generally punitive instead of rehabilitative. Young people are treated like hardened criminals, despite the fact that many are in detention for minor, nonviolent crimes, and that their behavior is often related in some way to physical abuse, sexual abuse, or neglect at home.

APPENDIX VII:
POST-PRISON CONSEQUENCES

The harsh consequences of a criminal conviction do not end with the term of imprisonment; parole conditions, discriminatory laws, and social stigma can last a lifetime.[280] People exit prison to face enormous challenges remaking their lives on the outside. Beyond the psychological impact of isolation and potential abuse, imprisonment damages or destroys familial bonds and community ties, and can disrupt education, employment, and the development of professional skills. Further, a number of federal and state laws curtail the rights of persons convicted of crimes by restricting their ability to vote, find housing or employment, or continue to provide and care for their children and families. This appendix examines state laws and state application of relevant federal law affecting persons released from prison, based largely on two studies published by the Legal Action Center: *After Prison: Barriers Facing People With Criminal Records*, completed in 2004,[281] and the follow-up report published in 2009.[282]

Public Access to Criminal Records

Increasingly, states are making arrest and conviction records available to the public online. While some states bar or limit discrimination based on these records in specific circumstances, such as hiring for employment, unfettered internet access to them undermines such limitations and makes redressing discrimination difficult or impossible.[283] With widespread public access to criminal-record information, convictions that have little bearing on an individual's capacity to successfully perform a job or be a satisfactory tenant nevertheless provide grounds for an employer or landlord to refuse employment or housing, and they can often do so without any accountability.[284] As of 2009, thirty-five states published criminal records online or otherwise allowed internet access to them.[285]

Additionally, criminal-record reports may contain errors and misleading information, such as arrests listed as convictions or arrest records that fail to state whether a conviction resulted.[286] Most individuals are neither aware of the frequency of such errors nor qualified to interpret records that are often inaccurate, incomplete, and complex.[287]

Though not without qualifications, some states allow individuals to seal, dismiss, or expunge conviction records, and others allow the sealing or expungement of arrests that did not lead to conviction. In 2009, twenty-five states allowed some conviction records to be expunged or sealed.[288] States that allow the expungement of convictions place the burden of demonstrating rehabilitation on the convicted individual, and often limit the remedy to certain enumerated offenses or first-time offenses only. Generally, in order to pursue expungement, one must have completed and fully complied with the terms of probation or parole.

An expungement does not always mean that a conviction will disappear from a criminal record. In some cases, the record may remain with a qualification, such as "expunged" or "dismissed." Additionally, expungement may permit an individual to deny the existence of a conviction on certain applications, but not on all: employment applications with more stringent requirements, such as those for state-licensed occupations, law enforcement, or jobs that entail working with children, do not qualify. Applications for public assistance or low-income housing also do not qualify.

Parenting

Since the 1980 Adoption and Child Welfare Act, states can only receive federal child-welfare funds on the condition that state agencies make "reasonable efforts" to keep children with their families, and, where removal could not be prevented, to facilitate family reunification.[289] In 1997, however, Congress passed the Adoption and Safe Families Act (ASFA), specifying situations in which state agencies are not required to make reasonable efforts to prevent removal or facilitate reunification. (The legal details and application of ASFA are explained in Appendix V, above.) This may impose a punishment beyond the sentence determined at court, and can also effectively punish children of the individual sentenced, destroying existing families and established networks of care and support.

ASFA also prohibits persons with certain convictions from adopting children or becoming foster parents, and mandates that states run criminal-background checks on prospective adoptive or foster parents before receiving federal funds.[290] ASFA recommends that states forbid persons convicted of child abuse, neglect, spousal abuse, crimes against children, and violent crimes from ever becoming adoptive or foster parents, and that states institute a five-year ban for persons convicted of physical assault, battery, or drug-related felonies.[291] In 2009, thirteen states uniformly barred persons with criminal records from becoming adoptive or foster parents,[292] while thirty-eight states considered prior convictions when determining a potential adoptive or foster parent's suitability.[293]

Driver's Licenses

A valid driver's license can be essential for obtaining and maintaining meaningful employment. Additionally, a number of states require a driver's license on payment of child support, traffic tickets and fines, and restitution, or payment of fines imposed as part of a criminal sentence.[294]

In 1992, Congress amended the Federal Highway Apportionment Act to make a portion of the federal highway funds granted to states contingent on the state's adoption of a law revoking or suspending driver's licenses for people convicted of drug offenses, effective for at least six months after the conviction. This would apply to any criminal offense involving the possession, distribution, manufacture, cultivation, sale, or transfer of drugs; the attempt or conspiracy to commit these offenses; or driving under the influence of a controlled substance.[295] As of 2009, twenty-eight states automatically suspended or revoked driver's licenses upon some or all drug convictions,[296] while twenty-three did so only for driving-related offenses.[297] All but eleven states offered some type of restricted license, allowing certain persons with suspended or revoked driver's licenses to travel to treatment programs, school, or work.[298] Persons with criminal convictions may find themselves in a catch-22 if these restrictions render them unable to commute to find or keep a paying job, especially if that job is necessary to meet court-imposed financial obligations.

Restrictions on the commercial driver's licenses necessary to drive buses, trucks, and commercial vehicles present another barrier to employment for persons with conviction records; details can be found in the discussion of employment and occupational licensing, below.

Employment

Most of the employment laws that affect persons convicted of crimes exist at the state rather than the federal level. Generally, employers are permitted to inquire about criminal convictions during the application process and may consider them during hiring decisions. State laws prohibit employers from hiring convicted persons for positions in certain fields, such as child care, education, security, nursing, and home healthcare.[299] However, businesses covered by Title VII of the Civil Rights Act, a federal employment anti-discrimination law, cannot deny employment based on conviction unless it is justified a "business necessity." According to a policy statement issued by the Equal Opportunity Employment Commission, three factors determine a business necessity when a discrimination complaint undergoes review: "the nature and gravity of the offense; the time that has passed since the conviction and/or completion of the sentence; and the nature of the job held or sought."[300]

Further, state occupational licenses can be required for upwards of a hundred types of occupations in a given state, and are as varied as accountant, nurse, registered nurse's assistant, ambulance driver, barber, bail bondsman, cosmetologist, bus driver, contractor, longshoreman, taxi driver, and radiologist.[301] Each occupation is governed by a state licensing board with different standards for licensing and revocation. License applications almost always require a criminal-background check, and are often denied on the basis of criminal convictions. As of 2009, twenty-six states had no standards governing the relevance of conviction records in licensing decisions, and twenty-five states required individualized determinations of relevance.[302]

Voting

States have the power to determine whether someone with a prior conviction can vote. Forty-eight states place some sort of restriction on the right to vote for persons convicted of a felony.[303] As of 2009, Kentucky and Virginia permanently disenfranchised persons convicted of any felony.[304] Seven more states permanently disenfranchised persons convicted of certain felonies or with multiple convictions.[305] Twenty-six states restored voting rights to persons with felony convictions after the completion of parole or probation,[306] and in fourteen states persons still on probation or parole were able to vote.[307]

Financial Aid for Education

The federal Higher Education Act governs scholarships, low-interest loans, and work-study programs for college students.[308] Before 2005, students convicted of any drug-related offense were ineligible for such programs. Since then, Congress has amended the act to bar only students who were receiving financial aid at the time of their conviction. No other type of offense, including violent offenses and sex offenses, results in a flat denial of federal financial aid eligibility.[309]

The 2007 Second Chance Act authorized federal, state, and local grant programs to fund education and other services for people released from prison. In 2008, an amendment to the act authorized grants supporting higher education programs in prison.[310] Supported by these changes and spurred by the high cost of imprisonment in the face of budget crises, many states have expanded re-entry programs in recent years.[311] For example, state officials in Michigan have cited a focus on job-placement programs as a major factor in the 15 percent reduction of the state's prison population over the past four years, which saved the state over $200 million.[312] However, following the passage of the federal budget for fiscal year 2011, money allotted for the Second Chance Act was cut by $32 million.[313] The effects of the recent budget cut remain to be seen.

Public Housing

As discussed above, increasing public access to arrest and conviction records facilitates discrimination against housing applicants by private landlords. Criminal convictions also present a barrier to obtaining low-income, government-subsidized housing, including tenant-based subsidies such as Section 8, project-based subsidies, and government-owned housing.

Although local housing agencies administer these programs, federal law sets specific restrictions on them related to criminal convictions.[314] For example, federal law requires local housing authorities to bar persons from residing in federally subsidized housing if they have been convicted of methamphetamine production or certain sex offenses.[315] Laws passed in 1996 and 1998 also allow housing authorities to deny housing to anyone who has ever engaged in "drug-related" activity.[316] Following the implementation of these laws, the number of applicants denied housing because of "criminal backgrounds" doubled.[317]

Outside of these federal laws, determining the relevance of convictions for one's public-housing eligibility is left not to state law, but to local housing authorities. They may decide which types of convictions make an applicant ineligible, how long a ban on eligibility will last, and whether some demonstration of rehabilitation can overcome a conviction-based ban. In 2002, for example, a Supreme Court decision upheld a local Public Housing Authority's right to evict entire families based on the one-strike policy, regardless of any prior knowledge of drug use on the part of the leaseholder.[318] According to the Legal Action Center's 2009 study, which surveyed the policies, but not the practices, of the housing authorities in the largest cities in each state, forty-eight states provided for individualized determination of the eligibility of an applicant, and three states had flat bans on persons with a wide range of convictions.[319]

Benefits and Public Assistance

According to experts, welfare assistance serves as a "pivotal transitional mechanism" for impoverished families, providing them with the most basic necessities for daily living and access to anti-poverty resources including drug treatment, education, and employment.[320] The 1996 Personal Responsibility and Work Opportunity Reconciliation Act instituted a lifetime ban on federal food stamps or TANF (Temporary Assistance for Needy Families) for anyone convicted of a drug offense,[321] and mandated that a state looking to opt out of or modify this ban must adopt specific legislation doing so.[322] By 2009, nine states had permanently denied benefits to anyone convicted of a drug offense,[323] another nine states had passed legislation to eliminate the ban entirely,[324] while thirty-three states had modified the ban in some way, allowing persons with drug convictions to obtain benefits if they met certain requirements. These included having been convicted of a possession-only crime, meeting a waiting period, or participating in treatment.

A 2002 study published by the Sentencing Project revealed the disproportionate impact of the lifetime welfare ban on mothers of color and, potentially, their children: "First due to racially biased drug policies and enforcement of drug laws, drug offenses account, in large part, for the rapid growth in the number of African-American women and Latinas under criminal justice supervision. Second, as a result of race- and gender-based socioeconomic inequalities, African-American and Latina mothers are highly susceptible to poverty and as such, are disproportionately represented in the welfare system."[325]

APPENDIX VIII: BARRIERS TO COMMUNICATION FROM PRISON

Limits on communication from prison have had a broad and deep impact on the ability of people inside to protest human rights violations and receive redress. The limits on visitation, mail, phone calls, recording equipment—and in some cases outright media bans—severely restrict the flow of information out of prison. U.S. courts have consistently upheld communications restrictions, citing a necessity for public safety. Combined with the extreme difficulty of litigating abuses in prison, this leaves prison officials free to control the discussion about prison conditions and to act largely with impunity.

The Supreme Court has given prison administrators wide latitude to abridge constitutional rights "inconsistent with proper incarceration": "The very object of imprisonment is confinement," the Court wrote in *Overton v. Bazzetta*. "Many of the liberties and privileges enjoyed by other citizens must be surrendered by the prisoner."[326] The Court has viewed prison administration as the province of the executive and legislative branches of government, and substantially deferred to prison officials to determine the goals of proper incarceration and the measures necessary to achieve them.[327]

Since 1987, challenges to communication bans on the grounds that the ban violates a prisoner's constitutional rights have been made by testing the policy against four criteria, which have become known as the "Turner factors" (after the verdict of that year's *Turner v. Safely*). The court must consider: (1) whether there is "a valid, rational connection between the prison regulation and the legitimate governmental interest put forward to justify it"; (2) "whether there are alternative means of exercising the right that remain open to prison inmates"; (3) "the impact accommodation of the asserted constitutional right will have on guards and other inmates, and on the allocation of prison resources generally"; and (4) "the absence of ready alternatives" to the regulation.[328]

This hands-off approach to judicial review effectively weighs the scales of justice in favor of the state. While, in theory, the Turner standard does not absolutely foreclose persons in prison from challenging restrictions on their access to the outside world—or those in the outside world from access to information about conditions in prison—in practice its implementation has subjected these individuals to severe legal limitations as well as surveillance and censorship of all forms of communication. These have included not only the in-person visitation sometimes necessary for a journalist to gain the trust of a person in prison, but also communication by telephone and mail.

Limits on Visitation, Interviews, and Mail

Obstructions to information from prison precede *Turner v. Safely*. In 1974, a California regulation prohibiting media members from interviewing individuals in prison faced a constitutional challenge, on the grounds of the freedom of the press.[329] In response, prison administrators argued that, prior to the enactment of the policy in question, wider press access had granted certain individuals in prison influence and notoriety, making them "virtual public figures within prison society."[330] Ultimately, the administrators claimed, this created disorder that contributed to a 1971 escape attempt from San Quentin prison and resulted in the deaths of three prison staff members and two inmates.

The Supreme Court's verdict gave weight to the administrators' argument, rejecting the freedom-of-the-press challenge and finding that "newsmen have no constitutional right of access to prisons or their inmates beyond that afforded the general public."[331] The Court found that other "reasonable and effective" methods of communication—such as mail and visits with family and friends—remained available to persons in prison, and deferred to the judgment of prison officials to uphold limits on speech. The recommendation of substituting other methods of communication for media interviews with people in prison was repeated in a similar case later the same year.

In another case, after media requests to inspect a California jail following the 1978 suicide of a prisoner there had been denied,[332] the Supreme Court again upheld jail administrators' restrictions. Instead of granting the requested permission to take photographs, make sound recordings, and interview persons in jail, administrators offered a limited number of public tours of some areas of the jail, which did not including the portion of the facility where the suicide occurred, and on which recording equipment and interviews were prohibited.[333] Unlike the cases earlier in the decade, however, jail administrators did not cite any specific prior negative experience with media access, but argued nevertheless that media access would create "jail celebrities" and disrupt operations, order, and security.[334] As in those previous cases, the Court upheld the restrictions, deferring to jail officials' judgment regarding the potentially negative effects of media access.[335] Briefly, the Court also noted the availability of mail as a method of communication with people in prison, as well as the media's ability to interview attorneys representing persons in prison and recently released individuals.[336]

The Turner factors' "reasonableness standard" mentioned above—and the deference to prison administrators that it suggested—was formally adopted as a precedent in 1989.[337] Thereafter, this standard would be applied whenever an alleged violation of the constitutional rights of a prisoner reached court. In the 1989 case, the Court upheld the validity of a federal prison regulation authorizing prison officials to stop publications from entering the prison if they were judged detrimental to institutional security.[338] The Court, applying the Turner factors, ruled the objective of protecting prison security as "central to all other corrections goals" and that substitute publications were available, upheld the policy,[339] and deferred to the judgment of prison administrators in evaluating the potential effect of certain publications—though it "found comfort" in the fact that the decisions of what publications to exclude were individualized.[340]

More recently, a 2003 case in Michigan[341] challenged regulations that restricted visits to clergy members, the attorney of the person in prison, or persons on an approved visitor list.[342] In cases where parental rights had been terminated, the regulations prohibited visits from children who were minors, and otherwise allowed only visits from minors who were the children, stepchildren, siblings, or grandchildren of the person in prison.[343] The regulations banned visitors other than attorneys and clergy members in cases where the person in prison had committed multiple substance-abuse violations, though he or she would have the opportunity to reapply for visitation rights after two years.[344] Deciding this case, the Supreme Court remarked at length on an increase in the overall prison population in Michigan during the 1990s, which had resulted in increased visitation that strained prison resources and heightened challenges to maintaining order and preventing drug smuggling during visits.[345] Using a relatively brief analysis of the Turner factors, the Court found that the restrictions on visitation by minors bore a sufficient relationship to "maintaining internal security and protecting children from exposure to sexual or other misconduct or accidental injury"[346]: "The regulations promote internal security, perhaps the most legitimate of penological goals... by reducing the total number of visitors and by limiting the disruption caused by children in particular. Protecting children from harm is also a legitimate goal."[347]

The plaintiffs had argued that the exclusion of underage nieces and nephews, as well as children for whom parental rights had been terminated, bore no rational relationship to the maintenance of internal security,[348] but the Court rejected this contention: "to reduce the number of child visitors, a line must be drawn, and the categories set out by these regulations are reasonable."[349]

The substance abuse restrictions, too, according to the Court, had a legitimate goal: deterring alcohol and drug abuse.[350] Looking for "alternative means" that the regulation did not suppress, the Court noted that people in Michigan prisons could send messages to those who were not allowed to visit through those who were, as well as communicate by mail or telephone:[351] "Alternatives to visitation need not be ideal... they need only be available."[352] Further, the Court determined that wider visitation would require "significant reallocations of the prison system's financial resources and would impair the ability of corrections officers to protect all who are inside a prison's walls,"[353] and impose too heavy a restriction to the penological goal.

In these cases, the substantial deference given to prison administrators regarding regulations and policies abridging the First Amendment rights of persons in prison imposes an almost insurmountable burden on plaintiffs looking to challenge and overturn those rules. Prison administrators have been granted extremely wide latitude to articulate penological goals, of which prison "security" and "order" have appeared to be the broadest and most vague. The Supreme Court has noted repeatedly that imprisonment, by its very nature, represents the curtailment of fundamental constitutional guarantees, including freedom of speech.[354] And even before facing the analytical obstacles required for a Turner challenge, a person in prison—largely cut off from the world outside and receiving information heavily filtered through the very institution they are challenging—begins with the disadvantage of lacking the institutional expertise of prison officials, which could be put to use to determine or argue against claims of administrative cost and projected security concerns.

Limits on Telephone Communication

Prison phone regulations effectively restrict communication from prison through limitations on the time and frequency of phone calls, restrictions on recipients of outgoing phone calls, telephone surveillance and monitoring, and the high prices charged by prisons and telecommunications companies for telephone use. Though the Supreme Court has not applied the Turner standard to constitutional challenges of prison phone regulations, its treatment of these challenges has been similarly deferential to prison administration.[355]

First Amendment challenges have largely been based on the exorbitant costs imposed upon prisoners, as well as on their families and friends on the outside, through the collect-call and debit-call systems. Although the Federal Communications Commission (FCC) objects to the collusion between states and phone companies to raise the prices of calls from prison, widespread reform of the high rates charged has been stalled by Supreme Court decisions ruling that the FCC does not have the power to enforce change. Consequently, a handful of recent advocacy successes—including yearly price reductions in Georgia and an Indiana contract that abolished connecting fees—have occurred on the state level, largely through decisions by state Departments of Corrections and Public Service Commissions.

The Supreme Court has yet to address whether the right to make phone calls from prison is protected by the First Amendment, and the federal courts of appeal are currently split on the constitutional right of a person in prison to make telephone calls.[356]

In one case, *Arsberry v. Illinois*,[357] people in Illinois prisons alleged that the state's practice of contracting with only one telephone company for each jail or prison and its receipt of half of the revenues for each contract violated the First Amendment. The court agreed that the contractor's rates were "exorbitant," but held that the "primary use" of the phone by persons in prison was not protected speech: "any regulation direct or indirect on communications can have an effect on the market in ideas and opinions, but that possibility in itself does not raise a constitutional issue."[358]

Additionally, recording and monitoring prison telephone conversations does not violate the First or Fourth Amendment rights of persons in prison according to current constitutional case law. Elsewhere, a different federal court[359] held that a defendant's recorded jail telephone calls were admissible at trial, and that the practice of recording such calls withstood Fourth Amendment scrutiny. By the very nature of the phone call—outgoing from a jail—the court found the defendant to have no reasonable expectation of privacy, and thus Fourth Amendment protections were not triggered.[360] Additionally, the defendant was found to have implicitly consented to the taping of his phone calls when he was informed during his booking into custody that they would be recorded.[361] In other cases,[362] the Federal Bureau of Prisons' practice of recording all prison telephone calls has been upheld with the same rationale used in mail- and visitation-restriction cases: "legitimate governmental interest in order and security of penal institutions justifies the impositions of certain restraints on inmate correspondence."[363] The court accorded the "expert judgment" of prison administrators' "wide-ranging deference" in upholding the regulation, remarking only that the restrictions furthered "one or more of the substantial governmental interests of security, order, and rehabilitation"[364] and that the procedures were "generally necessary."[365]

State and Federal Regulations at a Glance

The following is a summary of prison regulations affecting communications between persons in prison and members of the media, based on the Program Statements of the Federal Bureau of Prisons and the administrative policies and regulations of the District of Columbia and fifteen states: Alabama, Arizona, California, Colorado, Idaho, Illinois, Louisiana, Massachusetts, Michigan, Nevada, New York, Ohio, Texas, Virginia, and Washington.

VISITATION: All of the prison regulations surveyed distinguish between general prison visitation and media access by providing either an exclusive definition of who may visit, specific media visitation regulations, or both. Regular visitation is generally limited to an approved list of family and friends who have established a relationship with the person in prison prior to his or her confinement, or a small number of visitors who need not have established a prior relationship but fit specific classifications—such as attorneys and clergy or spiritual advisors—and to whom other special regulations usually apply.[366] Members of the media, who often lack a relationship to persons in prison before their imprisonment, are by definition excluded from this type of contact. In some states, such as New York and Michigan, members of the media who have no prior acquaintance with the inmate may visit in accordance with regular visitation regulations, which prohibit cameras and tape recorders and limit the use of paper and pens.[367]

Most of the prison regulations surveyed provide a set definition of "media" persons, to whom special visitation and interview regulations apply, but the definition can vary state to state.[368] Some[369] include only those persons whose "principal employment" is to gather or report news for newspapers of general circulation, news magazines with a national circulation, national or international news services, or FCC-licensed radio or television programs,[370] but others provide a separate definition for media who don't fit into this more traditional category or explicitly include freelance reporters, documentary filmmakers, and nonfiction authors.[371] Media representatives who do not fit the most restrictive definition of "news media" are often required to provide prison administrators with specific information about their employment and project in order to gain visitation or interview access.

Generally, media representatives who meet the definition provided in the relevant regulations must request access to a prison facility in advance, often in writing, and sometimes with a specific request to use cameras or other recording devices.[372] Permission to visit is ultimately subject to the limitations prison administration considers necessary for maintaining order and security, and granted at the discretion of the institution head or the Public Information Officer.

INTERVIEWS: Of the states surveyed, only Idaho and California uniformly bar "specific-person face-to-face interviews" between media representatives and a person in prison.[373] Idaho, instead, allows interviews by collect telephone call from the person in prison to the media representative,[374] and California allows "random face-to-face interviews," including ones that are unplanned but occur with people "encountered while covering a facility activity or event... as stipulated by the institution head."[375]

In all other states, the discretion to grant an interview with a specific person in prison rests with the institution head or someone specifically designated with that authority,[376] as well as the written consent of the person to be interviewed. Other expressed reasons for the denial of an interview request have included the following: the person in prison is involved in a pending court action (Ohio);[377] he or she has been identified to be in need of mental health services (Nevada);[378] and he or she is serving sanctions of disciplinary action (Washington).[379] In Michigan, media representatives may visit face-to-face with a person in prison under the regular visitation rules, and may bring paper and a writing utensil with them, but meetings for reasons other than a personal visit require specific approval: "Due to the unique security concerns and disruption presented by the use or possession of a camera or other audio or visual recording device within a facility," the state explains, "such requests will be granted only in limited, unique circumstances."[380]

Some jurisdictions explicitly allow for telephone interviews, but limit their duration to fifteen[381] or thirty minutes.[382] Others, however, prohibit telephone interviews,[383] or forbid prisoners from "conduct[ing] interviews where they discuss the crimes they have been convicted of."[384]

TELEPHONE COMMUNICATION:[385] Persons in prison are generally not allowed to receive incoming telephone calls.[386] Outgoing phone calls are treated by prison administrators as a privilege, and thereby subject to additional restrictions for disciplinary purposes.[387] Regulations on prison phone use typically fall into three categories, described below.[388]

First, some rules restrict outgoing phone calls to a limited list of recipients. In federal prison, for example, individuals may call people included on a list of no more than thirty people.[389] In Massachusetts, prison rules allow a list of up to ten non-attorneys.[390] New York prison rules allow a list of up to fifteen phone numbers.[391]

The second group of regulations limits the frequency and duration of phone calls individuals may make. Unless subject to disciplinary sanction, persons in federal prison are accorded one telephone call per month.[392] Regarding this call, "an inmate who has sufficient funds is allowed at least three minutes... [and] The Warden may limit the maximum length."[393] In Wisconsin, individuals in prison are also allowed only one call per month, limited to six minutes.[394] Other states, such as Louisiana, Massachusetts, and New York, delegate time limits and telephone access to the discretion of detention facilities,[395] although in New York, "no call shall exceed thirty minutes."[396]

Third, phone calls from prison are not free of charge, and the cost must be paid by either the person placing the call—for example, by purchasing minutes at the commissary[397]—or by the call recipient on the outside. The phone systems, operated by telecommunications companies that contract with state corrections departments, are in effect granted what scholars have called "statewide prison monopolies," and are able to charge persons in prison and their loved ones outrageously high rates.[398] A fifteen-minute collect call from a state prison to another location in the same state can cost as much as $17.41,[399] an amount which can then be split between the telecommunications company and the state. "In exchange for exclusive contracts guaranteeing a steady high volume of expensive collect calls, states receive commissions ranging from eighteen to sixty percent—i.e. kickbacks—from prison phone-service providers," Attorney Madeleine Severin has argued.[400]

As mentioned above, prisons routinely monitor and record phone calls.[401] As with all other restrictions on access to the outside world, prison administrators justify this surveillance and the resultant censorship as necessary to maintaining prison security, preventing escape attempts and other misconduct, and promoting rehabilitation.[402]

MAIL CORRESPONDENCE: Because the process of requesting an interview with a specific person in prison usually requires written correspondence, regulations on prison mail have a direct impact on media access to prisons and on the ability to continue with contact by telephone or in person. Security policies that allow or require a prison administration to open and read incoming and outgoing prisoner mail encourages censorship, self-imposed or otherwise, especially of communications that would be critical of the prison or its staff.

Mail correspondence is usually divided between general and special or confidential mail. General mail is opened, inspected, and read, ostensibly to prevent the reception of contraband and other material considered detrimental to safety, security or the rehabilitative and penological goals of the prison. Special or confidential mail is generally defined as correspondence to or from United States government officials, officers of the court, or attorneys and legal services organizations.[403] The Federal Bureau of Prisons also grants "special" classification to outgoing correspondence to members of the media, but not to incoming mail sent by them. Often—for example, in federal prison—special or confidential incoming mail is opened in the presence of the addressee and inspected for contraband, then either "scanned" or not read at all.[404]

There is no limit to the number of letters a person in prison may send or receive, as long as that individual bears the relevant mailing costs. In most of the jurisdictions surveyed, regulations specifically provide for the provision of some postage to "indigent" persons in prison.[405] Most jurisdictions, however, limit the number of stamps or pre-stamped envelopes that someone in prison may receive in a single piece of mail, and many states flatly prohibit the reception of stamps or prepaid envelopes through mail to prison. New York, for example, prohibits receiving stamps through the mail with the exception of postage-prepaid, pre-addressed envelopes from a court or attorney,[406] and District of Columbia regulations state that the Department of Corrections "shall not accept envelopes mailed to inmates for use in future correspondence."[407]

APPENDIX IX: RAPE IN U.S. PRISONS, AND HOW TO STOP IT

How widespread is sexual abuse? According to recent reports by the Bureau of Justice Statistics (BJS), a branch of the Department of Justice, there were only 7,444 official allegations of sexual abuse in detention in 2008, and of those, only 931 were substantiated. These are absurdly low figures. But perhaps more shocking is that even when authorities confirmed that corrections staff had sexually abused inmates in their care, only 42 percent of those officers had their cases referred to prosecution; only 23 percent were arrested, and only 3 percent charged, indicted, or convicted. Fifteen percent were actually allowed to keep their jobs.

Published in December 2007 and June 2008, the BJS reports were extensive studies: they surveyed a combined total of 63,817 inmates in 392 different facilities. Sexual abuse in detention is difficult to measure. Prisoners sometimes make false allegations, but sometimes, knowing that true confidentiality is almost nonexistent behind bars and fearing retaliation, they decide not to disclose abuse.

Using a snapshot technique—surveying a random sample[408] of those incarcerated on a given day and then extrapolating only from those numbers—the BJS found that 4.5 percent of the nation's prisoners—i.e., inmates who have been convicted of felonies and sentenced to more than a year—had been sexually abused in the facilities at which they answered the questionnaire during the preceding year: approximately 60,500 people. Moreover, 3.2 percent of jail inmates—i.e., people who were awaiting trial or serving short sentences—had been sexually abused in their facilities over the preceding six months, meaning an estimated total, out of those jailed on the day of the survey, of 24,700 nationwide.[409] Overall, the more severe forms of abuse outnumber the lesser ones in both surveys.

The prison survey estimates not only the number of people abused, but the instances of abuse. Inmates who said they had been sexually abused were asked how many times. Their options were 1, 2, 3–10, and 11 times or more; answers of "3–10" were assigned a value of 5, and "11 or more" a value of 12. We know of no reason to think that answers of "3–10" should be skewed so far toward the low end of the range, however—and inmates are sometimes raped many more than twelve times.

In 2011, however, the Justice Department published revised estimates, which were considerably higher. In 2008, the Justice Department now says, more than 216,600 people were sexually abused in prisons and jails and, in the case of at least 17,100 of them, in juvenile detention. Overall, that's almost 600 people a day—twenty-five an hour.

The department divides sexual abuse in detention into four categories. Most straightforward, and most common, is rape by force or the threat of force. An estimated 69,800 inmates suffered this in 2008.[410] The second category, "non-consensual sexual acts involving pressure," includes 36,100 inmates coerced by such means as blackmail, offers of protection, and demanded payment of a jailhouse "debt." This is still rape by any reasonable standard. Finally, the department estimates that there were 45,000 victims of "abusive sexual contacts" in 2008: unwanted touching by another inmate "of the inmate's buttocks, thigh, penis, breasts, or vagina in a sexual way." Overall, most victims were abused not by other inmates, but by corrections staff.

The numbers from the Justice Department count people who were abused, not instances of abuse. People raped behind bars cannot escape their attackers, though. Between half and two thirds of those who claim sexual abuse in adult facilities say it happened more than once; previous BJS studies suggest that victims endure an average of three to five attacks each per year.[411] The department's estimate probably remains too low. It is based on extensive surveys conducted by the BJS (which is a part of the Department of Justice) in which inmates were able to report abuse anonymously. Some inmates probably fabricated such reports, creating "false positives," and some who had been abused probably decided not to report it, creating "false negatives." Since it is impossible to know how many errors of either kind there were, the department chose simply to take the BJS results at face value.

Even if the updated figures are low, the department's estimate is of epidemic numbers. It shows that there is a human rights crisis in our own country. The people raped in our prisons are our fellow citizens, family members, and neighbors. Beyond the physical injuries often sustained during an assault,[412] and beyond the devastating, lifelong psychological damage inflicted on survivors, rape in prison spreads diseases, including HIV.[413] Of all inmates, 95 percent are eventually released[414]—more than 1.5 million every year carrying infectious diseases, many of them sexually communicable[415]—and they carry their trauma and their illnesses with them, back to their families and their communities.

Most Sexual Abuse of Inmates Doesn't Happen in Prison

What little attention the BJS reports on adult victims received in the press at the time of their release had mostly been devoted to the prison study, not the one on jails. However, this misses the true implication of the BJS reports, and the jail study is very likely the more important of the two. This is partly because the study of jails answers more questions, and does more to help us understand the dynamics of sexual abuse in detention. But there is another, starker reason why the jail study is the most important: jail is where most inmates get raped.

On first glance at the reports it doesn't look this way. But—and this is what the press seems to have missed—because the early BJS numbers came from snapshot surveys, they represent only a fraction of those incarcerated every year. People move in and out of jail very quickly. The number of annual jail admissions is approximately seventeen times higher than the jail population on any given day.[416] Many people go to jail repeatedly over the course of a year; the number of people who go to jail every year is quite different from the number of admissions. Surprisingly, no official statistics are kept on the number of people jailed annually.[417]

Further complicating the matter, snapshot techniques like the BJS's will disproportionately count those with longer sentences. If Joe is jailed for one week and Bill for two,

Bill is twice as likely to be in jail on the day of the survey. Presumably, the longer you spend in jail, the more chance you have of being raped there. But even that is not as simple as it seems. Because those raped behind bars tend to fit such an identifiable profile—to be young, small, mentally ill, etc.—they are quickly recognized as potential victims. Very likely, they will be raped soon after the gate closes behind them, and repeatedly after that. The chance of being raped after a week in jail is likely not so different from the chance of being raped after a month. Probably more significant (at least statistically) is the difference in the number of times an inmate is likely to be raped.

In 1994, in *Farmer v. Brennan*, the Supreme Court declared that "having stripped [inmates] of virtually every means of self-protection and foreclosed their access to outside aid, the government and its officials are not free to let the state of nature take its course." Rape, wrote Justice David Souter, is "simply not 'part of the penalty'" we impose in our society.[418] But for many hundreds of thousands of men, women, and children, whether they were convicted of felonies or misdemeanors or simply awaiting trial, it has been. Most often, their assailants have been the very agents of the government who were charged with protecting them.

The Way to Stop Prison Rape and the Will for Reform

One of the most pernicious myths about prisoner rape is that it is an inevitable part of life behind bars. This is simply wrong. As the variance in the BJS findings shows, it can be prevented. In well-run facilities across the country it is being prevented—and this shouldn't be surprising. After all, the government has extraordinary control over the lives of those it locks up. Stopping sexual abuse in detention is a matter of using sound policies and practices, and passing laws that require them.

The commissioners of the National Prison Rape Elimination Commission convened expert committees, made an exhaustive review of available research, held numerous site visits and public hearings, and submitted draft versions of the standards for public comment. At every step they consulted corrections leaders, survivors of sexual assault in detention, researchers, advocates on behalf of prisoners, academics, legal experts, and healthcare providers. Finally, on June 23, 2009, six years after the passage of PREA, the commission published its recommendations. (Staff and board members from Just Detention International [JDI], the only U.S. NGO dedicated solely to ending sexual abuse in detention, served on all eight of the expert committees appointed by the commission. Members of JDI authored this essay.)

The commission wrote four distinct sets of standards, for different types of detention facilities. Reading them, one is repeatedly struck by how straightforward and plainly sensible these recommendations are—and, therefore, by how astonishing it is, and how appalling, that such basic measures haven't already been standard practice for decades.

The commission's first standard for all facilities stipulates that every corrections agency have "a written policy mandating zero tolerance toward all forms of sexual abuse." Staff and inmates must "understand what constitutes sexual abuse, know penalties exist for perpetration by prisoners or staff, and believe management will treat all incidents seriously." Staff must be trained to identify early warning signs that someone is at risk of sexual abuse, prevent abuse from occurring, and respond appropriately when it does occur. "Mandatory reporting policies are powerful antidotes to the code of silence." The standards also require that inmates be taught their rights, not only to be free from sexual abuse, but to be free from retaliation if they report it.

Every inmate when first arriving at a facility is put through a classification process, meant to assess the security risk he poses. In most corrections facilities, inmates are not classified by their risk of being subject to sexual abuse. But as we saw from the BJS studies discussed above, such risk can be objectively assessed according to a number of well-known factors—including age and size, or the fact that an inmate is entering prison for the first time, and that his or her crime was not violent.

One of the commission's most important standards requires that all inmates be screened in order "to assess their risk of being sexually abused by other inmates or sexually abusive toward other inmates." These screenings must rely on specific criteria that have been shown to be relevant to sexual violence. The results must then be taken into account when deciding where inmates will be lodged. The report's standards on "inmate supervision" and "assessment and use of monitoring technology" explain in detail how to do so.[419] "Without this process, vulnerable individuals may be forced to live in close proximity or even in the same cell with sexual assailants." It happens frequently.[420]

The commission's standards call for coordinated responses to sexual abuse from security staff, investigators, the head of the facility, and medical and mental health practitioners. The immediate safety of the survivor must be the first priority—and since those raped in prison are so often abused repeatedly, often by multiple rapists, there is great urgency to this. But survivors also face very serious longer-term health concerns, both physical and mental,[421] and the report proposes detailed standards on the care they should get.

The commission is equally concerned with the nature of the investigations that must follow every report of sexual abuse. The standards insist that agencies collect and carefully consider data on sexual abuse from all their facilities, and that facilities conduct "sexual abuse incident reviews":

> These reviews reveal patterns, such as vulnerable locations, times of highest risk, and other conditions... [They] generate information administrators need to make efficient use of limited resources, deploy staff wisely, safely manage high-risk areas, and develop more effective policies and procedures.

The commission's standards require

> facilities to monitor prisoners and staff who report abuse for at least 90 days to ensure that they are not experiencing retaliation or threats. If threats or actual retaliation do occur, the facility must take immediate action to stop the threatening behavior.

How much of a difference would the commission's standards make if adopted and enforced nationally? It's impossible to say with any precision. But as Jason DeParle wrote in the *New York Review of Books* in 2007, "Since 1980 the murder rate inside prisons has fallen more than 90 percent, which should give pause to those inclined to think that prisons are impossible to reform."[422] While the dynamics of sexual violence are quite different from those of homicide, both problems shrink or grow behind bars depending on the effectiveness of a facility's management.

The BJS studies suggest that sexual abuse has been nearly eradicated in some facilities already, and the policies and practices through which those institutions have achieved such success, as codified in the standards, are basic, commonsense measures. We believe that the incidence of prisoner rape would be cut dramatically if they were adopted everywhere—perhaps by as much as half over the next decade. As the BJS studies show, that would mean tens of thousands of people every year—perhaps as many as 100,000, or even more—who would be spared atrocious abuse.

The commission's recommended standards were submitted to U.S. Attorney General Eric Holder, who by law had until June 23, 2010, to review them and make any changes he deemed necessary. He missed that deadline. The standards that the Department of Justice has proposed, taken all together, fall far short of the commission's recommendations. During the review period, Attorney General Holder faced pressure to weaken the standards. The Department of Justice's review of the NPREC recommendations resembles the commission's in many ways, but what had been an open and inclusive process under the NPREC became largely closed. We know which agencies participated in the Justice Department's internal working group on the standards—including officials from the Bureau of Prisons, who are also opposed to important aspects of the commission's recommendations[423]—but we still do not have a list of the group's members.

Prisoner rape is one of the few issues on which there is no disagreement between Democrats and Republicans, or between the Christian right and liberals.[424] Nor is it simply an issue that pits corrections officers against the rest of the world. Good and dedicated corrections staff know that sexual abuse in detention is a terrible problem not only for its immediate victims, but for them as well, and for the country as a whole. In facilities where rape is common and unchecked by authorities, where the rules seem to have no force and animosity between inmates and staff is fueled, their safety is at risk. And they know that traumatized survivors and undeterred rapists may, on release, be more prone to recidivism themselves.

Addressing the Myth of the "Substantial Additional Costs" of Reform

The Justice Department's primary consideration in weakening the standards was expense. The government must fulfill its human rights obligations: this is a constitutional and moral imperative to which budgetary considerations are secondary, especially when, as the department affirms here, the measures in question will not "have [a significant] effect on the national economy."[425] On the other hand, PREA stipulated that no standards should be issued "that would impose substantial additional costs compared to the costs presently expended by Federal, State, and local prison authorities," and the department was obligated to take that seriously.[426]

The commission was mindful of this throughout its work, however.[427] And PREA is not the only relevant law here. Under the Eighth Amendment, which forbids cruel and unusual punishment, every corrections system is already obligated to protect its inmates from sexual abuse. Rape is illegal everywhere, including detention facilities, and all fifty states have laws making sexual contact of staff with inmates a criminal offense; so does applicable international law.[428] Still, no one doubts that bringing corrections systems across the country into compliance with the standards will require money, and everyone acknowledges the importance of this consideration.

The Justice Department needn't rely on estimates of future costs. Instead, it could look to corrections systems that are already implementing the standards, to see what their actual costs are. JDI is working with three such systems right now to help them achieve compliance with the standards even before they are legally obliged to do so. All three systems face budget crises, and are unable to provide significant additional funding. Between them, they will give a good indication of what is possible at what cost nationally. Max Williams, director of the Oregon Department of Corrections, estimates that his system has achieved compliance with 70 percent of the standards already. As he told us, "In Oregon, we haven't had to hire any new staff as part of the effort to implement the standards. Instead, we have retrained and repurposed existing staff. We have made some hard dollar investments, in cameras, a database, etc., but those are tools we can use for much more than handling the problem of sexual abuse."[429]

In any case, it would be a mistake to consider the costs of implementing the standards without also taking account of the benefits. Even when the financial implications of prisoner rape are the only ones considered—and surely they are less important than the moral or simply human considerations involved here—the savings and tangible benefits of preventing rape are considerable. As the result of litigation when corrections staff have engaged in or allowed sexual abuse in their facilities, corrections systems have had to pay many millions of dollars in damages over the last few years.[430] When survivors of prisoner rape require medical care, as they often do, corrections systems must bear most of the costs. And people traumatized by sexual assault behind bars are often unable to resume economically productive lives after their release.[431]

The Washington Department of Corrections estimates that the cost of providing mental health treatment for victims of prisoner rape or sexual assault—which is different from immediate medical care—is approximately $9,700 per victim. Neither category of care includes treatment for HIV, hepatitis C, and other sexually transmitted infections, which are spread by prisoner rape and also impose great costs on prison health services. Quite apart from the horror it inflicts on the victim, failing to protect an inmate from sexual abuse contributes to the substantial legal costs our prison systems face. While it is extraordinarily difficult for an incarcerated victim to bring a civil lawsuit—the 1996 Prison Litigation Reform Act (PLRA) was enacted with the explicit purpose of limiting prisoners' ability to be heard in court—prisons have still had to pay hundreds of millions of dollars in damages and fees to inmates who can establish that officials were "deliberately indifferent" in failing to protect them.

When inmates do report sexual abuse in prison, they are often put in "administrative segregation," isolated housing that can entail being locked alone in a tiny cell for up to twenty-three hours a day. It is enormously expensive. In California, for example, it costs an additional \$14,600 per year[432] to house a prisoner in administrative segregation.

Preventing prisoner rape will also help inmates successfully re-enter their communities when they're released from prison (as almost all will be, eventually). Not only will recidivism be decreased and the enormous costs of re-incarceration lowered, this will lower the costs of disability payments, public housing, and other government-subsidy programs. Former inmates who have not been sexually abused are far more likely to become members of the legitimate workforce and pay taxes. Severe financial, emotional, and social burdens are removed from the families who support former inmates if their loved ones are released from prison without the lasting trauma of sexual abuse. And the children who depend on those former inmates will also do better.

Apart from costs, we believe that there is also another and perhaps more important reason why some corrections officials are opposed to the commission's recommendations: the prospect that their compliance with the standards would be closely monitored.

The commission proposed a standard requiring that independent audits of every detention facility be made at least every three years.[433] This standard also requires that data collected by these audits be made public. And the commission strongly endorsed a resolution of the American Bar Association recommending that federal, state, and territorial governments adopt effective systems of external oversight.[434] Although effective oversight is not by itself enough to stop sexual abuse in detention, it is an indispensable part of any solution, and few reforms would do more to improve prison conditions generally. If the commission's standards and recommendations are approved and enforced, they will greatly strengthen our systems of oversight.

This, we believe, is what the opponents of reform truly fear. Will Harrell, the former independent ombudsman of the Texas Youth Commission, who was appointed after pervasive sexual abuse of its juvenile detainees by staff was revealed in 2007, told us in an e-mail:

> Administrators whose perspective was formed under the tradition of public exclusion are deeply resistant to independent, external oversight. They fear the loss of control over the flow of information. They fear potential embarrassment or scandal. But… the public must watch the watchmen.

Max Williams told us, "Many officials are afraid that these audits are designed to be a 'gotcha,' a 'we're going to zing you.' That's what they are worried about."

To a certain extent, such fear is understandable. Even good corrections officers feel embattled by dangerous inmates who badly outnumber them. They also feel that they are underfunded and underpaid by the government, and ignored or reviled by the public. A sort of bunker mentality often grows among them, in which the most unforgivable act is reporting on a fellow officer. When that is the case, even in facilities where good people work, corruption spreads.

But no public institutions are more in need of transparency and accountability than prisons and jails. Without external scrutiny, sadistic and autocratic people can turn their facilities into private hells—as happened in Texas just a few years ago, when hundreds of children were raped night after night by their guards, and there was no help for them. Any decent system of oversight would have made that impossible.

APPENDIX X: TEN WAYS TO LEARN MORE ABOUT WOMEN IN PRISON

1. On decreasing the number of people in prison through ending mandatory minimums and three-strikes laws, see:
   —Families Against Mandatory Minimums (famm.org)
   —Drug Policy Alliance (drugpolicy.org)
   —Californians United for a Responsible Budget (curbprisonspending.org)
   —The Sentencing Project (sentencingproject.org)

2. On reform of the Adoption and Safe Families Act (ASFA) of 1997, which results in the termination of parental rights for women in prison, see:
   —Brennan Center for Justice (brennancenter.org)
   —The Sentencing Project (sentencingproject.org)

3. On reproductive justice in prison, see:
   —Sister Song (sistersong.net) Provides advocacy training.
   —Justice Now (jnow.org) Fights to end illegal sterilizations of imprisoned women.

4. On the shackling of pregnant women in prison, and local organizing on this issue, see The Rebecca Project for Human Rights' guide, at rebeccaproject.org/images/stories/policypapers/state_shackling_policies_memo.pdf.

5. On reducing excessive collect telephone charges for people in prison, see:
   —Citizens United for Rehabilitation of Errants (curenational.org)
   —The Campaign to Promote Equitable Telephone Charges (etccampaign.com)

6. On supporting lives uninhibited by post-conviction retribution for women after prison, see:
   —Legal Action Center (lac.org)
   —All of Us or None (allofusornone.org)

7. On starting a reentry initiative through the National Reentry Resource Center, see: (nationalreentryresourcecenter.org/topics/starting-reentry-initiative)

8. On donating books to empower women in prison, see the Women's Prison Book Project: (wpbp.org/book-donations)

9. On promoting nonviolent solutions to child sexual abuse and domestic violence, see:
   —Generation 5 (.generationfive.org)
   —Creative Interventions (creative-interventions.org)

10. On donating to organizations fighting for justice in women's prisons, see:

NATIONAL:

The Rebecca Project for Human Rights (rebeccaproject.org)

Legal Services for Prisoners with Children (prisonerswithchildren.org)

ALABAMA:

Aid to Inmate Moms (inmatemoms.org)

CALIFORNIA:

Justice Now (jnow.org)

A New Way of Life (anewwayoflife.org)

GEORGIA:

SPARK Reproductive Justice NOW (sparkrj.org)

ILLINOIS:

Chicago Legal Aid to Incarcerated Mothers

MASSACHUSETTS:

Aid to Incarcerated Mothers

(catalogueforphilanthropy.org/ma/2003/aid_incarcerated_908.htm)

OREGON:

The Portia Project (theportiaproject.org)

NEW YORK:

Women on the Rise Telling HerStory (womenontherise-worth.org)

Women in Prison Project—Correctional Association of New York (New York)

(correctionalassociation.org/WIPP/index.htm)

ENDNOTES

[1] For a full list of interviewees, see Deborah LaBelle, et al., "Women in Detention in the United States: Preliminary Report for Rashida Manjoo, UN Special Rapporteur on Violence Against Women." 2011. ¶ 286.

[2] Universal Declaration of Human Rights, G.A. Res. 217A (III), U.N. Doc A/810 at 71 (1948), art. 8 (Dec. 10, 1948) ("Everyone has the right to an effective remedy by the competent national tribunals for acts violating the fundamental rights granted him by the constitution or by law").

[3] Rashida Manjoo, *Report of the United Nations Special Rapporteur on Violence against Women, Its Causes and Consequences*, ¶¶ 22–23 (April 2010) A/HRC/14/22, available at iansa-women.org/nde/446.

[4] U.S. Const. amend. VIII ("Excessive bail shall not be required, nor excessive fines imposed, nor cruel and unusual punishments inflicted").

[5] *Farmer v. Brennan*, 511 U.S. 825, 837 (1994) (holding that a prison official cannot be found liable under the Eighth Amendment for denying an inmate humane conditions of confinement unless the official knows of and disregards an excessive risk to inmate health or safety).

[6] *Id.* at 834; *Wilson v. Seiter*, 501 U.S. 294, 298 (1991) (holding that only those deprivations denying "the minimal civilized measure of life's necessities" are sufficiently grave to form the basis of an Eighth Amendment violation).

[7] See *Farmer*, 511 U.S. at 834; see also *Wilson*, 501 U.S. at 297.

[8] *Farmer, supra* note 11 at 832.

[9] *Rhodes v. Chapman*, 452 U.S. 337 (1981) (finding that double celling did not constitute cruel and unusual punishment as it did not lead to deprivations of essential food, medical care, or sanitation).

[10] See *Hill v. Pugh*, 75 Fed. Appx. 715, 721 (10th Cir. 2003) ("To the extent that [an inmate's] conditions are restrictive and even harsh, they are part of the penalty that criminal offenders pay for their offenses against society"); *Magluta v. U.S. Fed. Bureau of Prisons*, 2009 U.S. Dist. LEXIS 49170, *20 (D. Colo. 2009) ("ADX is a prison, after all, and confinement is intended to punish inmates, not coddle them").

[11] See *Wilson*, 501 U.S. at 296 (holding that "overcrowding, excessive noise… inadequate heating and cooling, improper ventilation, unclean and inadequate restrooms, unsanitary dining facilities and food preparation, and housing with mentally and physically ill inmates" taken together do not constitute cruel and unusual punishment).

[12] *Id.* at 304 (holding that prison conditions do not constitute "a seamless web for Eighth Amendment purposes. Nothing so amorphous as 'overall conditions' can rise to the level of cruel and unusual punishment when no specific deprivation of a single human need exists").

[13] *Estelle v. Gamble*, 429 U.S. 97, 104-07 (1976) (rejecting inmate's claim that prison doctors inflicted cruel and unusual punishment by inadequately responding to the prisoner's medical needs, since only the "unnecessary and wanton infliction of pain" implicates the Eighth Amendment; to meet this standard, a prisoner must show, at a minimum, "deliberate indifference" to "serious" medical needs); *Farmer*, 511 U.S. at 839-40.

[14] *Bell v. Wolfish*, 441 U.S. 520, 547 (1979) ("Prison administrators… should be accorded wide-ranging deference in the adoption and execution of policies and practices that in their judgment are needed to preserve internal order and discipline and to maintain institutional security").

[15] *Turner v. Safley*, 482 U.S. 78, 89 (1987).

[16] 18 U.S.C. § 3626 (1997).

[17] *Porter v. Nussle*, 534 U.S. 516, 524 (2002) ("Beyond doubt, Congress enacted §1997e[a] to reduce the quantity and improve the quality of prisoner suits; to this purpose, Congress afforded corrections officials time and opportunity to address complaints internally before allowing the initiation of a federal case").

[18] 18 U.S.C. § 3626 (1997).

[19] *Woodford v. Ngo*, 548 U.S. 81, 85 (2006) ("Prisoners must now exhaust all 'available' remedies, not just those that meet federal standards. Indeed… a prisoner must now exhaust administrative remedies even where the relief sought—monetary damages—cannot be granted by the administrative process").

[20] HUMAN RIGHTS WATCH, NO EQUAL JUSTICE: THE PRISON LITIGATION REFORM ACT IN THE UNITED STATES (2009) [hereinafter HUMAN RIGHTS WATCH (2009)] documenting cases dismissed in whole or in part because the prisoner submitted a form to the "inmate appeals branch" rather than to the "appeals coordinator" (*Chatman v. Johnson*, 2007 WL 2023544 [E.D. Cal. 2007]); filed an "administrative appeal rather than a disciplinary appeal" (*Richardson v. Spurlock*, 260 F.3d 495, 499 [5th Cir. 2001]); or wrote directly to the grievance body rather than filing a "service request" form (*McNeal v. Cabana*, 2006 WL 2794337, at *1 [N.D. Miss. 2006]), available at hrw.org/en/reports/2009/06/16/no-equal-justice-0.

[21] *Id.* (documenting application of the exhaustion requirement where non-compliance was due to dyslexia (*Williams v. Pettiford*, 2007 WL 3119548, at *3 [D.S.C. 2007]); illiteracy (*Ramos v. Smith*, 187 Fed. Appx. 152, 154 [3d Cir. 2006]); inability to read English (*Benavidez v. Stansberry*, 2008 WL 4279559, at *4 [N.D. Ohio 2008]); cerebral palsy (*Elliott v. Monroe Correctional Complex*, 2007 WL 208422, at *3 [W.D. Wash. 2007]); and mental illness (*Yorkey v. Pettiford*, 2007 WL 2750068, at *4 [D.S.C. 2007]).

[22] *Amador v. Andrews*, No. 03 Civ. 0650 (KTD) (GWG) (S.D.N.Y.).

[23] THE NATIONAL PRISON RAPE ELIMINATION COMMISSION, REPORT (2009) [hereinafter NPREC REPORT].

[24] As has been widely documented, survivors of violence, particularly sexual assault or abuse, may not report for a number of reasons. They may be experiencing PTSD, and they may be terrified of retribution, whether at the hands of other prisoners or correctional officers. Even outside of prisons, only a small fraction of sexual assault survivors report to the police or other public entities. The barriers to reporting within the prison context are necessarily more powerful by several orders of magnitude than those outside of prison, as prisoners may not have anyone they can trust or confide in and are trapped in the context where the abuse took place. See also NPREC REPORT, *supra* note 28 ("The Prison Litigation Reform Act… has compromised the regulatory role of the courts and the ability of incarcerated victims of sexual abuse to seek justice in court").

[25] For an extensive discussion of the inadequacies of grievance procedures in women's prisons, see,

e.g., Kim Shayo Buchanan, *Impunity: Sexual Abuse in Women's Prisons*, 42 Harv. C.R.-C.L. L. Rev. 45, 73 (2007); see also NPREC REPORT, *supra* note 25.

[26] See *Amador v. Andrews*, No. 03 Civ. 0650 (KTD) (GWG) (S.D.N.Y.), First Amended Complaint, Sept. 5, 2003 (describing how the policy of the New York correctional department is to take no action on a prisoner allegation of sexual abuse by a guard unless the prisoner provides either physical proof or DNA evidence).

[27] Buchanan, *supra* note 27, at 66–67.

[28] 18 U.S.C. § 3626 (1997).

[29] See, e.g., *Searles v. Van Bebber*, 251 F.3d 869, 876 (10th Cir. 2001) (holding that the PLRA's physical injury requirement barred a suit by a prisoner alleging a First Amendment violation: "The plain language of the statute does not permit alteration of its clear damages restrictions on the basis of the underlying rights being asserted... The statute limits the remedies available, regardless of the rights asserted, if the only injuries are mental or emotional").

[30] See Buchanan, *supra* note 27, ("On its face... the physical injury requirement appears to bar prisoner claims for sexual abuse if no physical injury results. For example, the text of this provision appears to bar claims that a prisoner was forced to perform or submit to oral sex... or was coerced into sexual compliance through threats or inducements without a beating").

[31] See, e.g., *Hancock v. Payne*, 2006 WL 21751, at *3 (S.D. Miss. 2006) ("In their Amended Complaint, the plaintiffs do not make any claim of physical injury beyond the bare allegation of sexual assault").

[32] P.L. 104–134, 110 Stat. 1321 (2006) (The PLRA caps attorney's fees in prisoner litigation at 150 percent of the damage award, and further provides that "No award of attorney's fees... shall be based on an hourly rate greater than 150 percent of the hourly rate established under section 3006A of title 18, United States Code, for payment of court-appointed counsel").

[33] HUMAN RIGHTS WATCH (2009), *supra* note 22, at 35.

[34] See HUMAN RIGHTS WATCH (2009), *supra* note 22, at 3 ("The effect of the PLRA on prisoners' access to the courts was swift. Between 1995 and 1997, federal civil rights filings by prisoners fell 33 percent, despite the fact that the number of incarcerated persons had grown by 10 percent in the same period. By 2001 prisoner filings were down 43 percent from their 1995 level, despite a 23 percent increase in the incarcerated population. By 2006 the number of prisoner lawsuits filed per thousand prisoners had fallen 60 percent since 1995").

[35] See Margaret Schlanger & Giovanna Shay, *Preserving the Rule of Law in America's Jails and Prisons: The Case for Amending the Prison Litigation Reform Act*, 11 U. Pa. J. Const. L. 139, 152-54 (2008), at 140 ("The PLRA's obstacles to meritorious lawsuits are undermining the rule of law in our prisons and jails, granting the government near-impunity to violate the rights of prisoners without fear of consequences"); see also *Buchanan, supra* note 27, at 72 ("A prison is virtually insulated from prisoner litigation to the extent that its grievance process is complex and time-consuming, its deadlines for filing a grievance are brief, and the threat of retaliation deters prisoners from using the process at all... [The] requirement invites technical mistakes resulting in inadvertent noncompliance with the exhaustion requirement, and bar[s] litigants from court because of their ignorance and uncounseled procedural errors").

[36] See LaBelle, *supra* note 1 and accompanying notes, at ¶ 18 (describing how some courts have interpreted sexual assault as not rising to the level of physical injury under the PLRA). (Adapted within Appendix I, above.)

[37] *Hemphill v. New York*, 380 F.3d 680, 686 (2d Cir. 2004) (in determining whether administrative remedies have been exhausted, the court considers 1) whether administrative remedies are actually available to the plaintiff; 2) whether the defendant should be estopped from asserting the defense of failure to exhaust because he/she inhibited the ability of the plaintiff to pursue administrative remedies; and 3) whether special circumstances excuse the plaintiff's failure to exhaust); see also Buchanan, *supra* note 35, at 73–74 (describing how many appellate courts have concluded that the physical injury requirement bars only actions for compensatory damages, and does not apply to actions for declaratory or injunctive relief or for nominal or punitive damages).

[38] See LaBelle, *supra* note 1, ¶¶ 42-51 (describing PREA in depth). (Adapted within Appendix I, above.)

[39] HUMAN RIGHTS WATCH, IN SUPPORT OF THE PRISON ABUSE REMEDIES ACT OF 2007; HEARING IN THE HOUSE JUDICIARY SUBCOMMITTEE (April 21, 2008), available at hrw.org/en/news/2008/04/21/support-prison-abuse-remedies-act-2007-hearing-house-judiciary-subcommittee.

[40] 42 U.S.C. § 15606 (2008).

[41] 42 U.S.C. § 15603 (2005).

[42] 42 U.S.C. § 15604 (2003).

[43] 42 U.S.C. § 15605 (2003). Since passage, the Bureau of Justice Statistics has awarded grants to over twenty-eight state departments of corrections to improve their practices. See PROJECT ON ADDRESSING PRISON RAPE, INVESTIGATING ALLEGATIONS OF STAFF SEXUAL MISCONDUCT WITH OFFENDERS: THE PRISON RAPE ELIMINATION ACT OF 2003 — OVERVIEW AND UPDATE (2008), available at wcl.american.edu/nic/conference_july_08_staff/modules/2_prea.pdf?rd=1 [hereinafter THE PRISON RAPE ELIMINATION ACT OF 2003 — OVERVIEW AND UPDATE]. While laudable, many of the states awarded grants had already received substantial assistance since at least 1996 from the National Institute of Corrections on similar issues. See PROJECT ON ADDRESSING PRISON RAPE, DATABASE OF TRAINING PARTICIPATION 1996–2008 (on file with Project on Addressing Prison Rape). The Bureau of Justice Assistance did not provide funding to agencies that had received little funding over the years to address sexual abuse in custody—specifically jails, lockups, juvenile agencies, and Native American communities. See THE PRISON RAPE ELIMINATION ACT OF 2003 — OVERVIEW AND UPDATE, *supra* note 109, at 16.

[44] 42 U.S.C. § 15607 (2003).

[45] Kevin Corlew, *Congress Attempts to Shine Light on a Dark Problem: An In-Depth Look at the Prison Rape Elimination Act of 2003*, 33 AM. J. CRIM. L. REV. 157 (2006).

[46] See NATIONAL INSTITUTE FOR CORRECTIONS/WASHINGTON COLLEGE OF LAW PROJECT ON ADDRESSING PRISON RAPE, AN END TO SILENCE: POLICIES AND PROCEDURES, available at wcl.american.edu/nic/policies.cfm#prea (last visited Nov. 18, 2010).

[47] CAL. PENAL CODE §§ 2635-2643 (2006); TEX GOV'T CODE ANN. § 501.172.

[48] Robert Dumond, *The Impact of Prisoner Sexual Violence: Challenges of Implementing Public Law 108-79*

the Prison Rape Elimination Act of 2003, 32 J. LEGIS. 142, 143-44 (2006).

[49] See Brenda V. Smith, *Reforming, Reclaiming or Reframing Womanhood: Reflections on Advocacy for Women in Custody*, 29 WOMEN'S RTS. L. REP. 1, 8–9 (2007).

[50] *Thornburg v. Abbott*, 490 U.S. 401, 404 (1989) (holding that prison regulations affecting a prisoner's First Amendment rights should be analyzed under the reasonableness standard set forth in *Turner v. Safley*, 482 U.S. 78, 89 (1987): "when a prison regulation impinges on inmates' constitutional rights, the regulation is valid if it is reasonably related to legitimate penalogical interests").

[51] *Pell v. Procunier*, 417 U.S. 817, 834 (1974).

[52] See Brenda V. Smith & Jaime M. Yarussi, *Prosecuting Sexual Violence in Correctional Settings: Examining Prosecutors' Perceptions*, 3 Crim. L. Brief 19, 19 (2008) [hereinafter *Examining Prosecutors' Perceptions*]; OFFICE OF THE INSPECTOR GENERAL, U.S. DEP'T OF JUSTICE, DETERRING STAFF SEXUAL ABUSE OF FEDERAL INMATES 9 (2005) [hereinafter OIG (2005)] available at justice.gov/oig/special/0504/final.pdf.

[53] See *Examining Prosecutors' Perceptions*, *supra* note 54; OIG (2005), *supra* note 54, at 22.

[54] Cheryl Bell, et al., *Rape and Sexual Misconduct in the Prison System, Analyzing America's Most 'Open' Secret*, 18 YALE L. & POL'Y REV. 195 (1999).

[55] Most early studies focused on the problem in men's prisons only. Cindy Struckman-Johnson & David Struckman-Johnson, *Sexual Coercion Reported by Women in Three Midwestern Prisons*, 39 J. SEX RESEARCH 217, 217 (2002). This may be in part due to the now debunked view that female inmates do not coerce each other into sexual contact. The first empirical studies on the prevalence of the problem in women's prisons were small sample-size studies conducted in the 1990s. See Agnes L. Baro, *Spheres of Consent*, 8 WOMEN & CRIM. JUST. 61 (1997) (finding chronic problems of custodial sexual abuse in a small women's facility in Hawaii); Struckman-Johnson, et al., *Sexual Coercion Reported by Men and Women in Prison*, 33 J. SEX RESEARCH 67 (1996) (conducting a survey of women in a small Midwestern women's facility).

[56] Bureau of Justice Statistics, *Sexual Victimization in Prisons and Jails Reported by Inmates, 2008–2009*, at 12 (2010) [hereinafter BJS (2008–2009)]. Women were significantly more likely than men to experience inmate-on-inmate victimization, 4.7 percent compared to 1.9 percent, and slightly less likely than men to experience staff sexual misconduct, 2.1 percent compared to 2.9 percent. *Id.* The number of female-staff-to-male-inmate incidents of misconduct came as a surprise to many advocates and researchers, who are currently grappling with its implications for questions of gender in men's and women's prisons. See Brenda Smith, *The Prison Rape Elimination Act: Implementation and Unresolved Issues* 12 AMERICAN UNIVERSITY, WCL RESEARCH PAPER No. 2008–49, available at papers.ssrn.com/sol3/papers.cfm?abstract_id=1129810; Lauren A. Teichner, *Unusual Suspects: Recognizing and Responding to Female Staff Perpetrators of Sexual Violence in U.S. Prisons*, 14 MICH. J. GENDER & L. 259, 276–90 (2008) (discussing the divide between social expectations and the rate of female staff sexual misconduct and discussing the differential treatment of female perpetrators).

[57] Two women's institutions, Taycheedah Correctional Institution (Wisconsin) and Fluvanna Correctional Center (Virginia) had exceptionally high rates of inmate on inmate incidents: 11.9 percent and 11.4 percent respectively. And Fluvanna Correctional Center, again, and Bayview Correctional Center (New York) had exceptionally high rates of staff sexual misconduct, 11.5 percent and 6 percent, respectively; BJS (2008–2009), *supra* note 58, at 8-9.

[58] Ashley G. Blackburn, et al., *Sexual Assault in Prison and Beyond: Toward an Understanding of Lifetime Sexual Assault Among Incarcerated Women*, 88 THE PRISON J. 351, 351 (2008).

[59] Struckman-Johnson & Struckman-Johnson, *supra* note 57, at 220.

[60] NPREC REPORT, *supra* note 25, at 20; see also, RAPE, ABUSE, AND INCEST NATIONAL NETWORK, REPORTING RATES, available at rainn.org/get-information/statistics/reporting-rates (last visited Nov. 17, 2010) (indicating that sexual assault is generally one of the most underreported crimes).

[61] See NPREC REPORT, *supra* note 25, at 7 (defining various terminology for the types of sexual abuse reported).

[62] Deborah Labelle, *Bringing Human Rights Home to the World of Detention*, 40 COLUM. HUM. RTS L. REV. 79, 105 (2008) ("In the course of committing such gross misconduct, male officers have not only used actual or threatened physical force, but have also used their near total authority to provide or deny goods and privileges to female prisoners, to compel them to have sex"); Buchanan, *supra* note 27, at 55 ("Guards often extend unofficial accommodations to favored inmates and use illegal forms of intimidation and force on others. In such a setting, the sticks and carrots guards may use to coerce sex from prisoners are plausible and effective"). Advocates, lawyers, and lawmakers all tend to agree, at least in principle, that due to the power structure of the prison, any sexual contact between staff and inmates is abusive, regardless of any "consent" given. See BJS (2008–2009), *supra* note 58, at 7.

[63] Studies estimate that up to 80 percent of women in prison have experienced prior sexual or physical abuse. See Angela Browne, et al., *Prevalence and Severity of Lifetime Physical and Sexual Victimization Among Incarcerated Women*, 22 INT'L J. L. & PSYCHIATRY. 301 (1999). For more information on the prevalence of histories of abuse, as well as the prevalence of mental health and substance-abuse problems, see Labelle, *supra* note 1, at ¶¶ 62–67 (adapted within Appendix III, above).

[64] NPREC REPORT, *supra* note 25, at 45.

[65] Brenda Smith, *Watching You, Watching Me*, 15 YALE J. L. & FEMINISM 225, 230 (2003). There are significant questions about whether or not Title VII, which makes employment discrimination on the basis of sex illegal, requires prisons to allow cross-gender supervision. However, courts have been willing to uphold policies limiting cross-gender supervisions when a sufficient record demonstrates that it is necessary to prevent sexual abuse. See *Everson v. Mich. Dept. of Corrections*, 391 F.3d 737, 748–49 (6th Cir. 2004).

[66] *U.N. Standard Minimum Rules for the Treatment of Prisoners*, Rule 53 (1955), available at ohchr.org/english/law/pdf/treatmentprisoners.pdf.

[67] BUREAU OF JUSTICE STATISTICS, SEXUAL VICTIMIZATION IN PRISONS AND JAILS REPORTED BY INMATES, 2007, at 7 (2007).

[68] See generally, Smith, *supra* note 67.

[69] *Id.* at 249. In *Bell v. Wolfish*, the Supreme Court held that privacy rights of prisoners are significantly diminished and upheld body cavity searches. 441 U.S. 520 (1979). However, the Court has not passed on the direct question of cross-gender body cavity searches. While the case law is not entirely coherent or unified on this question, courts have been more sympathetic to women inmates' challenges to cross-gender supervision than to men's. Smith, *supra* note 67, at 264.

[70] Letter from American Civil Liberties Union to Avi Zavaras, Exec. Dir., Colorado Dept. of Corr.

(Aug. 23, 2010), available at aclu.org/files/assets/Zavaras_ACLU_8-23-10.pdf.

[71] 40 percent of women who reported unwanted sexual touching indicated that it occurred during a strip-search or pat-down. BJS (2008–2009), *supra* note 58, at 24.

[72] HUMAN RIGHTS WATCH, ALL TOO FAMILIAR: SEXUAL ABUSE OF WOMEN IN STATE PRISONS 60 (1996).

[73] *Id.*

[74] 511 U.S. 825 (1994).

[75] See LaBelle, *supra* note 1, at ¶¶ 10–13.

[76] See *Boxer v. Harris*, 437 F.3d 1107, 1111 (11th Cir. 2006) (holding that ordering a male prisoner to masturbate under threat of reprisal was *de minimis* harm); *Austin v. Terhune*, 367 F.3d 1167, 1171 (9th Cir. 2004) (officer's actions of exposing himself and making offensive comments were not actionable under the Eighth Amendment); *Morales v. Mackalm*, 278 F.3d126, 132 (2d Cir. 2002) (plaintiff alleging that a female staff member asked her to have sex with her and to masturbate in front of her and other staff failed to state a constitutional claim); see also Dori Lewis & Lisa Freeman, *The Sexual Abuse of Women Prisoners: Much Concern But Little Progress From the Perspective of Plaintiffs' Counsel in Amador, et al. v. Andrews, et al.* 10 (Mar. 11, 2010) (unpublished memorandum) (on file with Yale Detention and Human Rights Clinic).

[77] National Institute of Corrections, *Sexual Misconduct in Prisons: Law, Agency Response, and Prevention* (1996), available at nicic.gov/pubs/1996/013508.pdf.

[78] Government Accountability Office, *Women in Prison: Sexual Misconduct by Correctional Staff* (1999), available at gao.gov/archive/1999/gg99104.pdf.

[79] *Cason v. Seckinger*, 231 F.3d 777 (11th Cir. 2000); *Women Prisoners v. Dist. of Columbia*, 877 F. Supp. 634 (D.D.C. 1994); *United States v. Michigan*, No. 97-CVB-71514-BDT (E.D. Mich. 1999) (settled); *United States v. Arizona*, No. 97-476-PHX-ROS (D. Ariz. 1999) (settled).

[80] HUMAN RIGHTS WATCH, *supra* note 74; AMNESTY INTERNATIONAL, NOT PART OF MY SENTENCE: VIOLATIONS OF THE HUMAN RIGHTS OF WOMEN IN CUSTODY (1999).

[81] Radhika Coomaraswamy, *Special Rapporteur on Violence against Women, Its Causes and Consequences, Report of the Mission to the United States of America on the Issue of Violence against Women in State and Federal Prisons*, U.N. Doc. E/CN.4/1999/68/Add. 2 (Jan. 4, 1999), available at unhchr.ch/Huridocda/Huridoca.nsf/0/7560a6237c67bb118025674c004406e9?OpenDocument.

[82] See, e.g., NPREC REPORT, *supra* note 25, at 49 ("In short, the landscape is changing. Reporting hotlines and zero tolerance posters are becoming commonplace").

[83] While federal laws cover roughly 201,142 offenders under federal supervision, state law covers the other 7,312,498 prisoners (state and local), probationers, and parolees under custodial supervision. See Heather C. West, *Prisoners at Year End 2009*, BUREAU OF JUSTICE STATISTICS (June 2010); Lauren Galze & Thomas Bonczar, *Probation and Parole in the United States, 2008*, BUREAU OF JUSTICE STATISTICS (2009). These state criminal laws create a baseline of liability for misconduct and provide important routes to other sanctions, including official misconduct, loss of license, and sex offender registration. See Brenda V. Smith & Jaime M. Yarussi, *Legal Responses to Sexual Violence in Custody: State Criminal Laws Prohibiting Staff Sexual Abuse of Individuals Under Custodial Supervision* (2009).

State criminal laws are also flexible instruments that can reflect the political and social priorities of the state. In its 2005 report, the OIG reaffirmed the important role that state laws play in addressing staff sexual misconduct by comparing the federal law to existing state laws. See Office of the Inspector General, U.S. Dep't of Justice, Deterring Staff Sexual Abuse of Federal Inmates (2005).

[84] See Brenda V. Smith, *Fifty State Survey of State Criminal Laws Prohibiting Sexual Abuse of Individuals Under Custodial Supervision*, NATIONAL INSTITUTE OF CORRECTIONS/WASHINGTON COLLEGE OF LAW PROJECT ON ADDRESSING PRISON RAPE (2009), available at wcl.american.edu/nic/documents/50StateSurveyofSSMLawsFINAL2009Update.pdf?rd=1.

[85] See Labelle, *supra* note 1, at ¶¶ 21–23.

[86] See Prison Rape Elimination Act, 42 U.S.C. § 15602 (2003). The first federal bill addressing staff sexual abuse in prisons, the Custodial Sexual Abuse Act, was introduced in 1998, but was at that time unsuccessful. See Violence Against Women Act of 1999, H.R. 357, 106th Cong., §§ 341–346 (1999); see also Press Release, Rep. John Conyers, Conyers Introduces Omnibus Bill to Stop Violence Against Women and Their Children (May 12, 1999), available at house.gov/conyers/pr051299.htm. The introduction of this legislation and its ultimate passage was driven by the work of human rights organizations (Human Rights Watch and Just Detention International [then Stop Prisoner Rape]); domestic civil rights organizations (the NAACP and the ACLU Prisoners Rights Project); and faith-based organizations (the Hudson Institute and Prison Fellowship Ministries). That work built on the earlier reports addressing staff sexual misconduct in custodial settings that were at the core of the Special Rapporteur's 1998 visit. See Brenda V. Smith, *The Prison Rape Elimination Act: Implementation and Unresolved Issues*, 3 CRIM. L. BRIEF 19, 10 (2008). Another significant impetus for the passage of the legislation was a concerted campaign to address male prisoner rape. The issue of male prisoner rape was highlighted in a 2001 report by Human Rights Watch. HUMAN RIGHTS WATCH, NO ESCAPE: MALE RAPE IN U.S. PRISONS (2001). As a direct result, Congressmen Bobby Scott (D-VA), Tom Wolfe (R-VA), Senator Jeff Sessions (R-AL), and Ted Kennedy (D-MA) sponsored "The Prison Rape Reduction Act." The legislation, when initially introduced in 2001, only addressed male-on-male sexual violence in custodial settings. See The Prison Rape Reduction Act, H.R. 1707, 108th Congress (2003). In 2002, the bill was amended to add provisions related to all forms of sexual violence in custody in all settings, both adult and juvenile, and to change its name to the Prison Rape Elimination Act. See Prison Rape Reduction Act of 2003: Hearing on H.R. 1707: Before the S. Comm. on Crime, Terrorism, and Homeland Security of the S. Comm. on the Judiciary, 108th Cong. (2003).

[87] See *id.* at 215.

[88] *U.N. Standard Minimum Rules*, *supra* note 68 at Rule 53.

[89] NPREC REPORT, *supra* note 28, at 16.

[90] See, e.g., Silja J.A. Talvi, *Women Behind Bars: The Crisis of Women in the U.S. Prison System* 87 (2007), at 86 ("I can say without any exaggeration that medical 'care' represents one of the absolute worst aspects of life in women's jails and prison."); Kathleen J. Ferarro & Angela M. Moe, *Women's Stories of Survival and Resistance, Women in Prison: Gender and Social Control* 71 (Barbara H. Zaitzow & Jim Thomas, eds., 2003) ("The lack of adequate healthcare was a major concern for the women in our study").

[91] See Talvi, *supra* note 92.

[92] *Id.*

[93] Vernetta D. Young & Rebecca Reviere, *Women Behind Bars: Gender and Race in U.S. Prisons* 86 (2006) (biological risks include higher rates of susceptibility to sexually transmitted diseases; acquired risks include likely exposure to prior violence and drugs).

[94] *Id.* at 85; Talvi, *supra* note 92, at 88.

[95] U.S. CONST. amend. VIII.

[96] *Estelle v. Gamble*, 429 U.S. 97, 103 (1976).

[97] *Id.* at 104–05.

[98] For more information on what constitutes a serious medical need, see ACLU NATIONAL PRISON PROJECT, KNOW YOUR RIGHTS: MEDICAL, DENTAL, AND MENTAL HEALTHCARE (2005), available at aclu.org/images/asset_upload_file690_25743.pdf.

[99] *Farmer v. Brennan*, 511 U.S. 825, 836-39 (1994).

[100] *U.N. Standard Minimum Rules*, *supra* note 68.

[101] *Id.*

[102] *U.N. Rules for the Treatment of Women Prisoners and Non-custodial Measures for Women Offenders*, Oct. 6, 2010, U.N. Doc. A/C.3/65/L.5 (2010).

[103] Talvi, *supra* note 92, at 79.

[104] Nancy Stoller, *Improving Access to Healthcare for California's Women Prisoners, Women and Girls in the Criminal Justice System: Policy Issues and Practice Strategies* 40–42 (Russ Immarigeon ed., 2006) (reporting instances of denial of medical care, such as a woman who was forced to wait more than a year for a mammogram despite family history of breast cancer, and a burn victim who was denied prescribed dressings and physical therapy despite having burns covering more than half her body).

[105] Ferraro & Moe, *supra* note 92, at 72.

[106] Interviews with advocates (on file with Yale Detention and Human Rights Clinic).

[107] Young & Reviere, *supra* note 95, at 96.

[108] *Id.*; see also Stoller, *supra* note 106, at 40–45.

[109] Ferraro & Moe, *supra* note 92, at 72.

[110] Talvi, *supra* note 92, at 84, 93.

[111] Michael Puisis, Clinical Practice in Correctional Medicine 32 (2006).

[112] *Id.*; see also Young & Reviere, *supra* note 95, at 97.

[113] Talvi, *supra* note 92, at 88.

[114] The greatest number of women in prison fall within the age range of twenty-five to forty-four, with an average age of twenty-nine. Cindy Banks, *Women In Prison: A Reference Handbook* 165 (2003); *Women in Prison,* PRISON ACTIVIST RESOURCE CENTER, Dec. 7, 2008, available at prisonactivist.org/articles/women-prison.

[115] Young & Reviere, *supra* note 92, at 89.

[116] Talvi, *supra* note 92, at 88.

[117] Ferraro & Moe, *supra* note 92, at 71.

[118] *Id.* at 102.

[119] *Id.* at 109.

[120] Interviews on file with Yale Detention and Human Rights Clinic.

[121] THE SENTENCING PROJECT, WOMEN IN THE CRIMINAL JUSTICE SYSTEM: BRIEFING SHEETS (2007), available at sentencingproject.org/doc/publications/womenincj_total.pdf.

[122] Stephanie Covington, *Women and the Criminal Justice System*, 17 WOMEN'S HEALTH ISSUES 180 (2007).

[123] BUREAU OF JUSTICE STATISTICS, SPECIAL REPORT: WOMEN OFFENDERS 8 (1999), available at bjs.ojp.usdoj.gov/content/pub/pdf/wo.pdf.

[124] Talvi, *supra* note 92, at 96.

[125] Young & Reviere, *supra* note 95, at 90.

[126] *Id.* at 91.

[127] See, e.g., Kendra Weatherhead, *Cruel but Not Unusual Punishment: The Failure to Provide Adequate Medical Treatment to Female Prisoners in the United States*, 13 HEALTH MATRIX 429, 441 (2003).

[128] TALVI, *supra* note 92, at 97.

[129] *Id.* "New Jersey... doesn't test prisoners for HCV until they begin to show symptoms of liver disease. Pennsylvania tests all of its prisoners, but the Oklahoma prison system has gone so far as to adopt a 'don't ask don't tell' policy as a way of avoiding costs affiliated with HCV treatment. Other state correctional systems, including those in New York and California, say they provide testing upon request and treatment only if a prisoner can meet certain criteria." *Id.* Despite regulations to the contrary, California charges a $5 co-pay for HCV testing, creating a significant disincentive to testing for women in prison. See Labelle, *supra* note 1, at ¶ 184 (discussing California's co-pay system and its effects on women in the California prison system).

[130] *Id.* at 98.

[131] *See id.* at 100–106; see also Brent Staples, "Treat the Epidemic Behind Bars Before It Hits the Streets," *NY Times*, June 22, 2004.

[132] THE SENTENCING PROJECT, *supra* note 123; Kendra Weatherhead, *supra* note 129, at 441.

[133] THE SENTENCING PROJECT, *supra* note 123.

[134] WOMEN'S PRISON ASSOCIATION, wpaonline.org/institute (last visited Nov. 19, 2010).

[135] Press Release, The National Center on Addiction and Substance Abuse at Columbia University, Behind Bars II: Substance Abuse and America's Prison Population 4 (2010), available at casacolumbia.org/download.aspx?path=/UploadedFiles/tw0t55j5.pdf.

[136] *Id.* at 41.

[137] Nunn, et al., *Methadone and buprenorphine prescribing and referral practices in US prisons systems: Results from a Nationwide Survey*, 105 DRUG & ALCOHOL DEPENDENCE 83, 83 (2009).

[138] *Id.*

[139] Women with histories of abuse are three times more likely to have an alcohol abuse disorder and four times more likely to have a drug abuse problem. The National Center on Addiction and Substance Abuse at Columbia University, *supra* note 137, at 47.

[140] *Id.*; see also Young & Reviere, *supra* note 95, at 82 ("Even with new knowledge about gender differences, most prison drug treatment programs are still based on a male model and modified only slightly for women").

[141] The National Center on Addiction and Substance Abuse at Columbia University, *supra* note 137, at 47.

[142] THE SENTENCING PROJECT, *supra* note 123.

[143] Green, et al., *Trauma Exposure, Mental Health Functioning, and Program Needs of Women in Jail*, 51 CRIME & DELINQUENCY 133, 141 (2005).

[144] Covington, *supra* note 124.

[145] THE SENTENCING PROJECT, *supra* note 123.

[146] See, e.g., Covington, *supra* note 124; Talvi, *supra* note 92, at 126 ("Women… who end up in prison… have very little access to any kind of real psychiatric care").

[147] THE SENTENCING PROJECT, *supra* note 123.

[148] Young & Reviere, *supra* note 95, at 105.

[149] Talvi, *supra* note 92, at 123.

[150] Young & Reviere, *supra* note 95, at 105–106.

[151] See Peter Scharff Smith, *The Effects of Solitary Confinement on Prison Inmates: A Brief History and Review of the Literature*, 34 CRIME & JUST. 441, 456–507 (2006); *Istanbul Statement on the Use and Effects of Solitary Confinement* (adopted on Dec. 9, 2007 at the International Psychological Trauma Symposium, Istanbul).

[152] Talvi, *supra* note 92, at 127 ("Women turn to each other for support and basic survival in ways that men don't do as often. So the isolation issue takes on an even deeper [meaning] for women") (quoting Ellen Barry of Legal Services for Prisoners).

[153] For a description of the conditions of women's segregation units and experiences of women struggling with mental health problems in them, see Talvi, *supra* note 92, Chapter 5: Trying to Stay Sane.

[154] *Id.* at 131.

[155] Ferraro & Moe, *supra* note 92, at 77.

[156] *Id.* at 77–78.

[157] *Flynn v. Doyle*, 672 F. Supp. 2d 858 (E.D. Wisc. 2009).

[158] *Id.* at 877.

[159] *Flynn v. Doyle*, No. 06-C-0537 (E.D. Wisc. June 15, 2010), available at aclu.org/files/assets/2010-8-23-FlynnvDoyle-Settlement.pdf.

[160] CENTER FOR REPRODUCTIVE RIGHTS, HUMAN RIGHTS ABUSES OF U.S. INCARCERATED PREGNANT WOMEN 6 (2009) (on file with Yale Detention and Human Rights Clinic) [hereinafter CENTER FOR REPRODUCTIVE RIGHTS SUBMISSION].

[161] Jenni Vainik, *The Reproductive and Parental Rights of Incarcerated Mothers*, 46 FAM. CT. REV. 670, 676 (2008).

[162] Jennifer Clark, et al., *Reproductive Healthcare and Family Planning Needs Among Incarcerated Women*, 96 AM. J. OF PUB. HEALTH 834, 834 (2006).

[163] *Roe v. Wade*, 410 U.S. 113 (1973); *Planned Parenthood v. Casey*, 505 U.S. 833 (1992).

[164] See Lorraine Kenny, *Women Don't Check Their Reproductive Rights at the Jailhouse Door*, WOMEN, GIRLS & CRIM. JUST. at 21 (2007); Diana Kasdan, *Abortion Access for Incarcerated Women: Are Correctional Health Practices in Conflict with Constitutional Standards*, 41 PERSP. ON SEXUAL & REPROD. HEALTH 59 (2009).

[165] Elective abortions are often defined as all abortions not necessary to save the life of the mother.

[166] See *Roe v. Crawford*, 514 F.3d 789 (8th Cir. 2008); *Doe v. Barron*, 92 F. Supp. 2d 694 (S.D. Ohio 1999); *Reprod. Health Serv. v. Webster*, 851 F.2d 1071 (8th Cir. 1988); *Roe v. Leis*, 2001 U.S. Dist. LEXIS 4348 (S.D. Ohio 2001); *Doe v. Arpaio*, 150 P.3d 1258 (Ariz. Ct. App. 2007).

[167] *Monmouth County Corr. Inst'l Inmates v. Lanzaro*, 834 F.2d 326 (3d Cir. 1987).

[168] *Doe v. Arpaio*, No. CV2004-009286 (Sup. Ct. Ariz. 2009).

[169] Carolyn B. Sufrin, et al., *Incarcerated Women and Abortion Provision: A Survey of Correctional Health Providers*, 41 PERSP. ON SEXUAL & REPROD. HEALTH 6, 10 (2009).

[170] *Id.* at 8.

[171] *Id.*

[172] Interview with Diana Kasdan, American Civil Liberties Union (on file with Yale Detention and Human Rights Clinic).

[173] AMERICAN CIVIL LIBERTIES UNION, STATE STANDARDS FOR PREGNANCY-RELATED HEALTHCARE AND ABORTION FOR WOMEN IN PRISON, available at aclu.org/state-standards-pregnancy-related-health-care-and-abortion-women-prison-map (last updated Oct. 28, 2009).

[174] Rachel Roth, *Do Prisoners Have Abortion Rights?*, 30 FEMINIST STUDIES 353, 368 (2004).

[175] *Id.* at 366–367.

[176] *Id.* at 372.

[177] NEW YORK CIVIL LIBERTIES UNION, ACCESS TO REPRODUCTIVE HEALTHCARE IN NEW YORK STATE JAILS 2 (2008), available at nyclu.org/files/rrp_jail_report_030408.pdf.

[178] The United States has ratified only the ICCPR, ICERD, and CAT.

[179] CENTER FOR REPRODUCTIVE RIGHTS, BRINGING RIGHTS TO BEAR: ABORTION AND HUMAN RIGHTS 2 (2008), available at reproductiverights.org/sites/crr.civicactions.net/files/documents/ BRB_abortion_hr_revised_3.09_WEB.pdf.

[180] U.N. Standard Minimum Rules, supra note 68, at Rules 22–26; see also UNITED NATIONS OFFICE ON DRUGS AND CRIME & WORLD HEALTH ORGANIZATION EUROPE, WOMEN'S HEALTH IN PRISON: CORRECTING GENDER INEQUITY IN PRISON HEALTH (THE KYIV DECLARATION) 23 (2009), available at unodc.org/documents/commissions/CND-Session51/Declaration_Kyiv_Women_60s_ health_in_Prison.pdf ("Women may also decide not to proceed with their pregnancy in prison, especially if they were previously unaware that they were pregnant").

[181] See Human Rights Program at Justice Now, Prisons as a Tool of Reproductive Oppression, 5 STAN. J. C.R. & C.L. 309 (2009).

[182] December 10, 2010. Response from California Prison Healthcare Services to Public Records Request from Justice Now. (On file with Justice Now).

[183] Katherine Gabel & Denise Johnston, Children of Incarcerated Parents 274 (1995); THE SENTENCING PROJECT, WOMEN IN THE CRIMINAL JUSTICE SYSTEM: INVOLVEMENT IN CRIME 3 (2007).

[184] Human Rights Program at Justice Now, supra note 183.

[185] Young & Reviere, supra note 95, at 89.

[186] AMERICAN CIVIL LIBERTIES UNION, supra note 175.

[187] Id. (Only eight states explicitly state that medical examinations shall be included in prenatal care, four mention HIV testing, six include advice on levels of activity and safety, nineteen mention prenatal nutrition but only ten actually require provision of appropriate nutrition, seven explicitly require an agreement with a specific community facility for delivery, two require that institutions track pregnancies and their outcomes, and seventeen provide for screening for high-risk pregnancies).

[188] Cajune v. Lake County, No. 9:2009cv00164 (D. Mont. filed Nov. 19, 2009).

[189] Press Release, American Civil Liberties Union, Mother Asks Court to Remedy Mistreatment of Pregnant Inmates by Detention Facility (Nov. 19, 2009), available at aclu.org/reproductive-freedom/ montana-mother-asks-court-remedy-mistreatment-pregnant-inmates-detention-facili.

[190] REBECCA PROJECT FOR HUMAN RIGHTS & NATIONAL WOMEN'S LAW CENTER, MOTHERS BEHIND BARS 23-25 (2010), available at rebeccaproject.org/images/stories/files/mothersbehind- barsreport-2010.pdf.

[191] CENTER FOR REPRODUCTIVE RIGHTS, supra note 162, at 1.

[192] Vainik, supra note 163, at 678.

[193] Id.

[194] Weatherhead, supra note 129, at 450.

[195] CENTER FOR REPRODUCTIVE RIGHTS, supra note 162, at 5.

[196] Letter from Ralph Hale, Exec. Vice Pres., American College of Obstetricians and Gynecologists,

to Malika Saada Saar, Rebecca Project for Human Rights (June 12, 2007), available at acog.org/departments/underserved/20070612SaarLTR.pdf.

[197] U.N. HUMAN RIGHTS COMMISSION, CONCLUSIONS AND RECOMMENDATIONS OF THE COMMITTEE AGAINST TORTURE, 36th Sess., U.N. Doc. CAT/C/USA/CO/2, at ¶ 33 (July 25, 2006) ("The Committee is concerned at the treatment of detained women in the State party, including gender-based humiliation and incidents of shackling of women detainees during childbirth [art. 16].""); *Concluding Observations of the Human Rights Committee: United States of America*, 87th Sess., U.N. Doc. CCPR/C/USA/CO/3/Rev.1, at ¶ 33 (Dec. 18, 2008).

[198] Radhika Coomaraswamy *Special Rapporteur on Violence against Women, Its Causes and Consequences, Report of the Mission to the United States of America on the Issue of Violence against Women in State and Federal Prisons*, U.N. Doc. E/CN.4/1999/68/Add. 2 (Jan. 4, 1999) (by), available at unhchr.ch/Huridocda/Huridoca.nsf/0/7560a6237c67bb118025674c004406e9?OpenDocument.

[199] *Nelson v. Corr. Med. Servs.*, 583 F.3d 522, 533 (8th Cir. 2009); see also *Women Prisoners of D.C. Dep't of Corr. v. District of Columbia*, 877 F. Supp. 634, 668-69 (D.D.C. 1994).

[200] Compare Vainik, *supra* note 163, with REBECCA PROJECT FOR HUMAN RIGHTS, SHACKLING FACT SHEET, available at rebeccaproject.org/images/stories/factsheets/ShacklingFactSheet_7-12-10.pdf.

[201] Fed. Bureau of Prisons, U.S. Dep't of Justice, No.5538.05, available at bop.gov/policy/progstat/5538_005.pdf.

[202] REBECCA PROJECT FOR HUMAN RIGHTS, *supra* note 2.

[203] CENTER FOR REPRODUCTIVE RIGHTS, *supra* note 162, at 2.

[204] Jodi Jacobson, *Schwarzenegger Vetoes Bill to Ban Shackling of Pregnant Women*, RH REALITY CHECK (Sept. 29, 2010), available at rhrealitycheck.org/blog/2010/09/29/schwarzenegger-vetoes-bill-shackling-pregnant-women.

[205] CENTER FOR REPRODUCTIVE RIGHTS, *supra* note 162, at 2.

[206] Phone calls can be prohibitively expensive in many states, including New York. Julie Kowitz Margolies & Tamar Kraft-Stolar, *When "Free" Means Losing Your Mother: The Collision of Child Welfare and the Incarceration of Women in New York State*, WOMEN IN PRISON PROJECT OF THE CORRECTIONAL ASSOCIATION OF NEW YORK ("In New York, inmates are permitted to make collect calls only, which cost 600 percent more than market rates for the general public").

[207] Jocelyn M. Pollack, *A National Survey of Parenting Programs in Women's Prisons in the U.S., in Women and Girls in the Criminal Justice System: Policy Issues and Practice Strategies* 19-1, 19-2 (2006) ("Most incarcerated mothers have minor children and were, before their incarceration, the primary caretakers of their children").

[208] REBECCA PROJECT FOR HUMAN RIGHTS, *supra* note 2.

[209] See, e.g., *Meyer v. Nebraska*, 262 U.S. 390, 399 (1923); *Skinner v. Oklahoma*, 316 U.S. 535, 541 (1942); see also *Stanley v. Illinois*, 405 U.S. 645, 651 (1972) ("The rights to conceive and to raise one's children have been deemed 'essential' basic civil rights of man, and rights far more precious than property rights. It is cardinal with us that the custody, care and nurture of the child reside first in the parents, whose primary function and freedom include preparation for obligations the state can neither supply nor hinder").

[210] *Santosky v. Kramer*, 455 U.S. 745, 753 (1982).

[211] *Lawrence v. Texas*, 539 U.S. 558 (2003).

[212] *Id.* ("Senator John H. Chafee, the Rhode Island Republican who was a leading sponsor of the legislation, said on the Senate floor before the measure passed by a voice vote: 'We will not continue the current system of always putting the needs and rights of the biological parents first.' Although that is a worthy goal, he said, 'it's time we recognize that some families simply cannot and should not be kept together'"); see also 105 P.L. 89 Sec. 101(a)(15)(A) (codified in 42 U.S.C. § 671[15][A]) ("the child's health and safety shall be the paramount concern").

[213] Katherine Q. Seelye, "Clinton to Approve Sweeping Shift in Adoption," *NY Times*, Nov. 17, 1997.

[214] 105 P.L. 89 Sec. 103(a)(3)(E) (codified in 42 U.S.C. § 675[5][C]).

[215] 105 P.L. 89 Sec. 101(a)(15)(D) (codified in 42 U.S.C. § 671[15][D]) (stating that states do not have to make a reasonable effort at reunification if a parent has subjected the child to aggravated circumstances as defined by state law, if the parent has committed certain violent crimes against another of his/her children, or if the parent has previously had his/her rights terminated).

[216] Margolies & Kraft-Stolar, *supra* note 208 (describing how incarcerated mothers with children in foster care are often unable to meet court-mandated family reunification requirements for contact and visitation with their children, and consequently lose their parental rights).

[217] See Lauren E. Glaze & Laura M. Maruschak, *Parents in Prison and Their Minor Children*, BUREAU OF JUSTICE STATISTICS (2008) (reporting that mothers [11 percent] were five times more likely than fathers [2 percent] to report that their children were in the care of a foster home, agency, or institution).

[218] See also *id.* (reporting that mothers were more likely than fathers to report living with at least one child prior to incarceration; that among parents in state prison who had lived with their minor children just prior to incarceration, mothers [77 percent] were almost three times more likely than fathers [26 percent] to report that they had provided most of the daily care for their children; and that more than four in ten mothers in state prison who had minor children were living in single-parent households in the month before arrest).

[219] *Id.* ("Eighty-eight percent of fathers reported that at least one of their children was in the care of the child's mother, compared to 37 percent of mothers who reported the father as the child's current caregiver").

[220] See Margolies & Kraft-Stolar, *supra* note 208; see also U.S. DEPARTMENT OF JUSTICE NATIONAL INSTITUTE OF CORRECTIONS, DEVELOPING GENDER-SPECIFIC CLASSIFICATION (2004) ("[The] distance creates barriers to family visitation, work and educational opportunities, and access to medical and mental health services").

[221] Barbara Bloom, Barbara Owen, & Stephanie Covington, *Gender Responsive Strategies: Research, Practice, and Guiding Principles for Women Offenders*, 7 NATIONAL INSTITUTE OF CORRECTIONS (2003); see also U.S. DEPARTMENT OF JUSTICE, NATIONAL INSTITUTE OF CORRECTIONS, DEVELOPING GENDER-SPECIFIC CLASSIFICATION (2004) (noting that in Florida, children of women offenders were less likely to visit their incarcerated parent: 57.1 percent of women offenders reported that their children would not visit them in prison, compared with 34.6 percent of male inmates); Glaze & Maruschak, *supra* note 270 (noting that 70 percent percent of parents in state prison reported exchanging letters

with their children, 53 percent had spoken with their children over the telephone, and 42 percent had a personal visit since admission).

[222] REBECCA PROJECT FOR HUMAN RIGHTS, *supra* note 245, at 13 ("Studies show that the children left behind as a result of maternal incarceration are vulnerable to suffering significant attachment disorders. They are more likely to become addicted to drugs or alcohol, engage in criminal activity, manifest sexually promiscuous behavior, and dangerously lag behind in educational development and achievement").

[223] *Id.* at 12 ("Family-based treatment programs... demonstrate consistently successful outcomes for children's health and stability, family reunification, reduced rates of recidivism, and sustained parental sobriety. Moreover, it is less costly than incarceration and achieves better outcomes than those achieved by maternal incarceration and a child's placement in foster care").

[224] *Id.* at 7.

[225] Marc Mauer, *Race to Incarcerate* (The New Press, 2006).

[226] About 38 percent of the incarcerated population is black and 20 percent is Hispanic. BUREAU OF JUSTICE STATISTICS, PRISONERS IN 2008 (2009), available at bjs.ojp.usdoj.gov/content/pub/pdf/p08.pdf. The rate of incarceration is far out of proportion with their share of the population. Black persons make up approximately 13 percent of the population; persons of Hispanic origin make up approximately 16 percent of the population. See U.S. CENSUS BUREAU, STATE AND COUNTY QUICK FACTS, available at quickfacts.census.gov/qfd/states/00000.html (last visited Nov. 21, 2010).

[227] See BUREAU OF JUSTICE STATISTICS, PREVALENCE OF IMPRISONMENT IN THE U.S. POPULATION, 1974–2001, at 1 (2003), available at bjs.ojp.usdoj.gov/content/pub/pdf/piusp01.pdf.

[228] *Id.* at 2.

[229] Dorothy E. Roberts, *The Social and Moral Cost of Mass Incarceration in African American Communities*, 56 STAN. L. REV. 1271, 1274 (2004).

[230] See David Cole, *No Equal Justice: Race and Class in the American Criminal Justice System* 4-5 (The New Press, 1999).

[231] Bruce Western & Christopher Wildeman, *The Moynihan Report Revisited: Lessons and Reflections After Four Decades: The Black Family and Mass Incarceration*, 621 ANNALS 221, 228 (2009).

[232] Michael Tonry & Matthew Melewski, *The Malign Effects of Drug and Crime Control Policies on Black Americans, in* 37 CRIME AND JUSTICE: A REVIEW OF RESEARCH 1 (Michael Tonry ed., 2008).

[233] Marc Mauer, THE SENTENCING PROJECT, RACIAL DISPARITIES IN THE CRIMINAL JUSTICE SYSTEM: TESTIMONY OF MARC MAUER 4 (Oct. 29, 2009), available at sentencingproject.org/detail/publication.cfm?publication_id=289&id=120.

[234] Michelle Alexander, *The New Jim Crow* 97 (2010) (citing data from U.S. Department of Health and Human Services, Substance Abuse and Mental Health Services Administration). Although the rates of imprisonment of black offenders compared to white has dropped somewhat in recent years, the numbers are still grossly disproportional. See Marc Mauer, THE SENTENCING PROJECT, THE CHANGING RACIAL DYNAMICS OF THE WAR ON DRUGS (2009), available at sentencingproject.org/search/dp_raceanddrugs.pdf.

[235] AMERICAN CIVIL LIBERTIES UNION, ET AL., CAUGHT IN THE NET: THE IMPACT OF DRUG POLICIES ON WOMEN AND FAMILIES 7 (2005), available at aclu.org/files/images/asset_upload_ file431_23513.pdf.

[236] For an in-depth discussion of how and why racial bias influences law enforcement and thus creates the wide racial disparity in prison, see Alexander, *supra* note 236, at Chapter 3: The Color of Justice. See THE SENTENCING PROJECT, RACIAL DISPARITY IN SENTENCING: A REVIEW OF THE LITERATURE (2005), available at sentencingproject.org/doc/publications/rd_sentencing_review.pdf (reviewing the numerous studies demonstrating a correlation between race and harsher sentencing in different contexts); AMERICAN CIVIL LIBERTIES UNION, ET AL., *supra* note 237, at 28 (describing a 2000 GAO report which found that U.S. customs agents at airports disproportionately singled out women of color for pat-downs, frisks, and strip-searches); NATIONAL CRIMINAL JUSTICE COMM'N, THE REAL WAR ON CRIME, 112 (1996) ("All else being equal, whites did better than African Americans and Hispanics at getting charges dropped, getting cases dismissed, avoiding harsher punishment, avoiding extra charges and having their criminal records wiped clean"). See generally Michael Tonry, *Malign Neglect, Race Crime and Punishment in America* (1995).

[237] Alexander, *supra* note 236, at 109. The law inflicted a mandatory five-year sentence for possession of only five grams of crack, while possession of 500 grams of powder cocaine was required to trigger an identical sentence. *Id.* The combined effect of this "race-neutral" law and federal enforcement practices "resulted in African Americans constituting 80 percent of those charged with crack cocaine offenses over a 20-year period." Marc Mauer, *The Impact of Mandatory Minimum Penalties in Federal Sentencing*, 94 JUDICATURE 6, 8 (2010). In August 2010 Congress passed a law lowering the crack-powder penalty ratio to about 18 to 1; the law is not retroactive. The Fair Sentencing Act of 2010, Pub. L. No. 111–220.

[238] THE SENTENCING PROJECT, *supra* note 238, at 5.

[239] AMERICAN CIVIL LIBERTIES UNION, ET AL., *supra* note 237, at 15. A hospital in Charleston, South Carolina, which served a predominately black population, engaged in "selectively drug test[ing] pregnant women whom staff deemed 'likely' to have a drug abuse problem and reported positive tests to the police, who then arrested the women." *Id.* Twenty-nine of the thirty women prosecuted were black. In *Ferguson v. South Carolina*, the Supreme Court held that the practice was unconstitutional. 532 U.S. 67 (2001).

[240] See *Whren v. United States*, 517 U.S. 806 (1996); *McClesky v. Kemp*, 481 U.S. 279 (1987); and *Armstrong v. United States*, 517 U.S. 456 (1996).

[241] Scholar Michael Massoglia's research demonstrates that incarceration has significant effects on later health outcomes and "indicate[s] that the penal system accounts for a sizeable proportion of racial disparities in general health functioning." Marc Mauer, *Two Tiered Justice: Race, Class, and Crime Policy, The Integration Debate: Competing Futures for American Cities* 169, 179 (Chester Hartman & Gregory Squires, eds., 2010) (citing Michael Massoglia, *Incarceration, Health, and Racial Health Disparities*, 42 L. & SOC. REV. 275 [2008]).

[242] Buchanan, *supra* note 27.

[243] For a full explanation of the hardships that accompany individuals once released from prison, see Alexander, *supra* note 236, at Chapter 4: The Cruel Hand.

[244] Erika Wood, *Restoring the Right to Vote* 3, BRENNAN CENTER FOR JUSTICE, (2009), available at

brennancenter.org/page/-/Democracy/Restoring percent20the percent20Right percent20to percent-20Vote.pdf.

[245] THE SENTENCING PROJECT, FELONY DISENFRANCHISEMENT RATES FOR WOMEN, 1 (2008), available at sentencingproject.org/doc/publications/fd_bs_women.pdf.

[246] See Labelle, *supra* note 1, at ¶¶ 92–95; see also THE SENTENCING PROJECT, INCARCERATED PARENTS AND THEIR CHILDREN: TRENDS 1991–2007 (2009), available at sentencingproject.org/doc/inc_incarceratedparents.pdf.

[247] *Id.* at 7.

[248] Nekima Levy-Pounds, *From the Frying Pan into the Fire: How Poor Women of Color and Children Are Affected by Sentencing Guidelines and Mandatory Minimums*, 47 SANTA CLARA L. REV. 285, 328 (citing U.S. Department of Health & Human Services data).

[249] Western & Wildeman, *supra* note 233, at 240–241.

[250] Although there are many terms used to refer to the indigenous peoples of the United States, we have chosen "Native American" because that is the term that appears to be used most frequently by activists and academics, particularly those of indigenous descent.

[251] NPREC REPORT, *supra* note 25 ("The Commission consulted informally with Native American leaders and heard distressing testimony at a public hearing about the conditions of tribal detention facilities... Correctional facilities in Indian Country are certainly within PREA's ambit. However, the time-consuming work of consulting with numerous and diverse sovereign nations and entities posed an insurmountable challenge. We encourage Native American leaders to adapt the standards to their cultures and communities").

[252] Todd D. Minton, *Jails in Indian Country, 2008*, BUREAU OF JUSTICE STATISTICS (2009), available at bjs.ojp.usdoj.gov/index.cfm?ty=pbdetail&iid=1748.

[253] U.S. SENTENCING COMM'N, SYMPOSIUM ON ALTERNATIVES TO INCARCERATION (2008).

[254] Luana Ross, *Inventing the Savage* (University of Texas Press), (1998) ("[American Indian women in prison are] labeled as deviant, often because of characteristics that are attributed to being 'Native' in a system that has no understanding, training, education, or interest in being burdened with the rights or needs of indigenous people").

[255] U.S. SENTENCING COMM'N (2008), *supra* note 255 ("We have somewhere between seven and ten generations of Native American people living on reduced reservations with very few natural resources, save for a few oil-based tribes, not many. They have the highest rates of alcoholism and chemical dependency. They have the lowest life spans for men and women. They have the highest infant mortality rate and high levels of unemployment. On Pine Ridge Indian Reservation, unemployment is routinely between 70 and 86 percent").

[256] *Cruz v. Beto*, 405 U.S. 319, 322 (1972) (finding that a Buddhist inmate must be given "a reasonable opportunity of pursuing his faith comparable to the opportunity afforded to fellow prisoners who adhere to conventional religious precepts").

[257] Laura E. Donaldson, *Speaking Out: Religious Rights and Imprisoned American Indian Women*, J. OF FEMINIST STUDIES IN RELIGION, Vol. 17, No. 2 (2001), at 57–59 ("The gains from *Cruz v. Beto* remain divided along gender lines... although Native men have had some success in forcing prisons

to build sweat lodges and hire Native counselors, the spiritual needs of Native women have remained unnoticed and unheard"); see also Ross, *supra* note 347 ("Native men... receive higher gate pay upon being released and have greater access to Native religious resources and Native counselors").

[258] *Id.* ("Even when near to home, prisons often refuse to hire Indian spiritual leaders to perform ceremonies for their female inmates. In Montana, for example, former Governor Stan Stephens dismissed a plan to hire Native religious leaders and counselors by stating that he would only implement it if tribes in the state assisted in the financing").

[259] Luana Ross, *Native American Voices: A Reader* 415 (Susan Lobo & Steve Talbot, ed., Longman) (1998), ("Without access to their traditions, many Native women become even more susceptible to the endemic violence and bitterness of the prison environment. They themselves assert that spirituality—and not tranquilizers or Euro-American counseling is the answer... to surviving").

[260] Steven W. Perry, *American Indians and Crime*, BUREAU OF JUSTICE STATISTICS (2004), available at justice.gov/otj/pdf/american_indians_and_crime.pdf.

[261] *Id.* at 5.

[262] Lisa Bhungalia, *Native American Women and Violence*, NATIONAL ORGANIZATION FOR WOMEN, available at now.org/nnt/spring-2001/nativeamerican.html.

[263] See Todd D. Minton, *Jails in Indian Country, 2008*, BUREAU OF JUSTICE STATISTICS 2 (2009) (illustrating that in 2008, approximately 81 percent of the Native persons in custody were in state custody, 10.5 percent were in federal custody and 7 percent were in jails in Indian country).

[264] 25 U.S.C. § 1302(7) (2010).

[265] Tribal Law and Order Act of 2010, Pub. L. No. 111-211, § 304(b) (2010).

[266] 18 U.S.C. § 1153 (2006).

[267] 18 U.S.C. § 1162 (2010).

[268] Lisa Bhungalia, *Native American Women and Violence*, NATIONAL ORGANIZATION FOR WOMEN, available at now.org/nnt/spring-2001/nativeamerican.html.

[269] See NPREC Report, *supra* note 25, at 7 (stating that "research on sexual abuse in correctional facilities consistently documents the vulnerability of men and women with non-heterosexual orientations and transgender individuals"); Allen J. Beck & Paige M. Harrison, *Sexual Victimization in Local Jails, Reported by Inmates*, BUREAU OF JUSTICE STATISTICS 6 (2008), available at bjs.ojp.usdoj.gov/content/pub/pdf/svljri07.pdf (estimating that 2.7 percent of heterosexual inmates alleged an incident of sexual victimization, compared to 18.5 percent of inmates identifying as homosexual, and 9.8 percent of inmates identifying as bisexual or "other").

[270] See NPREC Report, *supra* note 25, at 74 (noting that "lesbian and bisexual women... are targeted in women's correctional settings"); Robin Levi et al., *Unpublished Briefing Paper on Gender-Identity Based Violations in California Women's Prisons*, Justice Now, (2010).

[271] See *id.* at 73 ("The discrimination, hostility, and violence members of these groups often face in American society are amplified in correctional environments and may be expressed by staff as well as other incarcerated persons").

[272] Levi, *supra* note 272, at PINCITE.

[273] *Id.*

[274] NPREC REPORT, *supra* note 25, at 74.

[275] *Id.*

[276] See *It's War in Here: A Report on the Treatment of Transgender and Intersex People in New York State Men's Prisons,* The Sylvia Rivera Law Project (2007), available at srlp.org/resources/ pubs/warinhere; *Still in Danger: The Ongoing Threat of Sexual Violence Against Transgender Prisoners,* Stop Prisoner Rape & ACLU National Prison Project (2005), available at justdetention.org/pdf/stillindanger.pdf.

[277] *Farmer v. Brennan,* 511 U.S. 825, 834 (1994) (asserting that sexual assault is "not part of the penalty that criminal offenders pay for their offenses against society").

[278] See 42 U.S.C. § 15601(13) (2003).

[279] 18 U.S.C. § 5031 (2003) ("juvenile" is defined under United States federal law as "a person who has not attained his eighteenth birthday." But see 42 U.S.C. § 5633 (2006) (however, within certain guidelines, states may determine when and whether juveniles may be tried as adults and incarcerated in adult facilities).

[280] For non-citizens, the consequences of a criminal conviction are even more dire. Criminal and immigration courts are in separate systems, but a criminal conviction or sometimes merely an arrest can result in deportation and a lifetime ban on returning to the United States. The intersections of immigration and criminal convictions in the United States can be extraordinarily complex; this appendix focuses on the consequences of criminal conviction for U.S. citizens and legal residents only.

[281] Legal Action Center, *After Prison: Barriers Facing People With Criminal Records.* 2004. lac.org/roadblocks-to-reentry.

[282] Legal Action Center. *After Prison: Roadblocks to Reentry,* Update. 2009. lac.org/roadblocks-to-reentry/upload/lacreport/Roadblocks-to-Reentry--2009.pdf.

[283] Michelle Natividad Rodriguez, and Maurice Emsellem. *65 Million Need Not Apply: The Case for Reforming Criminal Background Checks and Employment.* The National Employment Law Project. March 2011: p. 5., available at nelp.org/page/-/65_Million_Need_Not_Apply.pdf?nocdn=1.

[284] Erica Goode, "Internet Lets a Criminal Past Catch Up Quicker," *NY Times.* April 28, 2011.

[285] Alabama, Alaska, Arizona, Arkansas, Colorado, District of Columbia, Florida, Georgia, Hawaii, Illinois, Indiana, Iowa, Kansas, Kentucky, Louisiana, Maine, Maryland, Michigan, Minnesota, Missouri, Montana, Nebraska, Nevada, New Jersey, New Mexico New York, North Carolina, Ohio, Oklahoma, Pennsylvania, South Carolina, Tennessee, Texas, Vermont, Washington, Wisconsin. *Id.*

[286] Rodriguez and Emsellem, *supra* 7.

[287] Legal Action Center 2004, *supra.*

[288] Arizona, Arkansas, California, District of Columbia, Illinois, Indiana, Kentucky, Maryland, Massachusetts, Michigan, Minnesota, Mississippi, Nebraska, Nevada, New Hampshire, New Jersey, New York, Ohio, Oklahoma, Oregon, Rhode Island, South Carolina, South Dakota, Utah, Washington. *Id.*

[289] 42 U.S.C. § 671(a)(15)(B). Patricia E. Allard, and Lynn D. Lu, *Rebuilding Families, Reclaiming Lives*, Brennan Center for Justice: p. 10, available at brennan.3cdn.net/a714f3bf3bc8235faf_4am6b84bh.pdf.

[290] 42 U.S.C. §§ 671(a)(20)(A)-(B).

[291] *Id.*

[292] Alaska, Connecticut, Idaho, Kansas, North Carolina, Mississippi, New Jersey, New Mexico, Pennsylvania, Rhode Island, South Carolina, South Dakota, Virginia. Legal Action Center 2004.

[293] Alabama, Arizona, Arkansas, California, Colorado, Delaware, District of Columbia, Florida, Georgia, Hawaii, Illinois, Indiana, Iowa, Kentucky, Louisiana, Maine, Maryland, Massachusetts, Michigan, Minnesota, Missouri, Montana, Nebraska, Nevada, New Hampshire, New York, North Dakota, Ohio, Oklahoma, Oregon, Tennessee, Texas, Utah, Vermont, Washington, West Virginia, Wisconsin, Wyoming. *Id.*

[294] E.g., New Jersey: N.J.S.A. § 39:4-139.1 et seq., 15. N.J.S.A. § 2A:17-56.43.16, N.J.S.A. § 39:4-203.2; N.J.S.A. § 2C:46-2.

[295] 23 U.S.C. § 159. Legal Action Center 2004, *supra.*

[296] Alabama, Arkansas, Arizona, Colorado, Delaware, District of Columbia, Florida, Georgia, Indiana, Iowa, Louisiana, New York, Maine, Michigan, Mississippi, Missouri, New Jersey, Ohio, Oklahoma, Pennsylvania, Rhode Island, South Carolina, South Dakota, Texas, Utah, Virginia, Wisconsin, Wyoming. *Id.*

[297] Alaska, California, Connecticut, Hawaii, Idaho, Illinois, Kansas, Kentucky, Maryland, Massachusetts, Minnesota, Montana, Nebraska, Nevada, New Hampshire, New Mexico, North Carolina, North Dakota, Oregon, Tennessee, Vermont, Washington, West Virginia. *Id.*

[298] These states do not offer any type of restricted driver's license: Alabama, Connecticut, District of Columbia, Maine, Michigan, New Hampshire, Oklahoma, Pennsylvania, Rhode Island, Vermont, Wyoming. *Id.*

[299] Council of State Governments, Reentry Policy Council. Policy Statement 21: Creation of Employment Opportunities, Report of the Re-Entry Policy Council: Charting the Safe and Successful Return of Prisoners to the Community. New York: Council of State Governments, January 2005.

[300] Equal Employment Opportunity Commission Policy Statement on the Issue of Conviction Records under Title VII of the Civil Rights Act of 1964, as amended, 42 U.S.C. § 2000e et seq. Available at eeoc.gov/policy/docs/convict1.html.

[301] E.g., New York State Occupation Licensing Survey, Legal Action Center, 2006, 4–20. available at lac.org/doc_library/lac/publications/Occupational%20Licensing%20Survey%202006.pdf

[302] Legal Action Center 2009, p. 10, *supra.*

[303] Maine and Vermont do not disenfranchise individuals convicted of a felony. Project Vote, "Felon Voting Rights State-by-State," May 2010. available at projectvote.org/felon-voting.html.

[304] *Id.*

[305] Alabama, Arizona, Delaware, Mississippi, Nevada, Tennessee, Wyoming. Id.

306 In Alaska, Arkansas, Florida, Georgia, Idaho, Iowa, Kansas, Louisiana, Maryland, Missouri, Minnesota, Nebraska, New Jersey, New Mexico, North Carolina, Oklahoma, South Carolina, Texas, Washington, West Virginia, and Wisconsin, persons on parole or probation cannot vote. In California, Colorado, Connecticut, New York, and South Dakota, persons on parole cannot vote, but persons on probation can. *Id.*

307 District of Columbia, Hawaii, Illinois, Indiana, Massachusetts, Michigan, Montana, New Hampshire, North Dakota, Ohio, Oregon, Pennsylvania, Rhode Island, Utah. Id.

308 20 U.S.C. § 1091(r).

309 Legal Action Center 2004, *supra.*

310 *Id.*

311 Steven Greenhouse, "States Help Ex-Inmates Find Jobs," *NY Times*, January 24, 2011.

312 *Id.*

313 U.S. House of Representatives Committee on Appropriations, Press Release, April 12, 2011. Available at appropriations.house.gov/index.cfm?FuseAction=PressReleases.Detail&PressRelease_id=285&Month=4&Year=2011. "FY 2011 Continuing Resolution Reductions," available at republicans.appropriations.house.gov/_files/41211ProgramCutsListFinalFY2011CR.pdf (under State and Local Law Enforcement Assistance).

314 Legal Action Center 2004, *supra.*

315 *Id.*

316 Marc Mauer. "Invisible Punishment, Block Housing, Education, Voting," May/June 2003, Joint Center for Political and Economic Studies, The Sentencing Project, p. 3. Avilable at sentencingproject.org/doc/publications/cc_mauer-focus.pdf

317 *Id.*

318 *U.S. Department of Housing and Urban Development v. Rucker,* (535 U.S. 125 [2002])

319 Legal Action Center 2004, *supra.*

320 Allard "Life Sentences," p. 8.

321 Personal Responsibility and Work Opportunity Reconciliation Act of 1996, Pub. L. No. 104-193. p. 2.

322 Legal Action Center 2004, *supra.*

323 The nine states that have a lifetime ban on benefits eligibility are: Alabama, Alaska, Georgia, Mississippi, Missouri, Nebraska, North Dakota, West Virginia and Wyoming. Legal Action Center 2009, *supra*, p. 11.

324 The nine states that have opted out of the ban entirely are: Connecticut, District of Columbia, Michigan, New Hampshire, New York, Ohio, Oklahoma, Oregon, Vermont. *Id.*

325 *Id.* at 2.

326 *Overton v. Bazzetta*, 539 U.S. 126,131 (2003).

327 *Turner v. Safley*, 482 U.S. 78, 85 (1987).

328 *Turner*, 482 U.S. 78 at 89–90. (1987)

329 417 U.S. 817, 819 (1974).

330 *Id.* at 831.

331 *Id.* at 834.

332 438 U.S. 1, 3 (1978).

333 *Id.*

334 *Id.* at 5.

335 *Id.*

336 *Id.* at 15.

337 490 U.S. 401, 413 (1989).

338 *Thornburgh*, 490 U.S. at 404.

339 *Id.* at 414.

340 *Id.* at 416.

341 *Overton v. Bazzetta*, 539 U.S. 126, 132 (2003).

342 *Id.*

343 *Id.* at 129.

344 *Id.* at 130.

345 *Id.* at 129.

346 *Id.* at 133.

347 *Id.* (internal citations omitted).

348 *Id.*

349 *Id.*

350 *Id.* at 134.

351 *Id.*

352 *Id.* at 135.

353 *Id.*

354 See *Pell*, 417 U.S. at 822; *Thornburgh*, 490 U.S. at 407; and *Overton*, 539 U.S. at 131.

355 Nicholas H. Weil, "Dialing While Incarcerated: Calling for Uniformity Among Prison Telephone Regulations," 19 WASH. U. J.L. & POL'Y 427 (2005).

356 *Id.* at 431-436; *Washington v. Reno,* 35 F.3d 1093, 1095 (6th Cir. 1994); *Johnson v. State*, 207 F.3d

650, (9th Cir. 2000) (finding that while people in prison had a right to use the telephone, the cost of doing so was not excessive).

357 244 F.3d 558, 561, 564 (7th Cir 2001).

358 *Id.* at 564. Also see *United States v. Footman*, 215 F.3d 145, 155 (1st Cir. 2000) (observing in dicta, "prisoners have no per se constitutional right to use a telephone").

359 *United States v. Van Poyck*, 77 F.3d 285, 290-291, (9th Cir. 1996).

360 *Id.* at 291.

361 *Id.*

362 Such as *United States v. Vasta*, 649 F. Supp. 974, 990 (S.D.N.Y. 1986).

363 Quoting *Procunier v. Martinez*, 416 U.S. 396, 412-13 (1974).

364 *Id.* (quoting *Procunier*, 416 U.S. at 413).

365 *Id.* (quoting *Procunier*, 416 U.S. at 414).

366 See Federal Bureau of Prisons, Program Statement 5267; Alabama Department of Corrections, Administrative Regulation 303; Arizona Department of Corrections, Department Order 911; Ohio Department of Rehabilitation and Corrections, Policy Number 76-VIS-01; Texas Department of Criminal Justice, "Offender Rules and Regulations for Visitation Handbook," August 2008, available at tdcj.state.tx.us/policy/policy-home.htm.

367 State of New York Department of Correctional Services, Directive No. 0401; Michigan Department of Corrections, Policy Directive 05.03.140.

368 Federal Bureau of Prisons, Program Statement 1480.05; Louisiana Department of Corrections, Department Regulation No. C-01-013; Nevada Department of Corrections, Administrative Regulation 120.02; Ohio Department of Rehabilitation and Corrections, Policy Number 01-COM-09; Washington State Department of Corrections, Policy Number 150.100; Massachusetts Department of Correction, 103 C.M.R. § 131.

369 Federal regulations and the laws of Louisiana, Nevada, Ohio, Washington, Michigan, and Massachusetts.

370 Federal Bureau of Prisons, Program Statement 1480.05; Alabama Department of Corrections, Administrative Regulation, 005; California Department of Corrections, 15 C.C.R. § 3261; Colorado Department of Corrections, Administrative Regulation 1350-01; District of Columbia Department of Corrections, Public Statement 1340.2B; Louisiana Department of Corrections, Department Regulation No. C-01-013; Michigan Department of Corrections, Policy Directive 01.06.130; Nevada Department of Corrections, Administrative Regulation 120.02; New York State Department of Correctional Services, Directive No. 0401; Ohio Department of Rehabilitation and Corrections, Policy Number 01-COM-09; Washington State Department of Corrections, Policy Number 150.100; Massachusetts Department of Correction, 103 C.M.R. § 131.

371 See for example Alabama Department of Corrections, Administrative Regulation 005; District of Columbia Department of Corrections, Public Statement 1340.2B.

372 Federal Bureau of Prisons, Program Statement 1480.05; Alabama Department of Corrections,

Administrative Regulation 005; Arizona Department of Corrections, Department Order 207; California Department of Corrections, 15 C.C.R. § 3261; District of Columbia Department of Corrections, Public Statement 1340.2B; Nevada Department of Corrections, Administrative Regulation 120.02.

[373] California Department of Corrections, 15 C.C.R. § 3261.5; Idaho Department of Correction, Directive Number 110.

[374] Idaho Department of Correction, Directive Number 110.

[375] California Department of Corrections, 15 C.C.R. § 3261.5.

[376] See Federal Bureau of Prisons, Program Statement 1480.05; Alabama Department of Corrections, Administrative Regulation 005; Arizona Department of Corrections, Department Order 207; Colorado Department of Corrections, Administrative Regulation 1350-01; District of Columbia Department of Corrections, Public Statement 1340.2B; Idaho Department of Correction, Directive Number 110 Illinois, "Society of Professional Journalism," available at spj.org/prison-IL.asp; Nevada Department of Corrections, Administrative Regulation 120; Ohio Department of Rehabilitation and Corrections, Policy Number 01-COM-09; Washington State Department of Corrections, Policy Number 150.100; Massachusetts Department of Correction, 103 C.M.R. § 131.00.; Virginia, "Society of Professional Journalism," available at spj.org/prison-VA.asp.

[377] Ohio Department of Rehabilitation and Corrections, Policy Number 01-COM-09.

[378] Nevada Department of Corrections, Administrative Regulation 120.

[379] Washington State Department of Corrections, Policy Number, 150.100.

[380] Michigan Department of Corrections, Policy Directive 04.01.110.

[381] Arizona Department of Corrections, Department Order 207.

[382] District of Columbia Department of Corrections, Public Statement 1340.2B.

[383] Colorado Department of Corrections, Administrative Regulation 1350-01; Ohio Department of Rehabilitation and Corrections, Policy Number 01-COM-09.

[384] Louisiana Department of Corrections, Department Regulation No. C-01-013.

[385] The section examining telephone regulations is not based on the survey of state and federal regulations and rules pertaining to the other portions of this memo.

[386] See La. Admin. Code tit. 22, pt. I, § 314(E)(4)(a); 103 Mass. Code Regs. 482.07(3)(a); N.J. Admin. Code § 10A:18-8.4; Utah Admin. Code r. 251-702-3(6) to -3(7).

[387] See 28 C.F.R. § 540.100 (regulating federal prisons): "The Bureau of Prisons extends telephone privileges to inmates as part of its overall correctional management. Telephone privileges are a supplemental means of maintaining community and family ties that will contribute to an inmate's personal development. An inmate may request to call a person of his or her choice outside the institution on a telephone provided for that purpose. However, limitations and conditions may be imposed upon an inmate's telephone privileges to ensure that these are consistent with other aspects of the Bureau's correctional management responsibilities. In addition to the procedures set forth in this subpart, inmate telephone use is subject to those limitations which the Warden determines are necessary to ensure the security or good order, including discipline, of the institution or to protect the public. Restrictions on

inmate telephone use may also be imposed as a disciplinary sanction."

[388] "Dialing While Incarcerated: Calling for Uniformity Among Prison Telephone Regulations," Nicholas H. Weil, 19 Wash. U. J.L. & Pol'y 427 (2005).

[389] 28 C.F.R. § 540.101(a)-(b).

[390] 103. Mass. Code Regs. 482.07(3)(c). See also, La. Admin. Code tit. 22, pt. I, § 314(E)(1)(c), (f) (limiting calls to a list of up to twenty numbers).

[391] N.Y. Comp. Codes R. & Regs. Tit. 7, §§ 723.2(a), 723.3(d)-(e).

[392] 28 C.F.R. § 540.100(b).

[393] Id. § 540.101(d).

[394] Wis. Admin. Code DOC § 309.39(3), (5) (also providing that more calls are allowed "where resources permit").

[395] La. Admin. Code tit. 22, pt. I, §§ 314(E)(2)(a), (3)(a); 103 Mass. Code Regs. 482.07(3)(e), (3)(h); N.Y. Comp. Codes R. & Regs. Tit. 7, §§ 723.3(b),.5(b)(2), (6).

[396] Id. See also Or. Admin. R. 291-130-0020(3), -00060(1) (calls may be terminated for illegal activity or plans for illegal activity, and prohibiting calls between 11 p.m. and 6 a.m.).

[397] See 28 C.F.R. § 540.105 ("Third party billing and electronic transfer of a call to a third party are prohibited. (b) The Warden shall provide at least one collect call each month for an inmate who is without funds... (d) The Warden may direct the government to bear the expense... under compelling circumstances..."); Utah Admin. Code r. 251-702-3(6) to 3(7) (allowing only collect calls); Wis. Admin. Code DOC § 309.39(4) (requiring calls to be collect "unless payment from... account is approved").

[398] Ben Iddings, "The Big Disconnect: Will Anyone Answer the Call to Lower Excessive Prisoner Telephone Rates?" 8 N.C.J.L. & TECH. 159 (2006), p.p. 161-62.

[399] Id. See also, "The Campaign to Promote Equitable Telephone Charges, Current Status by State," available at etccampaign.com/etc/current_status.php, visited May 2, 2011.

[400] Iddings, "The Big Disconnect," 8 N.C.J.L. & TECH. 159 at 162, quoting Madeleine Severin, "Is There a Winning Argument Against Excessive Rates For Collect Calls From Prisoners?," 25 Cardozo L. Rev. 1469, 1469 (2004).

[401] See Me. Rev. Stat. Ann. Tit. 15, § 712(2); 18 Pa. Cons. State. Ann. § 5704(13), (14); Wash. Rev. Code Ann. § 9.73.095(3)(a); Mass. Gen. Laws Ann. Ch. 272 § 99(B)(4).

[402] See United States v. Vasta, 649 F. Supp. 974, 990 (S.D.N.Y. 1986); U.S. Dep't of Justice, Office of the Inspector General, Criminal Calls: A Review of the Bureau of Prisons' Management of Inmate Telephone Privileges 43 (1999), available at usdoj.go/oig/special/9908.

[403] See Federal Bureau of Prisons, Program Statement, 5265.11; Alabama Department of Corrections, Administrative Regulation 448; California Department of Corrections, 15 C.C.R. § 3135; Colorado Department of Corrections, Administrative Regulation 300-38; Idaho Department of Correction, Directive Number 402.02.01.001; Illinois Department of Corrections, 20 A.C. § 525; Massachusetts Department of Correction, 103 C.M.R. 481; Michigan Department of Correction, Policy Directive 05.03.118; Nevada Department of Corrections, Administrative Regulation 750; New York State

Department of Correctional Services, Directive No. 4421; Ohio Department of Rehabilitation and Corrections, Policy Number 75-MAL-01; Virginia Department of Corrections, vadoc.state.va.us/offenders/prison-life/mail.shtm; Washington State Department of Corrections, Policy Number 450.100.

[404] See Federal Bureau of Prisons, Program Statement, 5265.11; Alabama Department of Corrections, Administrative Regulation 448; California Department of Corrections, 15 C.C.R. § 3135; Colorado Department of Corrections, Administrative Regulation 300-38; Idaho Department of Correction, Directive Number 402.02.01.001; Illinois Department of Corrections, 20 A.C. § 525; Massachusetts Department of Correction, 103 C.M.R. 481; Michigan Department of Correction, Policy Directive 05.03.118; Nevada Department of Corrections, Administrative Regulation 750; New York State Department of Correctional Services, Directive No. 4421; Ohio Department of Rehabilitation and Corrections, Policy Number 75-MAL-01; Virginia Department of Corrections, vadoc.state.va.us/offenders/prison-life/mail.shtm; Washington State Department of Corrections, Policy Number 450.100;

[405] California Department of Corrections 15 C.C.R. § 3138; Massachusetts 103 C.M.R. § 481; Michigan Department of Corrections, Policy Directive 04.02.120; Idaho Department of Corrections, Directive Number 402.02.02.001; Illinois Department of Corrections, 20 A.C. § 525.

[406] New York State Department of Correctional Services, Directive No. 4422.

[407] District of Columbia Department of Corrections, Public Statement 4070.4D.

[408] In the prison study, however, "the size measures for [state] facilities housing female inmates were doubled to ensure a sufficient number of women to allow for meaningful analyses of sexual victimization by gender." And inmates younger than eighteen were excluded from the surveys of adult facilities.

[409] Prison inmates had been in their current facilities for an average of 8.5 months prior to taking the survey; jail inmates had been in theirs for an average of 2.6 months.

[410] As a point of comparison, it may be worth noting that the latest National Crime Victimization Survey (NCVS) by the BJS, which excludes "Armed Forces personnel living in military barracks and institutionalized persons, such as correctional facility inmates," estimates that in 2009 there were 125,910 instances of rape and sexual assault in the United States. However, several caveats are necessary here: first, that the definitions of these crimes used in this study are not the same as those used in the surveys of prisoner rape; second, that the 2009 number was down significantly from the 2008 NCVS finding of 203,830 rapes and sexual assaults in the free community; third, as the BJS says in the 2009 NCVS, "The measurement of rape and sexual assault represents one of the most serious challenges in the field of victimization research." The 2009 National Crime Victimization Survey is available at bjs.ojp.usdoj.gov/content/pub/pdf/cv09.pdf.

[411] Of juvenile detainees reporting sexual abuse by other inmates, 81 percent said it happened more than once.

[412] According to the jail study, approximately 20 percent of those sexually abused also suffered other physical injuries in the process; approximately 85 percent of that number suffered at least one serious injury, including knife and stab wounds, broken bones, rectal tearing, chipped or knocked-out teeth, internal injuries, and being knocked unconscious.

[413] "In 2005–2006, 21,980 State and Federal prisoners were HIV positive or living with AIDS. Researchers believe the prevalence of hepatitis C in correctional facilities is dramatically higher, based on [the] number of prisoners with a history of injecting illegal drugs prior to incarceration. The incidence of

HIV in certain populations outside correctional systems is likely attributable in part to [sexual] activity within correctional systems. Because of the disproportionate representation of minority men and women in correctional settings, it is likely that the spread of these diseases in confinement will have an even greater impact on minority men, women, and children and their communities." (National Prison Rape Elimination Commission Report, p.p. 129–130). The commissioners seem to be saying here, as delicately as they can, that they suspect prisoner rape has contributed to the way HIV infection in this country has shifted demographically: i.e., to the way AIDS has changed from being a predominantly gay disease to a predominantly black one.

[414] National Prison Rape Elimination Commission Report, p. 26.

[415] National Prison Rape Elimination Commission Report, p. 134.

[416] See Todd D. Minton and William J. Sabol, *Jail Inmates at Midyear*, 2007, Bureau of Justice Statistics, 2008, p. 2; available at bjs.ojp.usdoj.gov/content/pub/pdf/jim07.pdf. Local jails made an estimated 13 million admissions during the twelve months ending June 29, 2007; the jailed inmate population on that day was 780,581. The same logic applies to the prison survey results, but there is much less turnover in the prison population. It also applies, more forcefully, to the results of the juvenile detention survey.

[417] Neither do there seem to be good statistics on the annual number of admissions to prison. We do know that as of June 30, 2008, counting both prisons and jails, the United States incarcerates about 2.4 million people on any given day. (See Bureau of Justice Statistics, "Jail Inmates at Midyear 2008—Statistical Tables," available at ojp.usdoj.gov/bjs/pub/pdf/jim08st.pdf. See also Heather C. West and William J. Sabol, *Prison Inmates at Midyear* 2008—Statistical Tables, Bureau of Justice Statistics, available at ojp.usdoj.gov/bjs/contentpub/pdf/pim08st.pdf.) This is more than any other country in the world, either on a per capita basis or in absolute numbers. Including those in immigration and youth detention and those supervised in the community (in halfway houses and rehabilitation centers, on probation or parole), more than 7.3 million people are in the corrections system on any given day. The cost to the country is more than $68 billion every year. (See National Prison Rape Elimination Commission Report, p. 2.)

[418] *Farmer v. Brennan*, 511 US 825 (1994).

[419] Best of all is "what's known in the profession as direct supervision": "In a direct supervision facility, officers are stationed in living units and supervise incarcerated individuals by moving around and interacting with them." This kind of regular contact gives officers a much better sense of what's going on in their facility than they can otherwise have. But even in facilities whose architecture makes this impossible, guards can make their patrols at unscheduled, hence unpredictable times. Electronic surveillance equipment can be put in known blind spots.

[420] Keith DeBlasio was sent to a minimum-security federal prison in West Virginia for fraud, but transferred to a higher-security facility in Michigan after complaining about corrections officials. There he was placed in a dormitory holding 150 inmates that had dozens of places that could not be observed and only one officer on duty at a time. A gang leader who had just served three days in segregation for brutally assaulting another inmate was made DeBlasio's bunkmate; according to DeBlasio's testimony before the commission, he raped DeBlasio "more times than I can even count" while fellow gang members stood watch. DeBlasio contracted HIV as a result. See the National Prison Rape Elimination Commission Report, p. 46, and DeBlasio's testimony to the commission, available at justdetention.org/en/NPREC/keithdeblasio.aspx.

[421] As the report says, "In non-correctional settings, one-third to one-half of rape victims consider suicide; between 17 and 19 percent actually attempt suicide." The lasting emotional trauma may be particularly severe "in a correctional facility, where victims may regularly encounter the setting where the abuse occurred—in some cases their own cell. It also may be impossible to avoid their abuser, causing them to continually relive the incident and maintaining the trauma."A coordinated response to sexual assault, typically through sexual assault response teams (SARTs), is common outside of corrections settings and widely regarded as best practice; therefore, an effective way to meet the commission's standard here, and one that leading agencies are already beginning to adopt, is for facilities to join their communities' SARTs. Prisoner rape survivors who are brought to outside hospitals, where victims' advocates from local rape crisis centers can meet them, are then able to receive the full range of care available to other victims; corrections investigators can benefit from the expertise of SART members who investigate and prosecute sex crimes in the community.

[422] Jason DeParle, "The American Prison Nightmare," The New York Review of Books, April 12, 2007, available at nybooks.com/articles/20056.

[423] Harley Lappin, director of the Bureau of Prisons, wrote to Judge Walton on July 7, 2008, that "we believe the Commission exceeded its mandate by recommending costly standards and broadening definitions contained within the Prison Rape Elimination Act."

[424] PREA, which was the first civil law ever to address the problem, passed unanimously in both chambers of a deeply divided Congress. Chuck Colson's Prison Fellowship Ministries and conservative think tanks such as Hudson Institute joined JDI (which was then called Stop Prisoner Rape) and other prisoners' advocates to demand congressional consideration in the first place. Ted Kennedy was the bill's champion, but Alabama Republican Jeff Sessions cosponsored it with him in the Senate; Republican Frank Wolf was joined by Democrat Bobby Scott in the House; and George W. Bush signed it. The commission itself was made up of five Republican and four Democratic appointees.

[425] The sentence reads, "The Department does not believe that these national standards will have an effect on the national economy, such as an effect on productivity, economic growth, full employment, creation of productive jobs, or international competitiveness of United States goods and services."

[426] However, as the department says, "Congress understood that such standards were likely to require Federal, State, and local agencies (as well as private entities) that operate inmate confinement facilities to incur costs in implementing the standards. Given the statute's aspiration to eliminate prison rape in the United States, Congress expected that some level of compliance costs would be appropriate and necessary."

[427] See the National Prison Rape Elimination Commission Report, p. 27.

[428] Sexual abuse in detention is considered torture under the International Covenant on Civil and Political Rights and the Convention Against Torture, both of which the United States has ratified.

[429] The commission writes in the report that the costs of complying with the standards will not be "substantial compared to what these agencies currently spend and are necessary to fulfill the requirements of PREA."

[430] After years of egregious abuse, forty-nine girls at the juvenile detention center in Chalkville, Alabama, brought charges that "male staff had fondled, raped, and sexually harassed them" (National Prison Rape Elimination Commission Report, p. 144). Fifteen employees were fired or resigned as a result of the allegations, and that litigation ended in 2007 with a $12.5 million settlement. In February

2008, "a jury in Ann Arbor determined that the Michigan Department of Corrections, the former director of the department, and the warden at Scott [Correctional Facility] knew about the 'sexually hostile prison environment,' where nearly a third of male officers allegedly engaged in sexual misconduct." Ten female inmates were awarded $15.4 million in damages; "more than 500 women who are or were incarcerated in Michigan prisons are [still] suing the State in a class action lawsuit" (National Prison Rape Elimination Commission Report, p. 51). Since the report was published, the series of lawsuits of which this was a part have resulted in a final settlement of $100 million. And these are only a few examples among many across the country.

[431] Tom Cahill, an Air Force veteran and a former chair of JDI's board, was jailed for twenty-four hours on a civil disobedience charge in 1967. His jailer put him in a crowded cell and told the others there that he was a child molester; that if they "took care of him" they would get extra rations of jello. Cahill told the commission:

> One of the prisoners turned and yelled out, "fresh meat." I turned and looked at the guard, and he was smiling. After lights out, that's when it started.
>
> Six or seven guys beat me and raped me while another two dozen guys just looked away. I remember being bounced off the walls and the floor and a bunk like a ball in a pinball machine. They put me inside a mattress cover and then set it on fire. Then someone urinated on it to put it out. I kept waiting for it to end, but it went on, and on, and on.
>
> After I was released from jail, I tried to live a normal life, but the rape haunted me. I was diagnosed with bipolar disorder. That one day I spent in jail has cost the government and the taxpayers at least $300,000.
>
> I've been hospitalized more times than I can count and I didn't pay for those hospitalizations, the taxpayers paid. My career as a journalist and photographer was completely derailed. For the past two decades, I've received a non-service-connected security pension from the Veterans' Administration at the cost of about $200,000 in connection with the only major trauma I've ever suffered, the rape.

See the National Prison Rape Elimination Commission Report, p.p. 2 and 47, and Cahill's testimony to the commission, available at justdetention.org/en/NPREC/tomcahill.aspx.

[432] David R. Shaw, "Prison Security Housing Mismanagement Costs State Money and Violates Inmate Rights," Office of the Inspector General for the State of California, January 15, 2009. Available at oig. ca.gov/media/press_releases/2009/Prison percent20security percent20housing percent20mismanagement percent20costs percent20state percent20money percent20and percent20violates percent20inmate percent20rights.pdf.

[433] The 2008 draft of the standard required annual audits, but this stricture was relaxed because of fierce protests from corrections officials.

[434] The American Bar Association resolution, which according to the report lists twenty requirements "that experts and practitioners generally agree are necessary to achieve true accountability and transparency," is available at abanet.org/crimjust/policy/cjpol.html#am08104b. It is resolution 104B from the 2008 annual meeting.

This project was made possible, in part, by grants from:

THE AKONADI FOUNDATION

For more information on the Akonadi Foundation, visit akonadi.org.

THE CALIFORNIA COUNCIL FOR THE HUMANITIES

*The Council is an independent non-profit organization and a state affiliate
of the National Endowment for the Humanities. For more information
on the Council, visit calhum.org.*

THE CULTURAL EQUITY GRANT PROGRAM OF THE SAN FRANCISCO ARTS COMMISSION

*For more information about the San Francisco Arts Commission,
visit sfartscommission.org.*

ACKNOWLEDGEMENTS

This project would not have been possible without the partnership and collaboration of Justice Now, a California-based human rights organization dedicated to building a movement among people in women's prisons to challenge violence and imprisonment. We worked closely with Justice Now to shape the vision and scope of the project, and we relied greatly on their decade's worth of experience building relationships with people in women's prisons, and their advocates. their reputation as a trusted organization among people inside was crucial to identifying, and gaining the trust and cooperation of potential narrators. Justice Now staff trained our interviewers to work with narrators in prison, arranged for access into the prisons, oversaw logistics of interviews, conducted interviews, helped develop the book's appendix, and contributed to content, editing, legal research and fact checking. Crucially, Justice Now also helped support narrators in prison in facing and resisting retaliation for their participation in this project. Without this support, the depth and candor of the narratives in this book would have been impossible to achieve. Special thanks is extended to Justice Now Direct Service Director Amanda Scheper, who led Justice Now's training and logistical support of Voice of Witness staff and volunteers, support of narrators in prison, and follow-up communications between narrators and interviewers. Her work made the depth and quality of this book possible.

We would also like to thank Tammica L. Summers, a poet currently in prison, whose poem "Dehumanization Resistance" provided the inspiration for the book's title. Her writing can be found on womenandprison.org.

About THE EDITORS

ROBIN LEVI is the human rights director of the Oakland-based nonprofit Justice Now, a California-based human rights organization dedicated to building a movement among people in women's prisons to challenge violence and imprisonment.

AYELET WALDMAN, an attorney and former public defender, is the author of *Red Hook Road* and *Bad Mother: A Chronicle of Maternal Crimes, Minor Calamities, and Occasional Moments of Grace.*

The VOICE OF WITNESS SERIES

Voice of Witness is a nonprofit book series, published by McSweeney's, that empowers those most closely affected by contemporary social injustice. Using oral history as a foundation, the series depicts human rights crises in the United States and around the world. This is the ninth book in the series. The other titles are:

SURVIVING JUSTICE
America's Wrongfully Convicted and Exonerated
Edited by Lola Vollen and Dave Eggers Foreword by Scott Turow

These oral histories prove that the problem of wrongful conviction is far-reaching and very real. Through a series of all-too-common circumstances—eyewitness misidentification, inept defense lawyers, coercive interrogation—the lives of these men and women of all different backgrounds were irreversibly disrupted. In *Surviving Justice*, thirteen exonerees describe their experiences—the events that led to their convictions, their years in prison, and the process of adjusting to their new lives outside.

ISBN: 978-1-934781-25-8 469 pages Paperback

VOICES FROM THE STORM
The People of New Orleans on Hurricane Katrina and Its Aftermath
Edited by Chris Ying and Lola Vollen

The second book in the McSweeney's Voice of Witness series, *Voices from the Storm* is a chronological account of the worst natural disaster in modern American history. Thirteen New Orleanians describe the days leading up to Hurricane Katrina, the storm itself, and the harrowing confusion of the days and months afterward. Their stories weave and intersect, ultimately creating an eye-opening portrait of courage in the face of terror, and of hope amid nearly complete devastation.

ISBN: 978-1-932416-68-8 320 pages Paperback

UNDERGROUND AMERICA
Narratives of Undocumented Lives
Edited by Peter Orner Foreword by Luis Alberto Urrea

They arrive from around the world for countless reasons. Many come simply to make a living. Others are fleeing persecution in their native countries. But by living and working in the U.S. without legal status, millions of immigrants risk deportation and imprisonment. They live underground, with little protection from exploitation at the hands of human smugglers, employers, or law enforcement. *Underground America* presents the remarkable oral histories of men and women struggling to carve a life for themselves in the United States. In 2010, *Underground America* was translated into Spanish and released as *En las Sombras de Estados Unidos.*

ISBN: 978-1-934781-15-9 379 pages Hardcover and paperback

OUT OF EXILE
The Abducted and Displaced People of Sudan
Edited by Craig Walzer
Additional interviews and an introduction by Dave Eggers
and Valentino Achak Deng

Millions of people have fled from conflicts and persecution in all parts of Sudan, and many thousands more have been enslaved as human spoils of war. In *Out of Exile*, refugees and abductees recount their escapes from the wars in Darfur and South Sudan, from political and religious persecution, and from abduction by militias. They tell of life before the war, and of the hope that they might someday find peace again.

ISBN: 978-1-934781-13-5 465 pages Hardcover and paperback

HOPE DEFERRED
Narratives of Zimbabwean Lives
Edited by Peter Orner and Annie Holmes Foreword by Brian Chikwava

The sixth volume in the Voice of Witness series presents the narratives of Zimbabweans whose lives have been affected by the country's political, economic, and human rights crises. This book asks the question: How did a country with so much promise—a stellar education system, a growing middle class of professionals, a sophisticated economic infrastructure, a liberal constitution, and an independent judiciary—go so wrong?

ISBN: 978-1-934781-94-4 304 pages Hardcover and paperback

NOWHERE TO BE HOME
Narratives from Survivors of Burma's Military Regime
Edited by Maggie Lemere and Zoë West Foreword by Mary Robinson

Decades of military oppression in Burma have led to the systematic destruction of thousands of ethnic minority villages, a standing army with one of the world's highest number of child soldiers, and the displacement of millions of people. *Nowhere to Be Home* is an eye-opening collection of oral histories exposing the realities of life under military rule. In their own words, men and women from Burma describe their lives in the country that Human Rights Watch has called "the textbook example of a police state."

ISBN: 978-1-934781-95-1 496 pages Hardcover and paperback

PATRIOT ACTS
Narratives of Post-9/11 Injustice
Compiled and edited by Alia Malek Foreword by Karen Korematsu

Patriot Acts tells the stories of men and women who have been needlessly swept up in the War on Terror. In their own words, narrators recount personal experiences of the post-9/11 backlash that have deeply altered their lives and communities. The eighth book in the Voice of Witness series, *Patriot Acts* illuminates these experiences in a compelling collection of eighteen oral histories from men and women who have found themselves subject to a wide range of human and civil rights abuses—from rendition and torture, to workplace discrimination, bullying, FBI surveillance and harassment.

ISBN: 978-1-936365-37-1 376 pages Hardcover and paperback

Thanks to the generosity and assistance of many donors and volunteers, Voice of Witness is currently at work collecting oral histories for a variety of new projects around the world. For more information about the series, or to find out how you can help or donate to the cause, visit the Voice of Witness website:

VOICEOFWITNESS.ORG